THE DEVELOPING WRITER

A Guide to Basic Skills

3rd Edition

Martin M. McKoski
The University of Akron

Lynne C. Hahn
The University of Akron

Scott, Foresman and Company
Glenview, Illinois
Boston
London

An instructor's manual is available for this text. It may be obtained through your local Scott, Foresman representative or by writing to Skills Editor, College Division, Scott, Foresman and Company, 1900 East Lake Avenue, Glenview, Illinois 60025.

Photographs

Cover: H. Armstrong Roberts
Part 1 Opener: Wayne Miller/Magnum (p. xx)
Part 2 Opener: Courtesy General Motors (p. 194)
Part 3 Opener: Courtesy Airstream, Inc. (p. 280)
Courtesy Ford Motor Co. (p. 211)
H. Armstrong Roberts (p. 212)
Scott, Foresman (p. 220)
Courtesy General Motors (p. 222)
Hank Walker/LIFE Magazine © 1955, Time Inc. (p. 225)
UPI/Bettmann Newsphotos (p. 227)
New York Public Library, Schomburg Center for Research in Black Culture (p. 228)
UPI/Bettmann Newsphotos (p. 232)
UPI/Bettmann Newsphotos (p. 235)
H. Armstrong Roberts (p. 237)
H. Armstrong Roberts (p. 241)
H. Armstrong Roberts (p. 245)
From *Googie,* Fifties Coffee Shop Architecture. Courtesy Reibsamen, Nickels & Rex, Architects. (p. 248)
UPI/Bettmann Newsphotos (p. 249)
UPI/Bettmann Newsphotos (p. 252)
Allan Grant Productions (p. 256)
H. Armstrong Roberts (p. 259)
Western History Collection, Natural History Museum of Los Angeles County. Seaver Center for Western History Research. (p. 262)
Bernard Hoffman, LIFE Magazine © 1955. Time Inc. (p. 263)
Scott, Foresman (p. 264)
Courtesy Peoples Gas Co. (p. 266)
Courtesy Westinghouse (p. 268)
Courtesy Sunbeam Corp. (p. 272)
Scott, Foresman (p. 275)
Courtesy Proctor Silex (p. 277)

1 2 3 4 5 6 MVN 92 91 90 89 88 87

Library of Congress Cataloging-in-Publication Data
McKoski, Martin M.
 The developing writer.
 Includes index.
 1. English language—Rhetoric—Problems, exercises,
etc. 2. English language—Grammar—Problem,
exercises, etc. I. Hahn, Lynne C. II. Title.
[PE1413.M34 1987] 808'.046'076 87-23538
ISBN 0-673-38025-4 (pbk.)

Preface

Our central purpose in the third edition of *The Developing Writer* remains the same as it was in the first two editions: to promote in student writers both confidence and control. The text uses essentially the same approach as the previous editions and is a product of methods and strategies that have worked successfully with our basic writers. It also reflects our philosophy that students be presented with only as much information as they need—and no more—thereby allowing them to gain necessary control. Confidence follows naturally. We also feel that if we as instructors are truly to reach our students, we must begin at their current levels of preparedness. For this reason, we have used actual writing by former basic writers for all of our models and exercises throughout the entire text. Identified as having been created by basic writing students, the paragraphs and sentences are tacit evidence that developing writers' efforts are worthwhile and that success is attainable.

FEATURES NEW TO THIS EDITION

In this third edition, we have revised our coverage of sentence combining and provided new student sentences for the sentence combining exercises. To further emphasize the writing process, we have included more models of actual student writing, given more attention to freewriting and topic selection, and added a new lesson on coherence. We have also included collaboration activities in most sections on "Improving a Paragraph." Further, our new reader, "Writing About Reading," was redesigned in accordance with current classroom practice in reader-response. Finally, the revised Instructor's Manual includes a description of the pedagogical theory underlying the text and suggestions for classroom use.

ORGANIZATION AND INTENT OF THE BOOK

The three-part structure of the book provides a flexible approach to building confidence and control in student writers. Each part is designed for a specific purpose.

Part One: Writing

Sentence combining exercises and writing assignments are placed at regular intervals throughout this section so that the sentence work will have a direct carryover into paragraph writing.

Sentence Combining. Like other skills, writing is learned through performance. For this reason, sentence combining is a useful way to present to students basic information about grammar and syntax, not as isolated rules, but as practice, directly related to their writing.

With each sentence combining lesson in the text, students are given sentences to combine ("Practice in Combining") and immediately afterward are required to write their own sentences based on the models ("Practice in Composing"). We find that unless students actually create their own sentences, as they do in "Practice in Composing," the direct transfer of skills may not occur. Each sentence combining lesson concludes with a review, in which students recombine, sentence by sentence, actual student paragraphs. They are then encouraged to find ways of integrating the structures with the appropriate punctuation into their own writing. This pattern prevails throughout Part One.

Freewriting. The series of freewritings that students are required to do in each writing assignment provides a nonpunitive and informal method for them (1) simply to get words on paper, (2) to discover a subject, and (3) to elaborate on that subject with details and examples. The freewriting approach we use is an adaptation of the technique as presented in Peter Elbow's *Writing Without Teachers* (New York: Oxford University Press, 1973).

Paragraphing. As students move from one writing assignment to the next, they learn to shape what at first are only rough paragraphs into ones that have topic sentences and unified, coherent, detailed supporting sentences. While the topics for the majority of the writing assignments elicit expressive writing, the writing is done in the standard expository paragraph form.

Improving a Paragraph. Each writing assignment concludes by calling students' attention to specific editing and proofreading skills: sentence combining, sentence completeness, adding pertinent or eliminating unrelated information, and making the order of sentences clear for a reader. Here, each student learns to write for a reader.

Writing Beyond the Paragraph.   Part One concludes with a brief section on the multi-paragraph paper, which is designed to provide a bridge to the college essay. This section will move students beyond the paragraph and will ready them for successive instruction, which usually includes longer pieces of writing.

Part Two: Writing About Reading

Since we know that reading and writing are interrelated skills and that our students so often will be required in their college classes to write about reading, we have included a reader with student and professional selections that are, we believe, relevant and stimulating to basic readers and writers.

The readings may be used for discussion, as opportunities for free-writing, or further practice in paragraph or multi-paragraph writing. Essentially, this section provides additional practice in writing but with one difference: here the students' ideas will come from reading or associations made from reading rather than from their own freewritings.

Part Three: Proofreading

These exercises will sharpen students' awareness of vitally important aspects of grammar and mechanics, or the areas that constitute correctness. Each lesson consists of recognition exercises, drill and application, and an actual writing assignment in which the newly learned aspect is used. The lessons can be used to supplement work in Part One as individual needs dictate.

Together, the three parts of *The Developing Writer* combine to give student writers the examples, instruction, and purposeful practice they need to develop writing control—and confidence.

Martin M. McKoski
Lynne C. Hahn

Acknowledgments

There are many who contributed to this third edition of *The Developing Writer*. Without their help this book would not have been completed. We are, however, particularly indebted to the following: our own developing writers at The University of Akron who enthusiastically agreed to let us publish their writing and provided the foundation of this text; our reviewers—Jan Delasara, Metropolitan State College; Karen Greenberg, Hunter College, CUNY; Dennis Lebofsky, Temple University; Deborah Pickering, Northern Illinois University; and Fran Zaniello, Northern Kentucky University—for their support and practical advice; Nancy McKoski for generously contributing her students' writing to our reader; Connie Millard for her expert clerical assistance and enthusiastic appreciation of our project; Marykay Ess for attending to the many necessary and time-consuming details; and Anne Smith, Patricia Rossi, and Lydia Webster, our editors, for their professional guidance and their faith in our work.

M. M. M.
L. C. H.

Contents

THE DEVELOPING WRITER

A Guide to Basic Skills

3rd Edition

Part One

Writing

The methods used in this section are designed especially with *you*, the developing writer, in mind. The exercises and examples were developed from writing done by students who at one time may have quaked at the thought of doing any "school" writing but who found that with practice they really could write, after all. And since writing is learned by actually writing, Part One, the heart of this workbook, is made up of two basic ingredients: sentence building exercises and writing assignments. These are integrated in such a way that the sentence work has a direct carryover into your writing.

Lesson One

Freewriting

GETTING STARTED AND DISCOVERING IDEAS

Student writers often say they have difficulty getting started with a piece of writing. In fact, reactions such as "I don't know how to begin" or "I don't have anything to say about the topic" are common to many students faced with a writing assignment. There is, however, a way to begin writing and at the same time to discover ideas to write about. This is called FREEWRITING.

To use this method, simply put your pen on the page, and, concentrating only on the assigned topic, write whatever comes to your mind. Try not to stop or take your pen from the page, even if you must repeat words that you have already written. While your pen is on paper, let your thoughts, your impressions, and your feelings about the topic flow freely, jotting down anything that seems related to the topic.

Here are a few student examples of FREEWRITING on the topic of "Childhood." Notice how different each is. Freewriting may take the form of single words, group of words, or even complete sentences. Some students explore freely and include many different ideas about the topic. Others seem to know already what they want to write about, and so their freewritings are more focused. Either way, freewriting gives you an easy way to begin writing and at the same time is a useful tool for exploring your thoughts and feelings. Because the students who wrote the examples that follow were thinking on paper to and for themselves only, they did not need to be concerned about a reader at that point.

2

My bear named Teddy with no mouth or nose and fur
I am drawing a total blank   always
sisters fighting   brother Bob's car that never
worked   Christmas presents   going for a tree
Williamsburg move   go to art shows
playing games with mom   bowling   Shelly
I saw cat Licorice   school   I warn
trauma   Oh that awful perm   ran away almost
because of it   picnic   fourth of July
Pittsburg   my aunts and uncles   Lisa Pickle
Geauga Lake   Cedar Point   the speed
roller coaster   oh that summer and times to Sea
World   same show over and over   getting
married   the crushes I had   what he looked
like   I remember Lynn and dolls and Halloween
my trick or treating   apples   need to
remember to by some apples   so good at this time
remember horrible peanut butter   apple
butter sandwiches   coffee   when we went to
get Christmas tree   spoiled rotten   Scoobie
Doo and Superman and the Monkeys   I Robin and
Steve   so many people   I God   you
remember Heidi and the clan   Jodie   ginger
bread   piano lessons   clarinet   fat
Brian   Scott   Jim   Mark   was weird
that teacher   all those teachers
couple of real good ones   kids are so mean
chocolate chip oatmeal cookies   those cookies
with weird stuff   I wonder how   working full
time   all those years   never even making
three dollars an hour   what a boss.

◆

What I remember about my childhood was when I was
about three years old and my mom and dad took my
brother and I to Sea World for the very first time I
could remember this giant bird cage with all of
these exotic birds in it. You could walk into it and
pet and hold the birds. My dad picked up a bird and
let my brother and I pet and feel the bird. I can

remember this little girl and her family had put the
birds on their head, shoulders, arms, and hands. I
can recall my mother refusing to hold a bird. So
when we were about to leave out of the exit I saw
this huge peacock and it was the same hieght as I
was and I looked over at it and it stared me right in
the eye and spread its feathers which looked like a
rainbow with eyes. Out as far as he could and then
made a funny noise and started to run behind me. At
that time I was terrified to death all I could do
was to think that this peacock was going to eat me,
so I started to run as fast as i could crying my eyes
out. All i could hear was my father running behind
me calling out my name but I didn't stop until he
caught me and picked me up. and when I finally came
back to earth all I could hear was laughter coming
from Dad, Mom and my brother. The only thing that
stopped me from crying was that my dad bought me
some cotton candy to eat.

◆

Gray house on street with the same name as mine
        father passed away when I was two   mother
raised five of us working in a candy store   my
first bike came from parts that were obtained from a
junkyard   Christmas was both good and bad for me
        Mom made most of our clothes   Christmas
meant store bought   It seems like every
Christmas I was in the hospital with pnumonia or in
my own bed with an oxygen tent   mother past away
when I was nine   my relatives cleaned out the
house of everything while we were staying at friends
houses the week of the funeral   left us with
nothing but the clothes on our back   then the
five of us went different places   some with
friends   some with relatives   no one knew
where anyone else was and no one cared   myself
        I was on my own   everyone thought I was
with someone else   so I lived in the gutters of
the city for the next three years   went to

school every day not thinking about being caught
        didn't have to worry   no body knew I was
missing   no one cared.

◆

    My childhood was exciting! I have had fun in
sports fishing, hunting, camping, of work I enjoyed
with my father in the woods, we cut trees for lumber
mills, for fence posts, and mine posts that were
used to hold up the roof of the coal mine.
    my father taught me the different types of trees,
also the different animals, and their habbits. he
has shown me the different kinds of insects the one
that most stands out in my mind is the Devils
Darning needles another is the Praying Mantis. I had
many trying times as well as good times. we lived in
poverty in my young life, yet we seemed to have
enough of the necessities of life. hardships were
taken as way of life. I often wonder why I would
hear Dad and Mom talking during the night, I now
know the plans and hopes that were changed or lost,
and the pain of disappointment they shared. Then
working together they would soften the impact that
we children would face.

◆

    Working for my aunt in her restaurant was fun but
embarrassing. That summer was the first time I had a
paying job and it made me feel very grownup. I did a
lot a fun things like helping with the menus. It was
really neat to decide what would be the special for
the day. I also worked out front waiting on
customers. Most of the people who came in worked at
the Lockheed aeronatics down the street. Most of
them were funny, and always joking around. Then the
worst day of my life happened   the regulars were
all there joking and kidding all of the girls. When
in walked this very large man. He had a beard,
mustache and looked very mean. I had always been

afraid that the clumsiness in me would sneak out,
and one day I would drop or spill something on
someone. On this day I did just that. The large mean
man decided on the special for the day, hot ham and
bean soup, and let me tell you   It was right off
the stove. As I was bringing his order one of the
regulars took that moment to pinch my behind. I let
out a squeel, and fell foward. The soup I was
carrying slid over the table right into the man's
lap. He jumped up and started to scream at me. The
whole place was roaring with laughter. I was never
so embarrassed in my whole life. I had a lot of fun
there but I will never forget how embarrassed I was
that day.

Writing Assignment

Using the same topic, "Childhood," try this on your own. Just *concentrate* on the topic and write as much as you can. Remember, relax, loosen up, and do not be concerned about "getting it right" the first time or about writing your thoughts and feelings correctly.

Lesson Two

Joining Sentences

JOINING SENTENCES WITH JOINING WORDS
(Conjunctions)

Two whole sentences that appear beside one another often express ideas that are so closely related that they are joined by the words, *and, but, or, for* (meaning "because"), *so, yet.* These JOINING WORDS (also called *conjunctions*), which are used to connect whole sentences, are preceded by a comma (,).

It's only been two weeks since the term started. I'm already finding it easier to put my thoughts down on paper.

can be written as

It's only been two weeks since the term started (, but) I'm already finding it easier to put my thoughts on paper.

The student who wrote these two sentences joined them with a comma and the word *but.* Notice that the second sentence does not begin with a capital letter because it is now joined to the first sentence.

Here is another example of two sentences brought together by a comma and a JOINING WORD.

Accomplishing the goals you set for yourself can be rewarding. It can give you confidence in your abilities.

can be written as

Accomplishing the goals you set for yourself can be rewarding(, and)
it can give you confidence in your abilities.

It is necessary here to be able to recognize what is considered a
whole or complete sentence in writing. For this, many students feel it is
best to trust their ears. They read a group of words *aloud* and listen for a
sound pattern that tells them whether or not it is a complete sentence.
This listening technique, however, takes time to develop.

All of the sentences provided in the sentence combining exercises
throughout Part One are complete sentences. If, then, you rely on your
understanding of language, and if you keep your ears pricked while you
are doing the sentence combining exercises, you will come to *hear* what a
complete sentence in writing sounds like. This technique, when applied
to the sentences you will be asked to write, will eventually lead you to
determine if *your* sentences are complete.

**Practice in
Combining**

Using a comma and a joining word from the choices below, combine
each of the following pairs of sentences, all written by students. In
selecting a joining word, choose one that sounds right to you and con-
veys what you want to say.

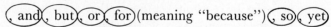

(, and)(, but)(, or)(, for) (meaning "because")(, so)(, yet)

As you write all the sentences in the exercises, read them aloud.

1. I can give you advice.
You will have to make up your own mind.

_____

_____

2. The sky grew dark.
Eerie silence covered the marsh.

_____

_____

3. His teeth are yellow.
He smells like an ashtray.

_____

_____

4. I missed out on a lot of good times with friends.
I was always out with my boyfriend.

_____

_____

5. After living with my grandparents for three months, I realized
just how important and special they were.
My love for them began to grow.

_____

_____

6. I love the way freshly fallen snow looks in the winter.
I hate the freezing temperatures.

_____

_____

7. When I met my first love, I got goose bumps.
That is the way I feel when I hear a guitar screaming vengeance.

_____

_____

8. I loved playing the guitar.
The sounds I could make with this instrument were like magic.

_____

_____

9. I was only two and a half years old at that time.
I remember it as if it were yesterday.

_____

_____

10. A college professor like that could never gain my respect.
Arrogance and insults are not the way to my heart.

_____

_____

11. Peanut butter is a staple in many American sandwiches.
After a steady diet of it, I began to wish I had never even heard
of George Washington Carver.

_____

_____

_____

12. We can work toward world peace.
We can prepare to meet the consequences of nuclear war.

_____

_____

13. She should stop feeling sorry for herself.
She will end up worse than she is now.

_____

_____

14. The light that filled the room was much too bright.
I dimmed it until a warm glow was all that was left.

_____

_____

15. This wasn't the first time a dog had wanted me for an entrée.
It was the worst.

_____

_____

16. I enjoy talking to older people.
They have so many interesting things to talk about and so much
information to pass on.

_____

_____

_____

17. I used imagination and forethought to make my subject
interesting.
The class didn't listen to my speech.

_____

_____

_____

18. The most influential person in my life has been my dad.
He has given me his views on life and made me aware of all the
possibilities that are available for my future.

_____

_____

_____

19. After becoming serious about studying in junior high, one "A"
　　came after another.
　　This made me extremely proud.

_____

_____

_____

20. I am terrified of needles.
　　I asked for laughing gas to make me feel relaxed and groggy.

_____

_____

Practice in Composing

Now write fifteen connected sentences of your own, using an appropriate joining word preceded by a comma. *Be sure to read aloud to check for sentence completeness.*

, and , but , or , for , so , yet

1. _____

_____

2. _____

_____

3. _____

_____

4. _____

_____

5. _____

_____

6. _____

_____

7. _____

_____

8. _____

_____

9. _____

_____

10. _____

_____

11. _____

_____

12. _____

_____

13. _____

_____

14. _____

_____

15. _____

_____

JOINING SENTENCES WITH *LONG* JOINING WORDS
(Long Conjunctions)

Whole sentences can also be connected by *long* JOINING WORDS.

Science has made many advances in curing and preventing disease. It has also made advances in destroying life.

can be written as

Science has made many advances in curing and preventing disease; however, it has also made advances in destroying life.

The federal government has cut the budget drastically. It is likely that more cuts will be necessary.

can be written as

The federal government has cut the budget drastically; furthermore, it is likely that more cuts will be necessary.

These *long* JOINING WORDS (also called *long conjunctions*) are used in the same way as the shorter joining words that you just practiced in the preceding lesson, but with one very important change, and that is in punctuation. **Long joining words are preceded by a semicolon (;) and followed by a comma.** They are somewhat more formal than the short joining words and can be used to add variety to your writing. The meaning of each of the *long* joining words is shown below.

; however,
; nevertheless,   } mean *but*

; furthermore,
; moreover,   } mean *in addition*

; consequently,
; therefore,   } mean *so*

Practice in Combining

Reading aloud, combine the following pairs of student sentences, using an appropriate *long* joining word and the punctuation that goes with it for each.

1. My writing is good.
   My spelling is "the pits."

   _____

   _____

2. Problems are a part of every individual's life.
   Good can come from difficult experiences.

   _____

   _____

3. The massive building had to be razed from the downtown area.
   Smoke and dust covered the entire city as the building crumbled
      down.

   _____

   _____

   _____

4. I started my diet today.
   I have been starting my diet all week long.

   _____

   _____

5. Because she expected me to succeed in most of my endeavors, I
      began to have a higher opinion of myself.
   Others began to react more positively toward me also.

_____

_____

_____

Practice in Composing

For each *long* joining word listed, write at least two connected sentences of your own. Make certain that you have included the correct punctuation. When you have finished, *read your sentences aloud, listening for completeness.*

(; however,) (; nevertheless,) (; consequently,) (; therefore,)

(; furthermore,) (; moreover,)

1. _____

_____

2. _____

_____

3. _____

_____

4. _____

_____

5. _____

_____

6. _____

_____

7. _____

   _____

8. _____

   _____

9. _____

   _____

10. _____

   _____

11. _____

   _____

12. _____

   _____

13. _____

   _____

14. _____

   _____

15. _____

   _____

FREEWRITING

There are a number of benefits to freewriting. First, it is relatively easy to do because you are writing only to and for yourself. Second, since it is not a finished piece of writing, freewriting can provide an opportunity to explore a topic, that is, to see the various thoughts, feelings, and impressions you have about it. In fact, it is often better to begin a paper by freewriting because it may encourage you to mull things over and do some thinking before your words and ideas are set in concrete. For example, sometimes the first thing you might think about is not always the best idea to write on. You may not care about it, may not know much about it, or it may be superficial and lead nowhere. Good writing rarely results from an idea you are not interested in or committed too.

Writing Assignment

Try freewriting on the topic "Reading and Writing in My Life." Remember, just concentrate on the topic and put on paper any ideas or feelings you have about it. At this point in the process, you are writing only for yourself, so don't be afraid to let yourself go.

FINDING ONE IDEA

Freewriting is only the first stage in the process of producing a paper. There are other stages that follow. After you finish freewriting, you must then decide on the one idea or point from your freewriting you will eventually share with a reader. This is important because in order to communicate, a writer must not confuse or distract a reader by writing about different ideas at the same time. Rather, *the writer must select one idea or point to communicate and explain it as fully as possible.*

You will recall from Lesson One that some students in their freewritings already seemed to know the one idea that they wanted to communicate so that their freewritings were more focused. Most writers, however, do not know until they have written, what they feel or think about something, so they use freewriting to explore various ideas and feelings they might have about a topic. If this is the case with you, to help determine one idea or point that is worthwhile to write about, you might ask yourself the following questions:

In your freewriting, is there an idea that seems to *stand apart* from the others, one that is particularly interesting or appealing to you, or one that is repeated frequently?

OR

Is there something in your freewriting that *sums up* your thoughts and feelings?
If not, can you *sum up* what your freewriting is about?

If your freewriting does not provide you with one worthwhile idea or if you have an idea but cannot write a lot about it, you will need to do more freewriting.

The student freewriting that follows shows how one student used freewriting to discover what it was that she wanted to write about.

```
    I've always been one who likes to write. I
remember in the 6th grade I had to write a story on
anything I wanted. I wrote a story on ''Flying
Dogs.'' I stretched my little 6th grade
imagination. My teacher loved it.       the class
roared.       I caught there attention
    I was so proud till the end       When I wanted to
say that flying dogs are pregnant for 9 months I
said they deliver for 9 months.       The classe
roared.       I was crushed. But laughed right along
with them. And soon I forgot my embarressment and
fell in love with the idea of writing. I've kept a
journal for about 9 yrs. then just every once in a
while. Writing in a journal is a way I release all
my thoughts. And no one can criticize me. I don't
let any one read them.
    I've always liked to read poems and true storys.
Other than that reading was always my weak point.
Until nine grade. I don't believe I read any except
the comic in the paper. But my 9th grade teacher Was
concerned for my class. none of us like to read So
she asked questions about our interest and got the
books on our interest. Soon the class was whipping
thru several books a month.
    Nursery rhymes, poetry, and true storys; were my
```

```
favorite. In the past two yrs. I've developed an
interest in mysteries.
    I find that the more I read. The more I want to
write. I'm excited about the classes that I'm taking
here at Akron U. they are related in many ways.
Reading and Writing. And I'm learning how to do them
both. One day I would like to write a childs book. I
also would like to help children to develope a love
for them both. I know that my children will not be
able to watch the TV as much as I did when I was
growing up. I'd rather them read and stretch there
imagination.
    I see that my reading skills are improving. And
so is my imagination and interest. I now want to do
some research and some writing. It has taken me 26
yrs. to realize that reading can be fun. And my love
for writing is now on an upswing.
```

In this case, as you can see, "in love with the idea of writing" stood apart for this student as particularly interesting or appealing and was what she wanted to write about. This, then, became her *central idea*.

FOCUSED FREEWRITING TO EXPLAIN THE CENTRAL IDEA

The next step in the writing process is to FREEWRITE again, but this time *for information that explains only the central idea*. Do this by concentrating on the central idea and jotting down information that is directly related to it. The information that is produced here can be the raw material for a future paragraph.

Here is what the student writer did in her second freewriting on her central idea, "in love with the idea of writing."

```
    Writing has always brought me enjoyment I like to
express myself and in writing I seem to do it a lot
better. To talk to someone used to be very difficult
for me. But when I write it down I get my thoughts
across without being persuaded to change my mind or
forget what I wanted to say. Writing down the way I
feel in a journal is always a release to me. if I'm
```

in a bad mood when I start I usually come out in a
good mood. When I write I can express my self
stretch my imagination and I can't really do that
when I talk. People don't always like to have a deep
conversation, I do. so I write it. I like to
communicate with people and writing stories,
letters, poems has always helped me. and if someone
reads something I wrote and gets my point I feel on
top of the world. Getting my point across has always
been hard for me. But writing makes it a lot easier.
I remember writing about flying dogs. the class
loved it and laughed.

I wrote a poem one time about two of my friends
that I introduced to each other. She loved it and
felt great that I would take the time to do it. I
felt great, because she did. I remember I wrote a
poem about the Cyprus tree while I was in Cyprus. I
sent it to my church paper and it was published in
the church paper. When I received the paper the best
feeling came over me. There it was my paper for
different congregations around the U.S. to see. One
day I was having a quarrell with my friend. Well she
was having it with me. I could not get a word in edge
wise. When I got home I wrote her a letter. She
called me when she received it. Having understood my
point of view and looking back on hers She was then
able to sort the problem talk reasonably and the
quarral was over. What a relief. So you see writing
has been an enjoy for me in many different ways.

What follows is a second student's freewriting on the topic "Reading
and Writing in My Life."

Writing for me was always a boring time consuming
experience, trying to think of what to say and how
to describe it to someone else was always the
problem for me. I never did like writing I could
never get the hang of it you had to rewrite my
paragraph a number of times to get it right
then I would hand in my paper and it would come back
all marked up with red ink and a message to redo the

paper   when I got the paper back I didn't want to
redo my work   I tried to do it and handed it in
if it's not right forget it   give me another
assignment   no matter how hard I try I could not
write very good   Writing causes me a lot of
aggravation from having to check word spellings all
the time and checking correct grammar   usage
along with editing my papers a number of times
changing the subject all the time in the middle of
my paragraph   always writing in first person
sentences and not using enough complex sentences
     spending a lot of time wondering what to write
     comming up with a good supportive topic
sentence and sticking to the topic sentence trying
not to repeat myself too many times.

     getting my assignments in on time   get fed up
with writing and quit for awhile   never did much
writing in school   found more interesting
things to do   writing was not interesting
it was work   too much work   took too much
effort   couldn't just spit out a fair paper in a
short time   always needed help   got writers
cramp too soon   writing was sloppy   never
neat or concise   never thought writing was
important   wish started writing sooner instead
of putting it off all the time.

This student felt that the one idea that summed up his freewriting
was "my writing isn't very good." This became the *central idea* of his
focused freewriting, which follows.

Most of my writings are not very good   spend
too much time on one paragraph   when someone
else reads my work they ask me if a seventh grader
wrote this because of small sentences and small
words   not college material for sure   want
to write like I have some sort of education
want my writing to read like a text book not a comic
strip   want my writing to be correct the first

```
or second time not the fifth      don't have that
much time to burn up doing all this unessary work
because I didn't take advantage of high school
classes      I am a college student        now I must
act, eat, think, write, dress, talk, like one      I
don't like writing about myself     don't do a good
job when I write about myself, I want my writing to
smack you in the face when you read it       you may
know what you are talking about but if I can't write
that way the reader (Employer) won't think that you
do so I may not get the job which I desire or I may
have to start at the bottom of the corporate ladder
in stead of jumping to the middle or the top just
from my inadequate letter on which the personnel
director based his findings which is not a good
impression of who the applicant really is
```

◆◆◆◆◆◆◆◆◆◆◆◆◆◆ Writing Assignment

Now read your freewriting on the topic "Reading and Writing in My Life" and decide, with the help of the following questions, what one idea or point is worthwhile to write about and will become the *central idea*.

In your freewriting, is there an idea that seems to *stand apart* from the others, one that is particularly interesting or appealing to you, or one that is repeated frequently?

OR

Is there something in your freewriting that *sums up* your thoughts and feelings?
If not, can <u>you</u> *sum up* what your freewriting is about?

If your freewriting does not provide you with one worthwhile idea or if you have an idea but cannot write a lot about it, you will need to do more freewriting.

Now do a focused freewriting for information that explains <u>your</u> *central idea*.

ATTACHING DEPENDENT CLAUSES
TO WHOLE SENTENCES

If you read the following groups of words aloud, you can hear that they are not whole sentences.

<u>Because</u> I'm still a kid at heart.
<u>When</u> I was late for class.
<u>After</u> I met with my teacher in conference.

Notice that each of these would be a whole sentence if you eliminated the introductory word, which is underlined. As the word groups appear above, however, they cannot stand alone and must be attached to whole sentences. Groups of words such as these that must be attached to whole sentences are called DEPENDENT CLAUSES.

I really get along with kids (because) I'm still a kid at heart.

OR

(Because) I'm still a kid at heart⊙   I really get along with kids.

The group of students I work with brought me up to date (when) I was late for class.

OR

(When) I was late for class⊙ the group of students I work with brought me up to date.

As the complete sentences above show, **if the dependent clause follows the sentence, no comma is used to separate the sentence from the clause. If, however, the clause precedes the sentence, a comma is used to separate the two.** If you read the sentence aloud, you can hear where the comma goes.

Practice in Combining

Combine each of the following pairs of sentences by attaching the second sentence to the first with a suitable introductory word or words from the list below. Your choice depends on what meaning you want to give the finished sentence. Also, the placement of the dependent clause before or after the first sentence depends on which way sounds better to you. *Remember to use a comma to separate the clause from the whole sentence if the clause appears first. Otherwise, no comma is used.*

after	as though	so that
although	before	when
as	because	while
as long as	even though	unless
as if	if	until
as soon as	since	

1. I never like it.
   You show off.

_____

_____

2. We will leave.
   I am finished.

_____

_____

3. I will die.
   You kiss me.

_____

_____

4. I finally realized I should just lie back, feet first, and let the river
   carry me.
   Someone on the rocks above finally threw me a line.

_____

_____

_____

© Scott, Foresman and Company

5. You know something is wrong.
   Everybody in your family is crying and sobbing.

   _____

   _____

6. My body felt strangely foreign.
   Something had invaded my muscles.

   _____

   _____

7. Against my will my father carried me back to my room and
   stayed with me.
   I went to sleep.

   _____

   _____

8. No one wants to hear the brutal truth.
   A euphemism would save his feelings.

   _____

   _____

9. Butterflies dance in my stomach.
   The dentist pokes my teeth to see if I have any cavities.

   _____

   _____

10. A fountain of tears rushed down my cheeks.
   I thought that I did not belong.

_____

_____

11. My stomach falls down to my toes, then settles somewhere
around my knees.
The jolt starts the elevator in motion.

_____

_____

12. I feel as though I am being watched.
I am on an elevator with just one other person.

_____

_____

13. Children will not learn to trust adults.
They are lied to.

_____

_____

14. I am proud of myself for finally attending college.
It took me a long time to get started.

_____

_____

15. The thought of sticking your hand back into a pail of dirty water
is gross.
You clean all of the dead bugs from your car's bumper and grill.

_____

_____

_____

16. His appearance startled me and caught me off guard.
He motioned to me and insisted that I come closer so he could
talk to me.

_____

_____

_____

17. He had me in the recruiter's office signing the preliminary
papers for my induction into the United States Army.
I knew what was really going on.

_____

_____

_____

18. My fist clenched, and my heart stopped.
I got off the bus at Fort Leonard Wood, Missouri, and saw that
big, ugly, red-eyed drill sergeant.

_____

_____

_____

19. Most passengers on the bus will choose to sit alone with their
eyes focused straight ahead and their legs close together.
They are sitting next to a person with a contagious, incurable
disease.

_____

_____

_____

20. I didn't realize I could learn what others could learn.
I began studying for the G.E.D.

_____

_____

**Practice in
Composing**

Write twenty sentences of your own that include dependent clauses,
using each of the introductory words at least once. Be sure to read your
finished sentences *aloud* to make certain they are complete.

after	as though	so that
although	before	when
as	because	while
as long as	even though	unless
as if	if	until
as soon as	since	

1. _____

_____

2. _____

_____

3. _____

_____

4. _____

_____

5. _____

_____

6. _____

_____

7. _____

_____

8. _____

_____

9. _____

_____

10. _____

_____

11. _____

_____

12. _____

_____

13. _____

_____

14. _____

_____

15. _____

_____

16. _____

_____

17. _____

_____

18. _____

_____

19. _____

_____

20. _____

_____

JOINING PARTS OF TWO SENTENCES WITH JOINING WORDS

Sometimes two complete sentences that express ideas that are closely related are written next to each other and contain many of the same words. In this case, it is often better to eliminate the repeated words before combining.

My self-respect went "down the tubes."
~~My~~ confidence ~~went "down the tubes."~~

would be rewritten as

My self-respect and confidence went "down the tubes."

You can "hear" that eliminating the repeated words and connecting the remaining information result in one improved sentence instead of two separate sentences.

Now I amount to something.
~~Now I~~ no longer feel negative about myself.

would be rewritten as

Now I amount to something and no longer feel negative about myself.

Notice that the joining word used in each of the rewritten sentences is *not preceded by a comma* because the joining word is not used to connect two whole sentences.

Practice in Combining

In each of the following pairs of sentences, eliminate the repeated words by drawing a line through them and connect the remaining information, forming a new sentence.

1. We have a lot of pride in our work.
We like to brag about it.

_____

_____

2. I sat in the bunker.
I watched the shells exploding on the horizon.

_____

_____

3. My mother helped me whenever I had a problem.
My father helped me whenever I had a problem.

_____

_____

4. My wits helped me to survive the ordeal.
My stamina helped me to survive the ordeal.

_____

_____

5. If we were rich, we would have nice clothes.
If we were rich, we would take luxurious vacations.

_____

_____

6. My husband, Hank, who is a gentleman, is also firm.
My husband is self-assured.

_____

_____

7. When it is time to clean up the popcorn maker, she disappears into the rest room until we are done.
When it is time to empty trash, she disappears into the rest room until we are done.

_____

_____

8. There is nothing to do inside an elevator but watch the floor indicator.
There is nothing to do inside an elevator but listen to all the strange noises.

_____

_____

9. I have learned things about myself that I had been carrying around with me for years.
I have conquered fears that I had been carrying around with me for years.

_____

_____

10. One's wedding day can be remembered as a haze of hurried, confusing details that never fell into place.
One's wedding day can be remembered as a joyous celebration that draws a peaceful, loving smile each time it is thought of.

_____

_____

_____

11. My bridesmaids had a great time remembering our single days' escapades and sharing our dreams for the future.
I had a great time remembering our single days' escapades and sharing our dreams for the future.

_____

_____

12. Our next-door neighbors, Mikki and John, let us use their garage for the band to set up in.
Mikki and John let us use their large carport drive as a dance floor.

_____

_____

**Practice in
Composing**

Using your own finished sentences from the preceding exercise as your guide, write out ten similar sentences of your own in the space provided below.

1. _____

_____

2. _____

_____

3. _____

_____

4. _____

_____

5. _____

_____

6. _____

_____

7. _____

_____

8. _____

_____

9. _____

_____

10. _____

_____

JOINING PARTS OF THREE OR MORE SENTENCES WITH JOINING WORDS

Three or more sentences that show related content and contain many of the same words can also be combined into one new sentence.

My hatred disappeared as I looked at him for the first time as a human being with pain and problems.

~~My~~ fear ~~disappeared as I looked at him for the first time as a human being with pain and problems.~~

~~My~~ anger ~~disappeared as I looked at him for the first time as a human being with pain and problems.~~

can be rewritten as

My hatred, fear, and anger disappeared as I looked at him for the first time as a human being with pain and problems.

The commas accomplish what you do with your voice when you read the sentence aloud. They mark pauses so that the sentence does not run together. **Furthermore, in this kind of sentence, with three or more items in a series, the joining word *and* is used after the final comma and before the last item in the series.**

Eugene raised the fishing pole high above his head.
~~He~~ cast the line as far as he could.
~~He~~ snagged another fisherman.

can be rewritten as

Eugene raised the fishing pole high above his head, cast the line as far as he could, and snagged another fisherman.

When joining parts of three or more sentences, be sure that all parts fit into the combined or finished sentence in the same way, as in the model sentences above.

My report was well written, neatly typed, and(had good logic in it.)

In this sentence, if you attach each item in the series to the first part of the sentence, you would have the following:

My report was well written.
My report was neatly typed.
My report was had good logic in it.

When you read it *aloud*, you can hear that "my report was had good logic in it" does not work. A successful version of this sentence would be "my report was logical." Thus all of the parts of the series are in parallel form: "My report was well written, neatly typed, and logical."

My best teacher was a man about forty years old, black hair, and wore glasses.

In the example above, each of the marked parts should fit with the beginning of the sentence, "my best teacher," to form a whole sentence.

My best teacher was a man about forty years old.
My best teacher black hair.
My best teacher wore glasses.

When reading *aloud*, you can hear, however, that "my best teacher black hair" does not make a complete sentence. A correct version, of course, would be, "my best teacher had black hair." The revised sentence would then read as follows: My best teacher was a man about forty years old, had black hair, and wore glasses.

Practice in Combining

Reading aloud, combine the following sentences, using the appropriate punctuation and joining word.

1. I felt used.
I felt disliked.
I felt plain old left out.

_____

_____

_____

2. At the library there are no ringing phones.
There are no chiming doorbells.
There are no distractions from the television set.

_____

_____

_____

3. I escape into the world of books for pleasure.
I escape for knowledge.
I escape for comfort when I have a problem.

_____

_____

_____

4. A boy is deep in some fanciful play.
A girl is deep in some fanciful play.
A shaggy sheepdog is deep in some fanciful play.

_____

_____

_____

5. The old man wore a tattered old wool coat on a blistery, hot,
sunny day.
He wore worn tennis shoes on a blistery, hot, sunny day.
He wore a black- and red-checked scarf on a blistery, hot, sunny
day.

_____

_____

_____

6. A young, teenaged girl stood watching the children playing.
A woman in her middle forties stood watching the children
   playing.
An elderly man stood watching the children playing.

_____

_____

_____

7. Jenny set the table.
She tossed the salad.
She peeled potatoes.
She put the roast into the oven.
She sat down to wait for her friend to arrive.

_____

_____

_____

8. After receiving several prank phone calls, I became frustrated.
After receiving several prank phone calls, I became worried.
After receiving several prank phone calls, I became really
   frightened.

_____

_____

_____

9. People screamed, trying to escape the rat.
   They jumped on top of the counters, trying to escape the rat.
   They rushed through the mall, trying to escape the rat.

   _____

   _____

   _____

10. When I feel wild, I listen to rock-and-roll music with a get-up-
    and-go spirit.
    When I feel enthusiastic, I listen to rock-and-roll music with a
    get-up-and-go spirit.
    When I feel energetic, I listen to rock-and-roll music with a get-
    up-and-go spirit.

    _____

    _____

    _____

Practice in Composing

Sentences that are combinations of three or more single sentences are easy to make and have an interesting sound to them. Write ten of your own. This time you might try some combinations that your classmates might find humorous, perhaps even silly.

1. _____

   _____

2. _____

   _____

3. _____

   _____

4. _____

_____

5. _____

_____

6. _____

_____

7. _____

_____

8. _____

_____

9. _____

_____

10. _____

_____

SENTENCE COMBINING REVIEW

In this exercise, combine the groups of sentences according to the various operations practiced in this lesson. *Each group of sentences will be rewritten as one sentence.*

If you are unsure of a certain operation and the *punctuation* used with it, refer to the examples.

The following exercise was developed from two student paragraphs. Combine the sentences, one after another, and reassemble the two paragraphs. As a check to *hear* whether or not your finished sentences are good ones, *read aloud* as you are working through them.

Sentence 1   My fear of speaking in front of others began several years ago.
I went to a weekly gathering at which the group members, taking turns, gave opinions on a selected topic of interest.

Sentence 2   I was new to the group.
Until then I hadn't had to speak.

Sentence 3   I was told I would be included in the group discussion.
I went from feeling calm and relaxed to feeling panicky.

Sentence 4   I sat there waiting my turn.
I felt my heart beating faster.
I felt a shortness of breath.
I felt my temperature dropping rapidly.

Sentence 5   I was frenzied.
The room was quickly becoming a blue haze around me.
I could no longer feel anything.

Sentence 6   At this point, I wouldn't have known if a needle had been pushed through my finger.
My body had turned numb.
My hands, normally very skilled and nimble, were completely useless to me.

Sentence 7   My turn came closer and closer.
I realized, immobilized by fear, that there would be no speaking for me.

Sentence 8   I was having an anxiety attack.
I thought I would die for sure.

Sentence 9   I quickly got up from my group.
I mumbled something about the bathroom.
I made my exit.

Sentence 10   My fear completely took over.
I never returned to the group.

_____

_____

_____

_____

_____

_____

Sentence 1　　In the middle of the afternoon on June 4, 1985, I was making my way toward home, whistling and humming some song.
I met a man who would change my life forever.

Sentence 2　　He wasn't much taller than I.
He seemed like a raging giant.

Sentence 3　　His appearance startled me.
His appearance caught me off guard.
He motioned for me to come closer.

Sentence 4　　My feet were hot and sore.
The shaded area of the building which he stood against looked very inviting from where I was in the blistering sun.

Sentence 5　　His short, black, well-cut hair, spelled "Army recruiter" with bold, obnoxious letters.
The shade felt so good that I had to stop.

Sentence 6　　The most distinct thing I noticed was the way his ribbons were placed above his left pocket.
I noted how neatly aligned they seemed.

Sentence 7　　He had me in the recruiter's office signing the preliminary papers for my induction into the U.S. Army.
I knew what was really going on.

Sentence 8　　Today I can write about it.
Today I can have a chuckle or two.

(Joining Word)   When I got off the bus at Fort Leonard Wood, Missouri, and saw that
                       big, ugly, red-eyed drill sergeant, my fists clenched.
                       My heart stopped.

Sentence 9   I could picture that recruiter's neck in my hands.
                       I could picture his eyes popping.

Sentence 10   Why, oh why couldn't I have stayed home that day?

_____

_____

_____

_____

_____

_____

_____

_____

_____

_____

_____

_____

_____

_____

_____

_____

_____

_____

_____

_____

_____

_____

_____

_____

Writing Assignment

In this writing assignment you will take your writing through all the stages of the writing process from freewriting for ideas to a finished paragraph to hand in. The general topic of this writing assignment is "My Recollections of School."

The following illustrates the development of one student's paragraph on this topic as she took it through the various stages.

FREEWRITING: GETTING STARTED, DISCOVERING IDEAS, AND FINDING ONE IDEA

```
   Made fun of        didn't dress well      English
teacher's smile never reached her eyes      Helped
tutor a friend in math in 5th grade      started my
```

```
m. period and was so embarrassed      The science
teacher was a man and didn't understand why I wanted
a nickel      He insisted I needed a dime for the
phone.      I liked English and math classes.      I
liked taking sentences apart apart apart      Went
out with another girl's boyfriend
      I didn't know but was called into school
counselor's office to discuss it.      I was called
to the office for wearing my clothes too tight.
      I explained to the principal I simply had
outgrown them and had none that fit.      I hated
history class, and I hated being called on.      I
never talked loud enough      There are not many
pleasant things I remember about school.
```

For this student writer, the idea in her freewriting that stood apart from the others—that is, the one that was particularly interesting or appealing to her—was the following.

```
      I was called to the office for wearing my clothes
too tight.
```

This, then, became the central idea for her second freewriting.

FOCUSED FREEWRITING TO EXPLAIN CENTRAL IDEA

```
      I was called to the principal's office for
wearing my clothes too tight. Seventh grade sat in
chair waiting for him to speak      I wiggled under
his stern gaze gruff voice ''It has been brought to
my attention that you have been wearing your clothes
too tight.'' Fear in my eyes      my head lowered in
shame      I looked him in the eye and told him the
truth. He was ashamed and embarrassed as I was. He
apologized.
```

WRITING A PARAGRAPH: THE PARAGRAPH FORM

The student writer formed the following paragraph by working directly from her second freewriting. As you can clearly see, she also added details and information not included in the freewriting. The first sentence of the paragraph was indented, and, unlike the freewriting, the .paragraph was written with *only complete sentences*.

My Recollections of School

In the seventh grade I was called into the principal's office. He met me at the door. He asked me to sit down in the chair opposite his desk. I wiggled under his stern gaze as I waited for him to speak. I jumped when I heard his gruff voice. ''It has been brought to my attention that you have been wearing your clothes too tight.'' As he waited for my answer, I sat with tears in my eyes. My head was lowered in shame. I raised my head. I looked him in the eye and told him ''I've outgrown them and can't afford new ones.'' I believe he then was as ashamed and embarrassed as I was. He quickly dismissed me with an apology and always treated me kindly thereafter.

IMPROVING A PARAGRAPH

After she completed her paragraph, her next and final step was to improve it by applying what she learned in Lesson Two about joining sentences.

My Recollections of School

In the seventh grade I was called into the

principal's office. He met me at the door. (and) He asked me to sit down in the chair opposite his desk. I wiggled under his stern gaze as I waited for him to speak. I jumped when I heard his gruff voice. ''It has been brought to my attention that you have been wearing your clothes too tight.'' As he waited for my answer, I sat with tears in my eyes. My head was lowered in shame. I raised my head, I looked him in the eye, and told him ''I've outgrown them and can't afford new ones.'' I believe he then was as

ashamed and embarrassed as I was~~x~~ ⋀ (because)he ~~He~~ quickly
dismissed me with an apology and always treated me
kindly thereafter.

For the student writer above, moving through the four-stage process
was relatively easy because she was satisfied with her central idea and
the memory was so vivid in her mind.

More often than not, this is not the case, as the next student example illustrates.

FREEWRITING

At the moment there is too many things that I can
remember about my school days. Except picking on a
teacher and called him chickenman. The reason we
called him that was that he had a big upper body and
a little legs. I mean they were real skinny. I also
remember trying smoking when I was in junior high
out in the school playyard. I was never so sick
after I tried to smoke in my life. I threw up The
only thing that I could think of was what I had ate
for lunch made me sick. So I never tried smoking
again. I think it must have been that same school. I
think it was the same year I tried to drink. I drank
a can of beer for my first try of alcohol I must
have been in the sixth grade. I remember my first
fight in school. It was with Lary and I was in the
5th grade. We got in a fight in the bathroom and the
playground well we got introuble when we fought out
in the playground. We got two cracks which was not
bad since it was detentions for fighting. I remember
winning an arts festival for school which I was
really happy to do. I remember my first girlfriend
which was in third grade. Then you no how third
graders were with being boyfriend and girlfriend.
Then as you mature I remember my first kiss which
was nice. What pops into mind right now, was how
easy it was for me to get A, B, and C's in high
school. The reason might be different of what you
think. I never had to do anything or do much work in

selected classes. History government, English,
Phys. Ed. and Biology. These teachers were all
coaches. They always and probably will still favor
athletes a jock as some people call them. I feel
this is not right because they are hurting the
students who participate in athletics. These
teachers do not look into the future enough, because
there is a great many great athletes that will never
play sports again after they get out of high school.
Except maybe some intermedial sports. I will give
you examples. I was in a History class that I never
once opened the book. My grades were straight A's
all the way across! My English teacher made us write
a essay at least three times a week. The length of
the essay would have to be 200 to 250 words   I
would usually turn in any where around 150 to 200
and would get a C on the paper. One night I sat down
and really tried to write a paper my mother and
girlfriend which is an excellent writer. Well it met
all of the requirements and was a pretty good paper.
When I got it back the grade I least expected was a
B+, but what I got was another C. I took the paper
home and showed my mom   she said that was good,
but she only saw the other papers I turned in that I
got C's on. So from then on I never tried in her
English class. And all I got was a C in that class.
My junior and senior English class is what I
remember most. I did not like this either. This
stinks too   I wish I could find something.

Although the one idea from the freewriting that he circled is about
boyfriends and girlfriends from third grade, his focused freewriting took
a slightly different direction. As you can see, he retold the history of his
romances all the way through school.

FOCUSED FREEWRITING

My topic is boy friend and girl friends during
grade school all the way up to high school. When I
was in kindergarden boys were a little scared of the
girls and vice versa. So we never really had

boyfriend and girlfriend relationships. So the first grade was about the same and then we hit the big second grade where boys and girls write each other notes and say they are boy friend and girl friend. Well in six grade you would maybe hold hands with a girl. That is if you are not shy. I was always really shy. Most of the girls in my school were more mature than the guys. They were usually the aggressor. But I feel in junior high it was the opposite meaning that the boys were the aggressor the girls were shyer or acted shyer. I was still shy in junior high. I really never had a girlfriend until I was a freshman. I really never could go out with the movies with her. Well we went out but my parents took us. So the girls always dated the older guys that drive a car. So we as freshman boys were kind of left out in the cold. Then when we got to our sophomore year we only concentrated on football because our school is very big on football. Our school strives on that sport. My junior year playing football a lot of girls liked me. Because I started when I was a sophomore and junior years. So I had a lot of girls that just wanted to go out with me. They were younger girls though. So I did take them out until the later half of my junior year when I found the girl of my dreams. She may not be pretty to everybody but she is beautiful to me. Her name is Tracy. Well I took her out when I was playing real heavy so I really did not see much of her. Then I asked her out again. now we have been seeing each other for two years. I think I would really be able to live with this lady for the rest of my life. But you never know. I am running out of things to say about girls and boys I hope this is long enough.

For one reason or another, perhaps because he felt the central idea in his focused freewriting was too broad, he decided to do a second focused freewriting. Because he was dissatisfied, he returned to his original intention, one he found more workable about his girlfriend from third grade.

SECOND FOCUSED FREEWRITING

```
Can you remember some grade school experiences?
Can you even remember your first romance? I can
remember my first romance. It was in the 3rd grade,
she was the prettiest thing I ever say. Her name was
Amy. She was the ripe age of 8 and I was 8½ as we
were in the third grade. She was a blond with blue
eyes. I was a little taller and much chubbier. The
first move I made on her was that I wrote her a note,
how exciting. I really did not expect a note in
return, but it was unbelievable she wrote me back.
Then I got the nerve to write another letter asking
if she would be my girlfriend. At lunch time I still
did not have a return, by this time I was getting
depressed. Right after lunch she gave me a note and
the answer was yes. I was never so happy as I wrote
her name on my books note books and even myself. The
romance did not last long. It lasted a whole 3
hours, but that is a long time for 3rd graders. That
was my first heartbreak, just to find many more to
come. I think I finally found something to write
about. I am getting to be happy. I had great times
as a little boy but this time was up there with the
exciting moments having your very first girl-
friend. Wow I could not believe that I actually had
a girlfriend.
```

This student used freewriting as a trial run, a chance to find out what worked for him and what did not. Even though it meant he had to abandon his initial focused freewriting, his willingness to explore paid off because what he did discover was an idea he really cared to write about.

After completing a rough draft, he produced the following paragraph to hand in, improving it by applying what he had learned about joining sentences and attaching dependent clauses, adding details and information, and making sure he had complete sentences.

IMPROVED PARAGRAPH

I can remember my first romance. I was the ripe age of eight and a half, and she was eight as we were in the third grade. I thought she was the cutest girl in the class, a petite blonde with blue eyes. I think Jenny was her name. I was the brown haired, blue eyed pudgy little boy who sat across the room from her. I thought, ''What should I do, write her a note or talk to her?'' I thought to myself, ''A note would be best,'' so I wrote it not expecting one in return. Before I knew it, there it was in my hand, her reply. I read the note, then decided to make my move. Again the note was written, this time with the important question on it, ''Would you be my girlfriend?'' This time the reply was a little slower to be returned. In fact, it was two hours later that I received the answer to my note. As a third grader this was my big moment. Would I have a girlfriend or would I not? I planned for the worst to happen, so I slowly opened it, waiting for fate to hit me, but it was not to be. The answer was yes. I was the proudest and happiest third grader that day; I was so happy I wrote her name on my desk, notebooks, and even myself. I looked like a human billboard. The life of a third grader has many ups and downs in one day. Three hours later the relationship was over. I guess that is pretty long for third graders. She was my first grade school romance and heartbreak.

Writing Assignment

Begin this writing assignment, first by freewriting on the topic "My Recollections of School." After you have completed the freewriting, select one idea or point to communicate and explain as fully as possible.

Once again, here are questions you might ask yourself to help determine one idea that is worthwhile to write about:

In your freewriting, is there an idea that seems to *stand apart* from the others, one that is particularly appealing to you, or one that is repeated frequently?

OR

Is there something in your freewriting that *sums up* your thoughts and feelings?
If not, can <u>you</u> *sum up* what your freewriting is about?

 If your freewriting does not provide you with one worthwhile idea or if you have an idea but cannot write a lot about it or if, like the student whose writing you just read, you become dissatisfied with the idea you have chosen, you will need to do more freewriting.

FOCUSED FREEWRITING

 When you have determined your central idea from your freewriting, then do a focused freewriting to get information that explains that central idea.

WRITING A PARAGRAPH

 When you decide on the information you want to include to explain your central idea, you are ready for the next stage, forming a paragraph from your focused freewriting.

 You might now want to add related details and information that are not included in your focused freewriting. You might also want to rearrange some of your information in an order that makes sense to you.

 Finally, make sure that the first word of the first sentence in the paragraph is indented about an inch and that, unlike your freewriting, your paragraph is written *in complete sentences only*.

 It might be a good idea to use the two student paragraphs above as a guide.

IMPROVING A PARAGRAPH

Once you have completed your paragraph, closely check it to see whether or not it can be improved by applying what you have learned about joining sentences with joining words or introductory words. Once again, the student paragraphs above may suggest some specific ways to do this.

Developing writing skills, both for effective sentences and effective paragraphs, takes patience and work. Good sentences and paragraphs do not simply "pop out" of the writer's mind, finished and polished, but are created, shaped, and reshaped through *freewriting for ideas, writing,* and *rewriting.*

You will develop the necessary skills for writing effective sentences and paragraphs as you practice taking your writing through these stages.

Lesson Three

Adding Descriptive Words

DESCRIPTIVE WORDS (Adjectives)

A whole sentence can be expanded with words that describe and add more detail. The following examples and exercises, which were originally student sentences, will give you practice in using and properly placing DESCRIPTIVE WORDS (also called *adjectives*).

Our teacher wore a pair of jeans, a plaid shirt, and a tie with a frog printed on it.
~~The jeans were~~ corduroy.
~~The plaid shirt was~~ drab.
~~The tie was~~ ugly.

With repeated and unnecessary words eliminated (the unnecessary words being *were* and *was*), the combined sentence is rewritten as

Our teacher wore a pair of *corduroy* jeans, a *drab* plaid shirt, and an *ugly* tie with a frog printed on it.

The words "jeans," "shirt," and "tie" are given more detail by describing them as *corduroy, drab,* and *ugly.*

Here is another whole sentence that was expanded with words that describe and add more detail.

The water of the deep protected the black coral.
The waters were icy.
The black coral was precious.

is written as

The *icy* waters of the deep protected the *precious* black coral.

Practice in Combining

Combine the following groups of sentences into one by eliminating repeated and unnecessary words (*is, are, was, were*) and placing the new information (descriptive words) appropriately in the first sentence of each group. *Reading aloud* and letting your ear be your guide, you will hear where the new word or words belong.

1. The husky pulled the sleigh over the tundra.
The husky was mighty.
The tundra was frozen.

_____

_____

_____

2. As my gaze shifts to the house, I notice the lumber that makes up the exterior.
The house is weatherworn.
The lumber is rough.

_____

_____

_____

3. There I was left to walk home with only a jacket in that weather.
The jacket was lightweight.
That weather was sub-zero.

_____

_____

_____

4. Bouncing from side to side, the mother led the child down the
aisle of the bus to the rest room.
The mother was young.
The child was anxious.
The aisle was crowded.
The bus was a Greyhound.
The rest room was for women.

_____

_____

_____

5. The desire for the taste of tobacco overcame me.
The desire was sudden.
The taste was harsh.
The tobacco was for cigarettes.

_____

_____

6. The only sounds I heard were the oars swishing in the water and
the plop of a frog jumping into the water's edge.
The oars were wooden.
The plop was occasional.

_____

_____

_____

7. My graduation day was nothing but confusion as I decided what to wear and checked all the other details.
The confusion was extreme.
The other details were vital.

_____

_____

_____

8. A woman with shoes and a scarf over her hair climbs on the bus with all the grace of an elephant climbing a tree.
The woman is extremely overweight.
The shoes are for tennis.
The scarf is multicolored.
Her hair is frizzy.
Her hair is blonde.

_____

_____

_____

9. My mother pushed bows, frills, and lessons, but I was a tomboy wanting jerseys, jeans, and a game of "chicken."
The lessons were for ballet.
The tomboy was bonafide.
The jerseys were for footballs.
The game was good.

_____

_____

_____

10. The car, a Chrysler, with an old engine, was running smoothly
when the police siren signalled me to pull over to the exit
ramp.
The car was mine.
The Chrysler was a 1970 model.
The engine was overhauled.
The siren was loud.
The exit ramp was deserted.

_____

_____

_____

Practice in Composing

Now write ten complete sentences of your own that include DESCRIP-
TIVE WORDS. Circle these descriptive words.

1. _____

_____

2. _____

_____

3. _____

_____

4. _____

_____

5. _____

_____

6. _____

_____

7. _____

_____

8. _____

_____

9. _____

_____

10. _____

_____

WRITING A DESCRIPTION

In the writing assignment that follows, you will describe a person who seems especially interesting to you. How clearly your reader will be able to "see" the person you describe depends on the thoroughness and accuracy of your details. The completed student paragraph below is an example of a successful description.

My grandfather is a seventy-eight-year-old man about five feet eight. He is far thinner than he used to be; therefore, his skin tends to hang from his bones. From hard work and the stress of raising six children, he has many face wrinkles. His eyes are drooping so much that the creases of his eyelids can no longer be seen. Under his eyes a pinky discoloring and puffiness shows through his dark-rimmed glasses. His cheeks are large and bulky from the fullness they used to have. Cracked at all times, his lips have lost their shape and structured appearance. His pores are large and seem to hold the dirt from all the hard labor he used to do. His huge, worn hands still contain grease in the nails and cuticles from last week's motor work. The skin on his hands is wrinkled, calloused, and scarred.

His left-hand thumb is somewhat of a stub with no
nail. Like a turtle's, his neck appears to have
.excess skin and a double chin. When he has shorts
on, his bony knees are hard not to notice above his
always-worn silk, black socks. As he walks, he takes
many deep breaths, for each step is a chore. To keep
a slow, even, and balanced pace, he puts his hands
behind him as he walks.

Noticing the kinds of descriptive details included in the above paragraph may be of some help to you now that you are about to begin the
process of composing your own paragraph.

FOCUSED FREEWRITING TO EXPLAIN THE CENTRAL IDEA

An assigned topic such as "A Particularly Interesting Person," may
not require the same probing or searching to discover ideas to write on
as other topics do. Such was the case for the student writer whose paper
is shown below. Because he knew the one person he wanted to write
about, he skipped the first freewriting for one idea. He began freewriting
instead for the information and details that resulted in the raw material
for his paragraph.

My Mother   medium size five feet four inches
tall round shoulders   olive complexion
gentle face with soft lines of age surrounding her
mouth, which was used to laughter, and her gray-
black eyes, which showed so much love or anger or
whatever emotion she felt. Her hair was laced with
more white than black making it look silver
fell astray on her forehead, and she was forever
brushing it back with her hand. She wore loafers and
housedresses with bib aprons covering them and
nearly always had flour on her hands.

Writing Assignment

Freewrite as much as you need to discover the person you want to write
on and to produce enough details so that the reader can "see" the person you are describing.

Alternate Topics

1. "A Place Where I Feel Comfortable"
2. "A Teacher in One of My Classes"
3. "Dinnertime at My House"

WRITING A PARAGRAPH: PLACING THE CENTRAL IDEA

Working directly from his freewriting, the student writer produced the following paragraph. You will notice that his paragraph, written in complete sentences only, contains much more information than the freewriting. You will also notice that *the paragraph begins with a statement of his central idea.* By making sure to place it in the first sentence of the paragraph, both the writer and reader can more easily stay on the subject and not become confused.

A Person I Remember

I want you to see Mamie, my mother, as I remember her. She has a medium frame. She stood five feet, four inches tall, with slightly rounded shoulders. Her clothing generally consisted of a colored housedress covered with a bib apron, and loafers. Mom's complexion was olive. Her hair, once black, was shaded with more white than black, making it look silver. Curls, which she was forever brushing back with her hand, fell over her forehead. Her face was lined from laughter, tragedies, and tears. Mom's mouth was full and ready to smile. Her nose was wide at the bridge with flared nostrils, but what I remember most were her spirited, gray-black eyes. They could grow black with anger as her dark brows drew together over them in a frown. They could sparkle with laughter or gently glow with love. My mother was a gentle, soft woman who knew how to love and whom I loved in return very much.

Writing Assignment

To write your paragraph, work directly from your focused freewriting. The information you jotted down in your focused freewriting may not yet be in an order that allows your reader to easily picture the person you are describing or to easily follow what you are saying. If this is the case, you may want to rearrange some of the details. *Also make sure that your paragraph begins with a sentence that states your central idea.*

IMPROVING A PARAGRAPH

Now that you have completed your paragraph, one good way to see whether or not you have drawn a clear enough picture for your reader is to read your paragraph aloud to a classmate or a partner to see whether she or he can picture the person (or place if you chose an alternate topic) you are describing.

It might be a good idea for your partner to close her or his eyes and concentrate as she tries to determine whether there are any missing details that might make your description more complete. After you have finished reading aloud, your classmate's feedback may help you determine if you need to add more information or descriptive words to your paragraph to make it come alive for your reader.

The next step is to improve it by applying what you have learned about joining whole sentences. The student paragraph below suggests some specific ways you might improve your paragraph.

A Person I Remember

I want you to see Mamie, my mother, as I
                                                                , and
remember her. She had a medium frame͙ ∧ She stood
five feet, four inches tall, with slightly rounded
shoulders. Her clothing generally
                    pastel
consisted of a ∧ colored housedress covered with
                                penny
a bib apron, and black ∧ loafers. Mom's
complexion was olive. Her hair, once black, was
shaded with more white than black, making it look
        Unruly
silver. ∧ Curls, which she was forever brushing back
with her hand, fell over her forehead.

gentle, weatherworn

Her/\face was lined from laughter, tragedies, and
tears. Mom's mouth was full and ready to smile. Her
nose was wide at the bridge with flared nostrils,
but what I remember most were her spirited, gray-
black eyes. They could grow black with anger as her
dark brows drew together

, (or)

over them in a frown_x/\They could sparkle with
laughter or gently glow with love. My mother was a
gentle, soft woman who knew how to love and whom I
loved in return very much.

Now, *read* the entire paragraph *aloud*, listening for sentence
completeness.

-ing DESCRIPTIVE WORDS (Present Participles)

DESCRIPTIVE WORDS take various forms. In the following sentence combining exercises, for instance, as in the model provided below,
the descriptive words end in *-ing*. The *-ing* descriptive words (or *present
participles*) are ones you are already familiar with and use to describe
everyday situations, for example, *crying* baby, *frightening* movie, *falling*
snow.

Our love affair was an experience.
~~The experience was~~ exhilarating.

is rewritten as

Our love affair was an *exhilarating* experience.

**Practice in
Combining**

Combine the following pairs or groups of sentences into one, and place
the *-ing* word or words appropriately. Again, let your ear be your guide.

1. Guns should never be portrayed as toys, for there is always
   danger when their use is taken lightly.
   The danger is life threatening.

_____

_____

2. Whistles sounded, friends hugged, and the class of '86 was set
   loose on society.
   The whistles were piercing.
   The society was unsuspecting.

   _____

   _____

3. Having a fear of doing things on my own was another stumbling
   block that I overcame.
   The fear was immobilizing.

   _____

   _____

4. Assertiveness training taught me to show facial expressions.
   The expressions were nonthreatening.

   _____

   _____

5. Many old people do not use their bodies as an excuse to stop
   living.
   Their bodies are aging.

   _____

   _____

6. I watched and listened as the chain saws shredded the oak.
   The chain saws were screaming.
   The oak was towering.

   _____

   _____

7. Buzzards wait patiently to spot the remains of another animal's kill.
The remains are decaying.

_____

_____

8. His hair and belly were sure signs of middle age.
His hair was thinning.
His belly was ballooning.
Middle age was approaching.

_____

_____

9. The lights and the music at the dance gave me a headache.
The lights were flashing.
The music was pulsating.
The headache was throbbing.

_____

_____

10. I have proven to myself that I am not the person I thought I was.
The person was nothing.

_____

_____

Practice in Composing

Now write ten complete sentences of your own that include *-ing* words that describe. Circle these descriptive words.

1. _____

_____

2. _____

_____

3. _____

_____

4. _____

_____

5. _____

_____

6. _____

_____

7. _____

_____

8. _____

_____

9. _____

_____

10. _____

_____

-ed DESCRIPTIVE WORDS (Past Participles)

Descriptive words also end in *-ed.* (They are called *past participles.*)

The words sounded awkward and clumsy.
~~The words were~~ rehearsed.

is rewritten as

The *rehearsed* words sounded awkward and clumsy.

Practice in Combining

Combine the following groups of sentences.

1. What made the occasion so meaningful was that it was such an experience.
   The experience was shared.

   _____

   _____

2. I used to feel like a kitten, but now that I am older, intimidation no longer bothers me.
   The kitten was frightened.

   _____

   _____

3. The teacher's concern for us radiated from her face.
   Her face was dimpled.

   _____

   _____

4. There are many questions on the subject of euthanasia.
   The questions are unanswered.

   _____

   _____

5. The dog gazed back at his owner with a look of contentment.
The dog was thoroughly combed and petted.
The owner was beloved.

_____

_____

6. When washing your car on a hot, sunny day, halfway through
the chore you must rewet the car.
The car is water spotted.

_____

_____

7. After the accident there was nothing left of my car but a heap of
metal, fenders, and torn upholstery.
The car was used.
The heap was twisted.
The metal was rusted.
The fenders were dented.

_____

_____

_____

8. Instant potatoes, meat, and vegetables were served to the guests.
The potatoes were whipped.
The meat was burned.
The vegetables were overcooked.
The guests were astounded.

_____

_____

_____

9. The wedding cake had three tiers with yellow daisies swirling
down the sides.
The tiers were heart shaped.

_____

_____

_____

10. The teacher read the test to the class.
The test was typed.
The class was shocked.

_____

_____

**Practice in
Composing**

Write ten complete sentences of your own in which you include *-ed*
words that describe. Circle these descriptive words.

1. _____

_____

2. _____

_____

3. _____

_____

4. _____

_____

5. _____

_____

6. _____

_____

7. _____

_____

8. _____

_____

9. _____

_____

10. _____

_____

PUNCTUATION WITH TWO DESCRIPTIVE WORDS

When two descriptive words appear beside one another and are not connected by the joining word *and*, but could be, a comma is used to separate the descriptive words so that they do not run together. This use of the comma accomplishes what you do with your voice when you read the sentence aloud.

The smells coming from the kitchen of the old house were like a link to the past.
~~The smells were~~ warm.
~~The smells were~~ comforting.

is rewritten as

The *warm, comforting* smells coming from the kitchen of the old house were like a link to the past.

Practice in Combining

Combine the following groups of sentences, using the model provided above as your guide. *Read* your combined sentence *aloud,* and let your ear tell you where the comma goes.

1. The slimeball, who must have crawled out from under a rock, sat
   down nearby and leered at me.
   The slimeball was greasy.
   The slimeball was creepy.

   _____

   _____

2. The tree's limbs toppled and crashed to the ground with a
   thundering roar.
   The limbs were huge.
   The limbs were knotted.

   _____

   _____

3. My puppy always seems to have an expression on his face.
   My puppy is cute.
   My puppy is curious.
   The expression is sad.

   _____

   _____

4. The girl watching the soap opera smiled at the situation being
   presented.
   The girl was young.
   The girl was beautiful.
   The situation was improbable.

_____

_____

5. Taking the driver's exam was an experience I will never forget.
The experience was nail-biting.
The experience was nerve-racking.

_____

_____

PUNCTUATION WITH THREE DESCRIPTIVE WORDS

When three or more descriptive words appear beside one another, the joining word _and_ is sometimes used after the final comma and before the last descriptive word in the series.

Twenty thousand rock fans jammed the concert hall.
The fans were pushing.
The fans were shoving.
The fans were screaming.

is rewritten as

Twenty thousand _pushing, shoving, and screaming_ rock fans jammed the concert hall.

You may prefer to omit the "and," depending on which version sounds better to you.

Twenty thousand _pushing, shoving, screaming_ rock fans jammed the concert hall.

Practice in Combining

Using the sentence above as a model, combine the following groups of sentences.

1. My ears are bombarded by the elevator's sounds.
The sounds are clanking.
The sounds are banging.
The sounds are whirring.

_____

_____

_____

2. We all look forward to our annual visit to my uncle's farm where
    we know we will spend a day together.
    The day will be happy.
    The day will be relaxing.
    The day will be fun-filled.

_____

_____

_____

3. His face has small laugh lines on the outside corner of each eye.
    His face is clean shaven.
    His face is well tanned.
    His face is oval.

_____

_____

_____

4. Three dozen night crawlers and a six-pack of beer were all we
    needed for a day of fishing.
    The night crawlers were long.
    The night crawlers were fat.
    The night crawlers were slimy.
    The six-pack was frosted.
    The beer was premium.

_____

_____

_____

5. When you finish washing the car, you admire how it gleams in the
  sun and try to ignore the clouds rolling in from the sky.
  The clouds are big.
  The clouds are black.
  The clouds are threatening.

_____

_____

_____

**Practice in
Composing**

Write five of your own sentences that include two descriptive words that
appear beside one another and are not connected by the joining word
and. In this case, the two descriptive words will be separated by a
comma.

  After you have written them, *read* all sentences *aloud* to check for
sentence completeness. If you have applied this listening technique, you
are probably beginning to *hear* what a complete sentence in writing
sounds like.

1. _____

_____

2. _____

_____

3. _____

_____

4. _____

_____

5. _____

_____

Now write ten sentences that include *three* descriptive words in a *series*, making sure to separate the three descriptive words with commas. Remember that you may choose to use the joining word *and* after the final comma and before the last descriptive word.

1. _____

_____

2. _____

_____

3. _____

_____

4. _____

_____

5. _____

_____

6. _____

_____

7. _____

_____

8. _____

_____

9. _____

_____

10. _____

_____

-*ly* DESCRIPTIVE WORDS (Adverbs)

There is another kind of descriptive word that also provides additional detail to a sentence. This descriptive word (also called an *adverb*) ends in -*ly*.

The coaches planned their strategy for Saturday's big game.
~~They~~ carefully ~~planned their strategy.~~

is rewritten as

The coaches *carefully* planned their strategy for Saturday's big game.

Practice in Combining

Combine the following groups of sentences, placing the -*ly* descriptive word or words appropriately in your finished sentence. The placement of the -*ly* descriptive word, either before or after the word it describes, will depend on which sounds better to you.

1. His hazel eyes reflect his emotions.
They openly reflect his emotions.

_____

_____

2. After concluding her piano recital, the young girl bowed and smiled.
The young girl smiled broadly.

_____

_____

3. One dark, lonely night, I crept up the stone path to the garden.
I secretly crept up the stone path to the garden.

_____

_____

4. The weak, tattered chair broke down with my heavy Aunt Emma in it.
The weak, tattered chair suddenly broke down.

_____

_____

5. Her high-pitched voice rang for hours in my ears.
Her voice was unusually high-pitched.

_____

_____

6. Drills prepare us to respond to any given situation.
Drills prepare us to respond automatically.

_____

_____

7. The father listened as his young son began to read his first library book.
The father listened patiently.
The son haltingly began to read.

_____

_____

8. I knew I would get the money somehow, but I had no idea
      where it would come from.
   I knew I eventually would get the money.

_____

_____

9. I walked up to the dance floor, but when the music started, I
      began popping to the beat and forgot all about the people
      watching.
   I nervously walked up to the dance floor.
   I quickly forgot all about the people watching.

_____

_____

10. We must prepare children for their adult lives, or one day the
       world will slap them in the face.
    We must adequately prepare children for their adult lives.
    The world will rudely slap them.

_____

_____

11. I smiled at him, and my cheeks changed to a glowing red.
    I sweetly smiled at him.
    My cheeks quickly changed to a glowing red.

_____

_____

12. The two friends laughed as they entered the fun house.
The two friends laughed hysterically.
They cautiously entered the fun house.

_____

_____

13. A Human Relations course was offered to help the company
operate.
It was offered to help the company run more smoothly.
It was offered to help the company run more effectively.

_____

_____

14. Row by row, the graduation procession progressed, and it seemed
forever until our turn came.
The procession slowly progressed.

_____

_____

15. Then we stood waiting in line, and with rubbery knees, took the
long walk across the stage.
We stood impatiently waiting.

_____

_____

**Practice in
Composing**

Write ten complete sentences of your own in which you include descriptive words that end in *-ly*. These *-ly* words sometimes precede and at other times follow the words they describe. When you read your sentences aloud, you will *hear* whether or not the *-ly* word is correctly placed. Circle these descriptive words.

1. _____

_____

2. _____

_____

3. _____

_____

4. _____

_____

5. _____

_____

6. _____

_____

7. _____

_____

8. _____

_____

9. _____

_____

10. _____

_____

SENTENCE COMBINING REVIEW

In this exercise combine the groups of sentences according to the various operations practiced in Lessons Two and Three which, you will recall, deal with joining sentences, attaching dependent clauses, and expanding whole sentences with descriptive words.

If you are unsure of a certain operation and the *appropriate punctuation* used with it, go back and consult the lesson in which the operation appears.

The following exercises were developed from student paragraphs. Combine the sentences, one after another, and reassemble the paragraphs. As a check to *hear* whether or not your finished sentences are good ones, *read aloud* as you are working through them.

Sentence 1

What I first noticed as I looked at my present were her eyes that seemed to be popping out of her face.
The present was for Christmas.
Her eyes were large.
Her eyes were coal black.
Her eyes were shiny.

Sentence 2

Her nose was surrounded by whiskers.
Her nose was small.
Her nose was pointed.
The whiskers were light brown.
She had ears that reminded me of velvet.
Her ears were extremely thin.

Sentence 3

Her teeth were razor sharp, I soon learned.
Her teeth were small.
Her teeth were beaver-like

Sentence 4

Her paws resembled a raccoon's.
Her paws were tiny.
Her paws were nimble.
Her legs, although strong, were as slender as matchsticks.
Her legs were very strong.

Sentence 5

She had a body that was covered with fur.
She had a large body.
She had a round body.
The fur was soft.
The fur was brown and white.
Bringing up the rear was a tail that looked comical.
The tail was short.
The tail was stubby.
The tail looked rather comical.

Sentence 6

I had never before had a hamster.
What a gift it was.
The gift was for Christmas.

_____

_____

_____

_____

_____

_____

_____

_____

_____

_____

_____

_____

_____

_____

Sentence 1   Frank is in his early thirties.
                        He is very athletic.
                        He is a good friend of mine.

Sentence 2   He is thin.
                        He is wiry.
                        He is about six feet tall.
                        He is often dressed in a runner's tee shirt.
                        He is often dressed in runner's shoes.
                        He is often dressed in jeans.
                        The jeans are casual.

Sentence 3   His hair is thinning on top.
                        His hair is short.
                        His hair is neatly kept.

Sentence 4   He has light green eyes.
                        They are large.
                        They are intelligent.
                        He has an uneven nose.
                        It is somewhat large.

Sentence 5   His life-style is kept as simple as the clothes he wears.
                        It is kept as useful as the clothes he wears.

Sentence 6   His hands hold his guitar with precision.
They hold it with care.
His hands are strong.
They are lean.

Sentence 7   I think of him.
I can almost smell his Pierre Cardin after-shave.

Sentence 8   His strength is quiet, his personality friendly and caring.
His nature is that of a kind man, who has learned to give and receive
  equally well.
It is that of a sensitive man.
It is that of a young man.

_____

_____

_____

_____

_____

_____

_____

_____

_____

_____

_____

_____

_____

_____

_____

_____

_____

_____

_____

Sentence 1

Pop is an image of a man who once was a tough guy in the early
     nineteen fifties.
The image is perfect.
The man is middle-aged.
The guy was teenaged.

**Sentence 2
(introductory
word)**

He lumbers through the house with his body.
His body is large.
It is six feet, one inch.
It is muscular.
He looks like a Hungarian king in his castle.

Sentence 3

Pop's nose is a feature.
It is his feature.
It is the most dominant.

Sentence 4

It is big.
It is round.
It is anchored by a moustache.
The moustache is mixed brown and gray.
It is neatly trimmed.

Sentence 5

His hair is thin with a touch of gray along his sideburns.
It is brown.

(joining word)

His eyes are squinted.
They are big.
They are brown.
They are always squinted.

(introductory word)

He never wears his glasses except when reading.

Sentence 6

He is outside working in the yard and a friend of his drives by and honks his horn.
He waves.
He yells "Hi."
Then he turns to me or Mom to ask, "Who the hell was that?"

Sentence 7

He doesn't wear his glasses.
He says glasses are for sissies and wimps.

Sentence 8

Also he cannot hear.
Most of the time he does not pay attention to anything around him.

Sentence 9

To keep his tough-guy image, he lifts weights.
He has been doing so for as long as I can remember.

(joining word)

For a man of fifty-three, his biceps are bigger than most twenty-year-olds.

Sentence 10

They have tattoos on them.
There are two tattoos.
They are very big.

Sentence 11

His left arm has a heart and the word "Mother" inscribed on it.
The heart is big.
The heart is red.
His right arm has a pillar covered with ivy and the word "Hunky" written in script diagonally across it.
The pillar is ancient.
It is Greek.

Sentence 12

Because of the details, you probably think my dad is a hard man.
The details are overpowering.
He is a rigid man.

(joining word) Actually, he is understanding and gentle.
He is an excellent father.

_____

_____

_____

_____

_____

_____

_____

_____

_____

_____

_____

_____

_____

_____

_____

_____

_____

_____

_____

_____

_____

_____

_____

_____

TOPIC SENTENCES AND SUPPORTING SENTENCES

In the previous writing assignment you learned that it was more effective to place your central idea in the first sentence of your paragraph. When you do this, you and your reader can more easily stay on the subject and not become confused. The next step is to shape this first sentence into what is called a TOPIC SENTENCE, which provides even more direction for you and your reader.

Notice what the topic sentence accomplishes in the student paragraph below on the general subject "A First Experience." It lets the reader know (1) *the topic* and (2) *the writer's opinion about* or *reaction to* the topic (what is being said about the topic). The remaining sentences of the paragraph provide details and examples to support the opinion or reaction. These sentences, which form the body of the paragraph, are called SUPPORTING SENTENCES

TOPIC

On my very first night at a P.T.A. meeting of a couple of hundred people I experienced one of my

OPINION OR REACTION

most (humiliating) moments ever. The main speaker had finished her presentation. I left my seat to go to the bathroom. Since the second half of the meeting would be starting shortly, and wanting not to miss anything, I was hurrying. That night I felt I was ''top shelf,'' for I was wearing my blue silk dress, my shiny blue boots, and lots of flamboyant bracelets on my arm that jangled as I walked. I really felt I was good-looking that night. On leaving the bathroom, I glided through several large groups of people up to my seat, which was in the front of the auditorium, right by the speaker. After I had been sitting down for a moment, a girl tapped me on my shoulder. Not expecting this, I jumped a mile and was fortunate I didn't go through the ceiling. As she bent down she whispered in my ear, ''Your dress is all up in the back.'' Without my knowing it, the entire back of my dress was caught and tucked way up in my belt, which left my whole derriere showing. My face turned red as a beet. I wanted to disappear off the face of the earth, or at least from this meeting room and all those smiling faces around me that I would be seeing at other meetings in the near future. God sure had humbled me at a time when my ego was sky high. Also along with that, my pride was really hurt when I realized I had on only plain white underwear instead of the nice, sexy ones I usually wore; furthermore, to add insult to injury, I had a nice big hole in my bloomers. Although that was an embarrassing moment for me, I will now always remember that old cliche that goes something like ''It's not the beautiful, glittering, wrapped package that counts, but what's underneath.'' Amen.

Practice with Topic Sentences

In the following sentences, underline the topic and circle the opinion or reaction. This exercise will give you practice with the two necessary ingredients for a topic sentence before you write your own.

1. Becoming a father was the greatest learning experience of my life.
2. My easygoing personality is what I like most about myself.
3. College is a good place to learn about yourself.
4. One of the things I am most proud of is that I am paying for my college education myself.
5. An unpleasant experience I had was when a huge white rooster attacked me.
6. I believe it is shameful to lie to a child.
7. Discipline is one of the most important things a child should learn in life.
8. My first date was one of the weirder experiences of my life.
9. Having my appendix removed was a scary experience.
10. One of the most important things I learned outside of school was not to meddle in other people's business.

Practice in Completing Topic Sentences

In the following exercise either the topic or the opinion or reaction is supplied for you. You are to supply the missing ingredient.

1. The most embarrassing moment in my life _____

   _____.

2. Learning to cope with peer pressure was _____.

3. My writing _____.

4. The teacher I liked the most _____

   _____.

5. Something I recently learned about myself _____

_____.

6. I like to _____.

7. The greatest problem of my most ineffective teacher was _____

_____.

8. I was proud when _____

_____.

9. My fondest memory is _____

_____.

10. A time I felt guilty was _____

_____.

FREEWRITING

In your previous freewritings you wrote to discover your central idea and to get information and details that explained that idea. Now you will be using your freewritings to discover

1. Your particular *topic*,

OR

2. Your *opinion* about or *reaction* to the topic (what it is you want to say about that topic),

AND

3. Details, examples, and reasons to support the opinion or reaction.

Writing Assignment

On your own paper, try several freewritings, or as many as are necessary, to produce enough raw material for a paragraph on the subject "A First Experience." With each freewriting you will come closer to saying what you want to say.

Alternate Topics:

1. "An Illness or Injury I Had"
2. "A Past Experience I Had"
3. "A Job or Chore I Have Had"
4. "An Unpleasant Experience I Had"
5. "An Embarrassing Moment I Experienced"

Once you have completed your freewritings, write out your topic sentence on the space provided below. Make sure that your sentence clearly states (1) *a topic* and (2) *an opinion about or reaction to the topic.* You will want to avoid topic sentences, such as the following which contain only one of the two ingredients necessary for a good topic sentence.

OPINION OR REACTION MISSING

topic
Last year I worked in a furniture factory.

This sentence is merely a statement of fact. While it has a topic—working in a furniture factory—it does not show the writer's opinion or reaction.

TOPIC MISSING

opinion or reaction
It was a very rewarding experience.

This sentence clearly states an opinion or reaction, but it does not let the reader know the topic being discussed.

Write your own topic sentence:

_____

_____

_____

Now go back and underline the topic and circle your opinion or reaction.

WRITING A PARAGRAPH: ADDITIONAL SUPPORTING INFORMATION

Now that you have arrived at a TOPIC SENTENCE and some supporting details from your freewriting, you may find that you need additional material *to support your opinion or reaction*. In any good communication, it is simply not enough for the writer or speaker to state thoughts, feelings, or opinions that he or she does not prove or support. A paragraph, then, should contain enough supporting *details or examples* for the reader to thoroughly understand your opinion about or reaction to the topic. Remember, it is the opinion or reaction that must be supported, not the topic.

One method for probing for additional supporting information is to ask, "What are my reasons for my opinion or reaction? Can I provide additional examples to prove that it is true?"

Writing Assignment

Working directly from your raw material, write your own paragraph, beginning with a clear TOPIC SENTENCE *that you prove* with SUPPORTING SENTENCES. You will recall that you are supporting your *opinion about* or *reaction to* the topic. Also work a few descriptive words into your writing and use what you have learned about joining whole sentences. For your new skills to carry over into your writing, you must consciously try to work these skills in.

IMPROVING A PARAGRAPH

Now that you have completed your paragraph, the next step is to improve it. First, read your topic sentence to a partner and ask what he or she thinks your topic and reaction are. It would probably be a good idea for your partner to jot down your reaction on a piece of paper. Then as your partner listens to you read your entire paragraph aloud, he or she might jot down key words or phrases from your supporting details and examples. The two of you will then determine together whether the details support the reaction in your topic sentence and whether you need additional information to develop your reaction.

Finally, check your use of descriptive words and your sentences to see whether there are any improvements you want to make. The student paragraph below might suggest some specific ways to do this.

TOPIC

<u>On my very first night at a P.T.A. meeting of a couple hundred people</u> I experienced one of my

OPINION OR REACTION

most (humiliating) moments ever.

After
∧The main speaker had finished her presentation⊙ I left my seat to go to the bathroom. Since the second half of the meeting would be starting shortly, and wanting not to miss anything, I was hurrying. That night I felt I was ''top shelf,'' for I was wearing my

swinging   sparkling

blue∧silk dress, my∧shiny boots, and lots of flamboyant bracelets on my arm that jangled as

extremely

I walked. I really felt I was∧good looking that night. On leaving the bathroom, I glided through several large groups of people up to my seat, which was in the front of the auditorium, right by the speaker. After I had been sitting down for just a moment, a girl tapped me on my shoulder. Not expecting this, I jumped a mile and was fortunate I didn't go through the ceiling. As she bent down she whispered in my ear, ''Your dress is all up in the back.'' Without knowing it, the entire back of my dress was caught and tucked way up in my belt, which left my whole derriere showing. My face turned red

⊙ and

as a beet χ∧I wanted to disappear off the face of the earth, or at least from this meeting room and all those smiling faces around me that I would be seeing at other meetings in the near future. God sure had humbled me at a time when my ego was sky high. Also, along with that, my pride was really hurt when I realized I had on only plain white underwear

⊙ colored

instead of the nice, sexy∧ones I usually wore; furthermore, to add insult to injury, I had a nice big hole in my bloomers. Although that was an

```
           excrutiatingly
           /\embarrassing moment for me, I will now always
           remember that old cliche that goes something like
           ''It's not the beautiful, glittering, wrapped
           package that counts, but what's underneath.'' Amen.
```

Now *read* the entire paragraph *aloud*, listening for sentence completeness. One useful approach for this is to read the paragraph *from the bottom up*. (For a more detailed explanation, see Lesson One, "Recognizing Incomplete Sentences," in Part Three.)

Lesson Four

Adding Descriptive Phrases

PREPOSITIONAL PHRASES

A whole sentence can also be expanded by adding a *group of words,* or what is called a *phrase.* This DESCRIPTIVE PHRASE, like the single-word additions of Lesson Three, is used to add more detail to a sentence.

I enjoy rock music.
~~The rock music is~~ from the early seventies period.

is rewritten as

I enjoy rock music (from) the early seventies period.

In the example above, the added DESCRIPTIVE PHRASE (also called a *prepositional phrase)* is introduced with the word *from.* All of the phrases in the first part of the lesson will begin with the prepositions *from, in, to, for, at, into, during, under, with, after, of, on,* and *without.*

Phrases introduced with these words should pose no problem for you because you use them frequently in speaking and writing. Once again, their placement in a sentence will be guided by how the finished sentence sounds to you when read aloud.

Here is another example:

My father showed disapproval.
~~My father showed disapproval~~ of my behavior.
~~My father showed disapproval~~ by his silence.

is rewritten as

My father showed disapproval ⟨of⟩ my behavior ⟨by⟩ his silence.

OR

⟨By⟩ his silence my father showed disapproval ⟨of⟩ my behavior.

Practice in Combining

Combine each of the following groups of sentences by placing the prepositional phrase or phrases appropriately in the first sentence.

1. Scared, I would pull the covers up, trying not to breathe so hard.
I would pull them up to my nose.

_____

_____

2. We read from a book on how to use our spare time.
During our five-minute break we read from a book.
The break was from class.

_____

_____

3. The world may end.
The world may end with people.
The people are in a state of mass hysteria.

_____

_____

4. He looked at me as he carefully cupped his hands.
He looked with a cigarette hanging.
It was hanging from his emotionless poker face.
He cupped his hands over his cards.

_____

_____

_____

5. Living in a room that used to be an attic, I heard a lot, and the
  wind seemed to echo.
  I heard a lot of eerie creaks.
  The creaks were along the floorboards.
  The wind was from the outside.
  The wind seemed to echo through my room.

_____

_____

_____

If you read your sentences aloud as you write, and listen carefully,
you will *hear* that the phrases can sometimes fit into different positions
in the sentence.

During the intermission we went to the refreshment stand for
popcorn and Coke.

OR

We went to the refreshment stand for popcorn and Coke during the
intermission.

Write two different sentences for each of the sets below by placing
the prepositional phrases in different positions, as done in the model
above. Include all of the information in each of the two sentences. Here
it is essential that you read the sentences aloud as you place the phrases.

1. The freeways are jammed.
  They are jammed at rush hour.
  They are jammed with high-speed vehicles.

a. _____

b. _____

2. I was left stranded.
I was left stranded with a dead battery.
I was left stranded in the early morning.
I was left stranded after a heavy snowfall.
I was left stranded in the middle of winter.

a. _____

_____

b. _____

_____

3. The noise echoed.
The noise was from the jumbo jet.
The noise echoed in my ears.
The noise echoed for days.
The noise echoed after I got off the plane.

a. _____

_____

b. _____

_____

4. Years ago we camped and fished.
We camped and fished on lazy June days.
We fished for smallmouth bass.
We camped and fished along the riverbanks.
We camped and fished in southern Ohio.

a. _____

_____

b. _____

_____

5. We huddled together.
   We huddled together during the gushing spring rain.
   We huddled together for protection.
   We huddled together under the nearest storefront awning.

a. _____

_____

b. _____

_____

Practice in Composing

Write five of your own sentences that include prepositional phrases that begin with some of the following prepositions: *from, in, to, for, at, into, during, under, with, after, of, on, without.*

1. _____

_____

2. _____

_____

3. _____

_____

4. _____

_____

5. _____

_____

RENAMING PHRASES (Appositives)

Here is another kind of descriptive phrase that is added to a whole sentence.

At the picnic we had strawberry shortcake.
~~It is~~ my favorite dessert.

After repeated or substituted words (here the word "It") and unnecessary words are eliminated, the combined sentence is rewritten as

At the picnic we had strawberry shortcake, my favorite dessert.

The patient had all four wisdom teeth extracted.
~~She was~~ a fourteen-year-old girl.

is rewritten as

The patient, a fourteen-year-old girl, had all four wisdom teeth extracted.

The models above show that this kind of phrase directly follows the word or words it describes. Notice also that besides describing, it _renames_ the word or words it follows, and, because it only renames, it is _not needed_ to convey the basic meaning or information of the sentence. In other words, the new information added by the phrase, while interesting, is only a sidelight and can be left out. **This _renaming phrase_ (also called an _appositive_), which is not essential to the sentence, is separated from the rest of the sentence by commas.** Notice, as in the first example above, that when the renaming phrase comes at the end of the sentence, it is set off by a comma and followed by a period.

Practice in Combining

Combine each of the following groups of sentences into one by first eliminating repeated or substituted words (_he, she, it,_ or _they_) and unnecessary words (_is, was,_ and _are_). Then place the remaining information, in this case, the renaming phrase, in the first sentence. Remember to use commas to separate the phrase from the sentence in which it appears.

1. Connie has an outgoing personality and a good sense of humor.
She is our department secretary.

_____

_____

2. There was a teacher who had some of the worst habits I have
    ever seen.
She was a six-foot, seven-inch marvel.

_____

_____

3. My teacher is sometimes overly concerned about us.
He is a worry wart.

_____

_____

4. My biggest fear hits me as elevator doors close behind me.
It is a form of claustrophobia.

_____

_____

5. My old neighborhood was torn down as part of the urban
    renewal project.
It was a haven for alcoholics and bums.

_____

_____

6. Angie McTovish McMikell was little more than a handful when
    we first met.
She was my pedigreed Scotch terrier.

_____

_____

7. An experience that changed the way I felt about something was the first time I rode a roller coaster at Cedar Point Amusement Park.
The roller coaster was the Gemini.

_____

_____

_____

8. I saw the Cadillac speed down the highway.
It was a big, white-finned model.

_____

_____

9. The company I work for offers a variety of self-help courses in an effort to better interpersonal relationships.
It is the Hillard Company.

_____

_____

10. My grandmother is an avid football fan.
She is a lively lady in her nineties.

_____

_____

11. Our car still runs beautifully.
   It is a Pontiac with over one hundred thousand miles on it.

   _____

   _____

12. The freshman math course is made even more unbearable by the instructor.
   It is my worst class by far.
   He is often a rude and inconsiderate man.

   _____

   _____

   _____

13. My classmates in English are helpful when it comes time to revise my themes.
   They are the partners I share my writing with.

   _____

   _____

   _____

14. Freewriting gives me a chance to think before writing.
   It is a good "warm-up" exercise.

   _____

   _____

15. The mechanic at the corner garage used to compete in the drag races on Highway 42.
   He is the best carburetor man around.
   It is the hottest strip in the state.

_____

_____

_____

Practice in Composing

Write ten sentences of your own that include renaming phrases. In each, be sure to use commas to set off this kind of phrase (since it is not needed to convey the basic meaning or information of the sentence).

1. _____

_____

2. _____

_____

3. _____

_____

4. _____

_____

5. _____

_____

6. _____

_____

7. _____

_____

8. _____

_____

9. _____

_____

10. _____

_____

Writing Assignment

On the topic "Something That Made Me Angry," freewrite to discover
1. your *topic* (exactly what it was that made you angry),
2. your opinion about or reaction to the topic (In this case, the reaction, anger, has already been given to you.),
3. details, examples, and reasons to support the opinion or reaction.

Try several freewritings, or as many as are necessary, to produce enough raw material for a paragraph. With each freewriting you will come closer to what you want to say.

Alternate topics:

1. "Something I Am (or Was) Proud of"
2. "A Fear I Have (or Had)"
3. "A Time I Had to Deal with Prejudice"
4. "The Worst Day of My Life"
5. "An Accurate (or Inaccurate) First Impression I Had"

In the course of your freewriting you might find it useful to question your opinion about or reaction to the topic in order to arrive at more supporting information. Some useful questions might be the following:

What are my reasons for my opinion or reaction?
Can I provide additional examples to further convince my reader?

WRITING A PARAGRAPH: TOPIC SENTENCE AND SUPPORTING SENTENCES

As you read through the finished student paragraph below, observe closely (1) what the topic sentence accomplishes and (2) what the supporting sentences accomplish.

Topic sentence

Supporting sentences

```
          OPINION OR REACTION      TOPIC
    I really got(mad)at my roommates recently for
making a mess out of our apartment. On a gloomy
Friday night a friend and I returned home from the
local bars to find my once-clean apartment a total
mess. As I walked through the door, my eyes stuck
out of my head like branches sticking out of trees.
The living room had a stenchy smell to it because
people had been smoking. I could feel the blood in
my veins pumping faster and faster. I was getting
very hot, but I knew to control my temper until my
roommates' guests, a bunch of real slobs, left. As I
started to walk through the living room, my shoes
stuck to the mucky floor. This made my Italian
temper start to show in my red hot face. I just
could not believe my eyes. I knew that if I saw any
more, I might become violent and hit the nearest
person. By this time everybody knew I was angry, so
they got their coats and left. After they had gone,
my stack blew. I gave my roommates a piece of my
mind, for if I hadn't, it would just happen again. I
pointed out the filthy living room, messy dining
room, and gross kitchen. They just sat there meekly
listening to me. I told them in a mean tone of voice
that the house had better be cleaned by the time I
got up in the morning or else.
```

◆◆◆◆◆◆◆◆◆◆◆◆ Writing Assignment

Working directly from your freewritings, write your paragraph on the topic "Something That Made Me Angry." Try to include in your paragraph at least one example of each of the two types of descriptive phrases practiced in this lesson, the prepositional phrase and the renaming phrase.

IMPROVING A PARAGRAPH: PROVIDING DETAILS FOR YOUR READER

There may be a general statement in your paragraph, either your topic sentence or one of your supporting sentences, that needs more detail or information so that your reader is convinced of what you are saying. A successful written communication is thorough and allows your reader to see and feel fully what you are saying.

Here is an opportunity to use a partner as a reader to help you determine if there are any statements in your paragraph that could be explained more fully. In spoken conversation a listener can question or help fill in details of what you are trying to say. In writing, however, you have to provide all the information that is needed. So here a partner can help you say all that you need to say in your paragraph by asking the kinds of questions that a listener would ask in a conversation. You can then answer them before you turn your paper in.

The second paragraph below shows the improvement that resulted with the addition of just a few specific details.

```
    Usually, I do not get angry, but when my parents
called and told me that I would have to move to
Ohio, I lost all self-control and flew into a rage.
At first, I could not believe it. I kept urging to
no avail that there was surely some way that I could
keep my residence in Texas. My parents did agree
that possibly there might be a way, but they sounded
pretty dismal about such thoughts. I guess it took a
while to hit me since I was in a state of shock, but
when I finally realized that I would have to move,
my eyes glistened with tears, and my voice started
to falter. As my parents tried to comfort me, my
anger rose to the boiling point. After a while, I
ended my conversation with my parents and bitterly
accepted it. I would be leaving Texas to start a
life in Ohio.
```

◆

```
    Usually, I do not get angry, but when my parents
called and told me that I would have to move to
```

```
Ohio, I lost all self-control and flew into a rage.
At first, I could not believe it. I kept urging to
no avail that there was surely some way that I could
keep my residence in Texas. My parents did agree
that possibly there might be a way, but they sounded
pretty dismal about such thoughts. I guess it took a
while to hit me since I was in state of shock, but
when I finally realized that I would have to move,
my eyes glistened with tears, and my voice started
to falter. As my parents tried to comfort me, my
anger rose to the boiling point. I wanted to let out
all of my suddenly frustrated feelings. I began to
yell at my parents and at Jessie, my friend, who was
staying over that night. I was very rude and
obnoxious. My words were insulting. I guess you
could say that I really came apart at the seams.
Jessie didn't know what to think as I screamed at
him and at my parents, arguing that I was not going
to leave Texas. I totally lost my self-composure,
but eventually I caught myself and tried to observe
some kind of calmness. After a while, I ended my
conversation with my parents and bitterly accepted
it. I would be leaving Texas to start a life in
Ohio.
```

Now go back over your paragraph and see if you can improve it by applying what you have learned in this lesson. After you have done that, *read* the entire paragraph *aloud*, listening for sentence completeness.

-ing DESCRIPTIVE PHRASES (Present Participial Phrases)

The *-ing descriptive phrase* is another way to expand a sentence with more detail and information.

The surgeon exposed the patient's rib cage.

~~The surgeon~~ carefully <u>made</u> the incision.

With the repeated "the surgeon" of the second sentence eliminated and *the underlined word changed into its* -ing *form,* the new information, "carefully making the incision," is then placed in the first sentence.

> Carefully making the incision, the surgeon exposed the patient's rib cage.
>
> OR
>
> The surgeon, carefully making the incision, exposed the patient's rib cage.

The *-ing* **phrase (present participial phrase), which is used to add more detail or information to a whole sentence, is separated from that whole sentence by commas.** Notice, as in the first example above, only one comma is used when the *-ing* phrase begins the sentence. While the phrase can be moved around in the sentence, it should be placed close to the word it describes.

Practice in Combining

Now try the following exercise. In the second sentence of each pair, eliminate repeated words, change the underlined word to its *-ing* form, and place that information in the first sentence close to the word or words it describes. Be sure to include appropriate punctuation.

1. I felt glued to the front seat.
I pulled into the driveway.

_____

_____

2. The loose papers became lodged in the wire fence.
They blew freely in the wind.

_____

_____

3. The crowd was really into the game.
It screamed and chanted about school spirit.

_____

_____

4. Customers are often unfair.
   They <u>condemn</u> the cashier for things he has no control over.

_____

_____

5. I felt a long, hard-shelled object crawl on my hand.
   I <u>reached</u> up to find the light switch.

_____

_____

6. I nearly died.
   I <u>realized</u> the hammering sound was really people smashing
   roaches.

_____

_____

7. The ant made its way across the vast space between the cracks
   in the sidewalk.
   It <u>crawled</u> slowly.

_____

_____

8. He no longer felt useful in his community.
   He <u>grew</u> old in a country that cares very little for old people.

_____

_____

9. I with my baby blue '66 Chevy II drove down Taylor Road. I <u>tried</u> to be cautious of the potholes in the dirty, gray, black asphalt.

_____

_____

_____

10. His eyebrows are thick and almost come together. They <u>give</u> him an almost Cro-Magnon appearance.

_____

_____

_____

11. She walked into the meeting. She <u>calmed</u> her nerves by breathing deeply.

_____

_____

12. My dad and I were sailing across the water when a big gust of wind blew past us. It <u>caused</u> the boat to tip on its side and <u>threw</u> my dad into the water.

_____

_____

_____

13. I was gasping for air. I <u>swallowed</u> water while calling out for help from my dad.

_____

_____

14. When she spoke, her beady black eyes showed her meanness.
She <u>looked</u> directly at you.

_____

_____

15. Ken grabbed a huge bottle of Draino and poured it all down the
clogged, smelly drain.
He <u>thought</u> quickly.

_____

_____

Practice in Composing

Now write ten of your own sentences that include *-ing* descriptive phrases. Make certain that they are descriptive phrases, as practiced above, and not *-ing* descriptive words as in Lesson Three. Remember to use commas for each descriptive phrase and to read your finished sentences aloud.

1. _____

_____

2. _____

_____

3. _____

_____

4. _____

_____

5. _____

_____

6. _____

_____

7. _____

_____

8. _____

_____

9. _____

_____

10. _____

_____

-ed DESCRIPTIVE PHRASES (Past Participial Phrases)

The *-ed descriptive phrase* (past participial phrase) is used in the same way as the *-ing* phrase, which means that it, too, needs commas to separate it from the rest of the sentence.

Lovers everywhere wonder why life is so brief.
~~Lovers everywhere are~~ clenched together in the heat of emotion.

is rewritten as

Lovers everywhere, clenched together in the heat of emotion, wonder why life is so brief.

OR

Clenched together in the heat of emotion, lovers everywhere wonder why life is so brief.

Practice in Combining

Combine each of the following pairs of sentences, using commas to separate the *-ed* descriptive phrase. Also remember that while the phrase can take various positions in the sentence, it should be placed close to the word or words it describes.

1. I woke up screaming.
   I was frightened for three weeks by nightmares.

   _____

   _____

2. I went out for a night to regain my composure.
   I was depressed by my poor grades.

   _____

   _____

3. I am a leader in an emergency when everyone else is running about in an erratic way.
   I am controlled and levelheaded.

   _____

   _____

4. I called the employment bureau and talked them into giving me the job that had been offered to my friend.
   I was not easily discouraged.

   _____

   _____

   _____

5. My sister and her boyfriend left for the wide open spaces of the Rocky Mountain high.
They were fed up with the rat race and confinement of city life.

_____

_____

_____

6. This excellent teacher would tell of past humorous experiences or easy ways for remembering often-used formulas.
She was determined to make math more enjoyable.

_____

_____

_____

7. I soon became comfortable at the university.
I was accepted by students the age of my own children.

_____

_____

8. I went to the movies to relax and regain my composure.
I was depressed by our argument.

_____

_____

9. The comma was in the right place.
It was placed after the -ed phrase.

_____

_____

10. I jumped up and dragged myself out of bed to answer the phone. I was rudely awakened by the ringing.

_____

_____

Practice in Composing

Now write five sentences of your own that include *-ed* descriptive phrases.

1. _____

_____

2. _____

_____

3. _____

_____

4. _____

_____

5. _____

_____

SENTENCE COMBINING REVIEW

In this exercise combine the groups of sentences according to the various operations practiced in Lessons Two through Four which, you will recall, deal with joining sentences, attaching clauses, expanding sentences with descriptive words, and expanding sentences with descriptive phrases.

If you are unsure of a certain operation *and the appropriate punctuation* used with it, go back and study the lesson in which the operation appears. In most cases, the operation asked for is clear. Where it might be unclear, a signal is provided in parentheses.

The following exercises were developed from student paragraphs. Combine the sentences, one after another, and reassemble the paragraphs. As a check to hear whether or not your finished sentences are good ones, *read aloud* as you are working through them.

Sentence 1

The time I auditioned for the part as a dancer was a moment.
The moment was embarrassing.

Sentence 2

At the age of sixteen, I was self-taught.
I had hopes of becoming a professional dancer.

Sentence 3
(-ed)

Several friends told me about an ad.
The friends were excited for me.
The ad was for dancing.
I decided to go for it.

Sentence 4

They came along for support.
The support was moral.
I was nervous about being in front of an audience.
I was really nervous.

Sentence 5
(-ing)

Once there I was shown a stage.
It <u>extended</u> across the whole back of the wall.
There were at least ten people sitting around it.

Sentence 6

I started off with a couple of dance routines.
They were slow moving.
They were interesting.
I became daring.
I became really daring.

Sentence 7

(-ing)

I miscalculated.
I put my foot down only halfway around.
I <u>swung</u> my leg around me once to the stage to make a full 360° turn.

Sentence 8

I went down with a plop.

The plop was ungraceful.

(-ing) I <u>landed</u> in the lap of the woman sitting in front of me.

(-ing) I <u>embarrassed</u> both of us to no end.

Sentence 9

I became fiery red.

(-ed) I was <u>abashed</u>.

I tried to concentrate on making sure the woman I landed on was not hurt.

Sentence 10

The whole time, I could see the smiles.

I could hear the chuckling.

The smiles and chuckling were around me.

Sentence 11

I just wanted to disappear into thin air.

(-ing) I <u>felt</u> extremely self-conscious.

I <u>knew</u> there was no way I could.

Sentence 12

Instead, I shrugged my shoulders.

I smiled sheepishly.

I sat down on the stage.

(-ing) I <u>waited</u> to hear my verdict.

_____

_____

_____

_____

_____

_____

_____

_____

_____

_____

Sentence 1   Miss Bluff was persistently courageous.
(renaming)   Miss Bluff was my fifth grade teacher.
                  She must have had a sense of humor.
                  The sense of humor was splendid.
(joining word) She faced us unfailingly each day.

Sentence 2   Miss Bluff wore her hair harshly pulled back.
(renaming)   Miss Bluff was a tall woman.
                  It was pulled back into a bun.
                  The bun was tight.
                  The bun was at the nape of her neck.

Sentence 3   She wore dresses.
                  They were long.
                  They were ill-fitting.
                  She wore glasses with lenses.
                  The glasses were wire-rimmed.
                  The lenses were extremely thick.

Sentence 4   Miss Bluff's eyesight was forever a source of ridicule.
                  Her eyesight was poor.
                  The ridicule was unmerciful.

Sentence 5   One day one of her students strategically placed thumbtacks.
                  The student was mischievous.
                  The thumbtacks were placed on her seat.

Sentence 6   Each of us waited as she began to sit down.
                  Each of us waited expectantly.
                  She innocently began to sit down.

Sentence 7   Suddenly, she sprang forward with dexterity.
The dexterity was unaccustomed.
She sprang forward with a roar of pain.

Sentence 8   Gales of laughter rose from her audience.
Her audience was attentive.

Sentence 9   With a look of anger on her face, she flung her arms about.
The anger was intense.
She flung them in fury.
She demanded to know who the culprit was.

Sentence 10   In a rage, she knocked her glasses off.
She knocked them off onto the floor.

Sentence 11   She frantically began searching while backing toward the trash can
than had just had ink dumped into it.
The searching was for her glasses.
The glasses were lost.
The trash can was large.
The trash can was yawning.

Sentence 12   What a sight it was as she made a landing.
It was a perfect three-point landing.

Sentence 13   She kicked.
(-ing)   She floundered in confusion.
She flung her arms.
(-ing)   She tried to loosen herself from her prison.
Her prison was round.
Her prison was metal.

Sentence 14   The laughter was deafening as the boys literally rolled.
The laughter was in the classroom.
The rolling was on the floor.
The rolling was in hysterics.

(joining word)
(-ing)
The girls were doubled over.
The girls <u>held</u> their sides in laughter.
The laughter was uncontrolled.

Sentence 15
Finally, another teacher came in to see what all the commotion was about.

(-ing) The teacher <u>heard</u> the din from within.

Sentence 16
He called us to order.
He called us to order with a voice.
The voice was low.
The voice was stern.
He helped Miss Bluff from her position.
Her position was ill-fated.

(-ing) He <u>returned</u> her lost glasses.

Sentence 17
Miss Bluff gained our respect as she brushed her hair back.
She straightened her dress.
She resumed her duties.
Her duties were demanding.
She resumed her duties with what dignity remained.

_____

_____

_____

_____

_____

_____

_____

Writing Assignment

As usual, begin this writing assignment by freewriting, this time on "What I Would Do Differently in My Life If I Had a Second Chance." With this subject, the opinion or reaction is already given to you (that is, doing something differently). What you will need to discover, though, is your particular topic and then your details, examples, and reasons why, which you will use for your supporting sentences.

Alternate topics:

1. "A Personal Characteristic I Would Like to Change"
2. "The Pressures of a Relationship I Have (or Had)"
3. "The Importance of Family Ties in My Life"

WRITING A PARAGRAPH

Once again, you might find it useful to refer to the student paragraphs below for guidance as you write your own paragraph. In addition to the topic sentence and supporting sentences, notice the use of the various types of descriptive phrases. Prepositional phrases appear frequently in all three student paragraphs. *-Ing*, *-ed*, and renaming phrases appear less frequently and must consciously be worked into writing. *-Ing* and *-ed* phrases are underlined, and the renaming phase is circled.

```
OPINION OR REACTION              TOPIC
(I strongly regret) not going to college right out
of high school. College was something that I thought
I wanted no part of; however, I was wrong. By the
time I was eighteen, I had all the school I could
handle; consequently, I found a good job, (an
assistant manager of a local business) and making
money for the first time seemed ''a dream come
true.'' I soon found out that money wasn't
everything and without a good education there
wasn't room for advancement. Nevertheless, my boss,
```

interested in his own welfare, always talked me out
of returning to school. Not realizing he was doing
this to benefit himself, I continued to be the
faithful employee. Now I realize I should have
followed my own conscience and returned to school
some time ago.

TOPIC
If I could turn back the clock and avoid

OPINION OR REACTION

getting married, (I would do it.) I was married at age
seventeen. Fresh out of high school, I was anxious
to experience the world. Then I fell hopelessly in
love with a man who I thought was my ''knight in
shining armor.'' I expected to be married and live
happily ever after. Unfortunately, I had no idea of
what was in store for me. At first, everything was
wine and roses. We were two silly kids in love with
love, enjoying all the romantic moments it had to
offer. We were carefree and gay and gazed at the
world through rose-colored glasses. But, as good
things usually do come to an end, so did my fairy
tale. After the novelty wore off, I felt like an old
married woman. I found myself thinking of past
dreams and ambitions. Feeling cheated, I finally
realized the mistake I had made in marrying so
young.

Writing Assignment

Now write your paragraph on the topic "What I Would Do Differently
in My Life If I Had a Second Chance." Include in your paragraph
some of the descriptive phrases practiced in this lesson. Also check to be
sure that your topic sentence is a good one and that you have enough
supporting details and reasons to communicate successfully with your
reader.

IMPROVING A PARAGRAPH: PROVIDING DETAILS FOR YOUR READER

Now go back over your paragraph and check to see whether you have written any general statements that need more support.

Do any statements need more details to fully convince your reader of what you are saying?
Will your reader fully see and feel what you are saying?

It might be a good idea to use a partner or a classmate to help you answer these questions as you did in the last writing assignment.

The second paragraph below shows the improvement that resulted with the addition of specific details.

```
    If I had a second chance to do something over
again in my life, it would be to go through high
school with a different attitude. Now that I realize
that high school provides the basics on which future
education is built, I know it would have been very
beneficial for me to study and do well. Not putting
enough time and effort into basic learning
processes is what made it hard for me in college.
When I was in high school, I didn't realize that
everything was a continuation from the previous
year's learning. I was too busy playing around and
having fun to understand why I had to study. There
are many things that I paid no attention to, and now
I regret that. This is why I really wish I could go
through high school again, knowing that what I would
be doing would benefit me in the years to come.
```

◆

```
    If I had a second chance to do something over
again in my life, it would be to go through high
school with a different attitude. Now that I realize
that high school provides the basics on which future
education is built, I know it would have been very
beneficial for me to study and do well. Not putting
enough time and effort into basic learning
```

processes is what made it hard for me in college. When I was in high school, I didn't realize that everything was a continuation from the previous year's learning. Each math class picked up where the last one left off, English papers became more complex through the years, and the sciences, which I cared nothing about, were just one big puzzle with each year being a new piece. I was too busy hunting and fishing with my brothers, riding around in cars with my friends, and lying in my room listening to my stereo to understand why I had to study. There are many things that I paid no attention to, and I regret that. This is why I really wish I could go through high school again, knowing that what I would be doing would benefit me in the years to come.

Lesson Five

Adding Descriptive Clauses That Begin with Who, Which, and That

WHO AND THAT DESCRIPTIVE CLAUSES
(Relative Clauses)

In Lesson Four a group of words called a phrase was used to expand a whole sentence. A whole sentence can also be expanded with a group of words called a *clause*. In the first part of this lesson each of the clauses will be introduced by the words *who* or *that*. Read the following sentences:

Those people probably never experienced anything bad.
~~Those people~~ say everything happens for the best.

After the repeated words are eliminated, the remaining information in the second sentence with the *introductory word "who" placed in front of it* forms the DESCRIPTIVE CLAUSE. This clause (called a *relative clause*) is then added to the first sentence. The whole clause is placed after the word described, which in this case is "people."

Those people (who) say everything happens for the best probably never experienced anything bad.

This particular descriptive clause is *not* separated from the rest of the sentence by commas because it is needed to identify the word it describes. In other words, the descriptive clause distinguishes the person or thing described from *other* persons or things.

The rule for choosing the right word to precede the clause is simple. If the word that the clause describes is a *person*, choose either *who* or *that*,

132

depending on which one sounds better to you. If the word described by the clause is anything other than a person, use *that*.

Here is an example using the introductory word *"that."*

The bike is being repaired.
~~The bike~~ has a flat tire.

is rewritten as

The bike that has a flat tire is being repaired.

This particular kind of clause would be a sentence if the word or words described by the clause were substituted for *who* or *that*. In the two examples below, you can *hear* that the clauses are complete sentences when the words "Those people" and "The bike" are substituted for *who* and *that*.

Those people
~~who~~ say everything happens for the best.
The bike
~~that~~ has a flat tire.

Practice in Combining

Combine the sentences provided below, making sure in each that the descriptive clause is preceded by the appropriate word and is placed immediately after the word or words it describes.

1. People make me really angry.
   They are rude.

   _____

   _____

2. I landed right in the lap of the woman.
   She was sitting in front of me.

   _____

   _____

3. My good friend Bob has brown eyes set close together and a
beard.
It is the color of wet sand on a sunny beach.

_____

_____

_____

4. Some people cannot be counted on.
They lie all the time.

_____

5. The product was a dark brown, four-sided wooden candle box.
I made the product.
It stood about ten inches high with a swinging stained-glass door
in front.

_____

6. His nature is that of a kind, sensitive young man.
He has learned both to give and receive.

_____

_____

7. The first time I drove a car was a terrible experience.
I will never forget the experience.

_____

_____

8. There is one person in my past.
   He influenced me by listening to my childish problems and being
   my counselor when I needed guidance.

_____

_____

_____

9. Because they had been reading horror stories all night, on the
   stroke of midnight the people jumped when a friend screamed
   out loud.
   They sat around the crackling fireplace.

_____

_____

_____

10. Making this box consisted of learning how to silk-screen pictures
   onto cut glass.
   I had designed the pictures.
   It fit the door.

_____

_____

_____

11. The beautiful young woman turned out to be my wife.
   She suddenly appeared in a seductive bikini.

_____

_____

12. The scratchings were made by animals.
    We heard the scratchings all winter long.
    They were trying to escape the terrible weather.

_____

_____

13. That part of the gulf coast will take years to rebuild.
    It was destroyed by the hurricane.

_____

_____

14. Explaining to my six-year-old brother that his puppy had died
        was a task.
    It was very difficult for me to do.

_____

_____

15. The most embarrassing situation that I ever had occurred as I
        entered a bar and tripped on the steps.
    It was for singles only.
    They led to a crowded dance floor and a huddle of gawking
        onlookers.

_____

_____

_____

Practice in Composing

Now write five sentences of your own that include clauses describing *persons*.

1. _____

_____

2. _____

_____

3. _____

_____

4. _____

_____

5. _____

_____

Write five sentences that include clauses describing *anything other than a person*.

1. _____

_____

2. _____

_____

3. _____

_____

4. _____

_____

5. _____

_____

FREEWRITING

By now you know how to freewrite and know its usefulness to you as a writer. You have learned that it often takes several freewritings to discover what it is you really want to say. In fact, sometimes what comes out first and easiest is not necessarily what we believe but what we have been told to believe, not what we really feel like writing but what we know is safe to write. If we want to get at our own *real* thoughts and feelings about something, we need to go beyond our first impressions and search deeper.

Writing Assignment

Freewrite as many times as necessary on the topic "What I Like Most About Myself," giving yourself an opportunity to pull out fresh information and to examine the *real* you.

Alternate topics:

1. "A Time When I Felt Like an Outsider"
2. "Something Important to Teach a Child"
3. "A Time I Had to Deal with Peer Pressure"
4. "Why I Would or Would Not Want to Donate My Body Organs to Others"
5. "The One Personal Belonging I Would Save—Excluding People or Pets—If My House Caught Fire"

WRITING A PARAGRAPH

Once you have completed your freewritings, you are ready to shape your paragraph. You might find it useful to refer to the student paragraph below for guidance. As you read through it, notice the underlined descriptive clauses practiced in this lesson.

What I Like Most About Myself

I feel that the very best quality <u>that I possess</u> is my ability to make other people smile. I guess you might say that I have what is called a ''sunny disposition.'' My good sense of humor often makes distressed people laugh despite their worries. For instance, if I am attending a rather boring, dull social gathering, I can make a remark <u>that tends to act as an icebreaker</u>; consequently, other people <u>who are tense</u> begin to relax. My ''icebreaking'' techniques are an unrehearsed part of my shining personality. I seem to possess this good sense of humor spontaneously and effortlessly. Perhaps this is an inborn quality because even as a toddling child I had an optimistic outlook on life. My ability to make other people smile has earned me many new friends.

Writing Assignment

Write a paragraph based on your freewritings. Include at least one example of the descriptive clause practiced in this lesson.

IMPROVING A PARAGRAPH: ELIMINATING UNRELATED INFORMATION

In the last few lessons you have learned that often you need to add specific details for your reader's sake. You also need to make sure that each of the supporting sentences in your improved paragraph relates *directly* to the opinion or reaction in your topic sentence.

Any other information—no matter how interesting—will distract the reader from the main idea you are communicating. The student paragraph below illustrates the improvement that resulted when unrelated sentences were eliminated.

I can remember feeling like an extremely self-conscious, lonely outsider the first time I went to my girlfriend's grandmother's house for Christmas dinner. ~~My family got up really early that morning to open our gifts. My parents gave me an expensive wristwatch since I was going to start college in January. After we all exchanged gifts and had breakfast, I left to pick up my girlfriend and head for her grandmother's house for the rest of the day.~~ Feeling painfully shy, I imagined each move I made while there would determine whether or not I would be accepted by her closest family members. Right from the start I didn't speak much or even attempt to be my normally relaxed, open, and sociable self. Thoughts of being evaluated socially, economically, morally, and physically raced through my mind. As my girlfriend introduced me to her aunts, uncles, grandmother, and grandfather, I tried my best to be a gracious, respectful guest. In fact, I concentrated on using good manners. But I can remember feeling as if I was being judged every second. It wasn't as if her family was asking me rude, personal, or embarrassing questions; actually they tried to make me feel quite welcome. Everyone said they were pleased to meet me and told me to make myself at home, ~~and it was a really nice place. The home was old and had a lot of comfortable antique furniture in it and smelled like cinnamon and pine. The Christmas tree took up one whole corner of the living room, and they said they had cut it down themselves.~~ However, I still could not relax, for I was worried about making a good first impression. As my girlfriend aimlessly wandered away, the house became very crowded. The farther away she moved, the more my feelings of being an outsider grew. I felt as if I was getting in the way of each and every Christmas hug and kiss. I felt as if the electrified buzz of Christmas joy was for everyone but me. I soon found myself an out–of–the–way seat in the corner. As I sat in the chair, I felt as if I was drifting out of the picture. I started to feel more and more withdrawn from the action. While everyone opened their presents and discussed each other's lives, I felt I was drifting into another dimension. I began to feel as if I was on the outside of the room, looking in on a special moment in time that I was not a part of. I started to feel as if the walls were closing in on me. Just at that time, one of the young boys had got a football and asked me if I wanted to go outside and play catch. His mother, trying to save me from being put on the spot by her son, said, ''No, son, it's cold out, and he might just want to relax.'' Feeling this was a perfect opportunity for me to elude my loneliness, I wasted no time in replying that it would be no problem. I told her I would be glad to play catch with him. The fact is, it could have been forty below zero outside, and I would have gone out to play catch anyway. I felt going outside would be a good way for me to relax. As I stepped outside, I vividly recall breathing a huge sigh of relief. I felt as if I could finally relax and stop trying to be conscious of every move I made.

You can clearly see that the eliminated sentences, while they are interesting and related in some ways to the general topic of Christmas and the grandmother's house, do not support the writer's *reaction*, "feeling like a self-conscious, lonely outsider." The writer's job here is to deal only with his stated reaction to the topic. Anything, then, that is not directly related to his discussion of feeling like an outsider is considered to be off the subject.

Once again, *a paragraph is not an explanation of the topic, but of the opinion or reaction.*

Carefully read through your finished paragraph and draw a line through *any* phrase or sentence that is *not* directly related to the opinion or reaction of your topic sentence.

You might get a second opinion by slowly reading your paper aloud to a partner, who can help you determine if any other sentences need to be eliminated.

WHO AND *WHICH* DESCRIPTIVE CLAUSES
(Relative Clauses)

There is another kind of clause that looks exactly like the one that you just practiced and is also used to add new information. It is, however, different from the other clause because it is *not needed* to identify the word it describes. In other words, the new information added by the clause, while interesting, is only a sidelight and is not essential. **This kind of clause is always separated from the rest of the sentence by** *commas*.

My mother taught me to become independent at an early age.
~~My mother~~ has quietly helped me throughout my life.

After the repeated words are eliminated, the remaining words from the second sentence, introduced by *who*, are placed appropriately in the first sentence.

My mother, who has quietly helped me throughout my life, taught me to become independent at an early age.

Once again, here is the rule for choosing the right word to precede the clause: When the word that the clause describes is a *person*, use *who*. A change, however, occurs when the clause is used to describe anything other than a person. The descriptive clause in this case begins with *which* instead of *that*.

Yellow daffodils, <u>which</u> burst from the thawing earth, signal the end of winter.

is rewritten as

Yellow daffodils, <u>which</u> burst from the thawing earth, signal the end of winter.

Practice in Combining

Combine the sentences provided below, making sure that in each set the descriptive clause is preceded by the appropriate word and is placed immediately after the word or words it describes. *Use commas to separate this extra information from the rest of the sentence.*

1. He had a cigarette in one hand, a gold earring dangling from his left ear, and unlaced black tennis shoes.
The tennis shoes happened to be mine.

_____

_____

_____

2. My sixty-year-old grandfather is an ornery, jolly person.
He has worked hard all his life.

_____

_____

3. My dog Hellyin is a German shepherd.
He weighs 110 pounds.

_____

_____

4. Several friends told me about the audition for the part of a dancer.
They were excited for me.

_____

_____

5. Bruce came toward me, smiling and waving.
He was a friend I had known since grade-school days.

_____

_____

6. Alcoholism interferes with one's physical, emotional, and
   spiritual health.
   It is a progressive disease.

   _____

   _____   _____

7. I believe a dope pusher has no sensitivity for any human's well-
   being.
   He believes only in himself and not in others.

   _____

   _____

8. I used to spend the weekend with Grandma Vaughn.
   She taught me how to add by playing dominoes with me.

   _____

   _____

9. Cornelia has lived through the horse-and-buggy era to the space
   age.
   Cornelia is a ninety-one-year-old lady.

   _____

   _____

10. I was watching the late show, so I started turning out the lights
   and pulling the blinds.
   The show was just about over.

   _____

   _____

11. My stepfather and sister wish they, too, had the opportunity to attend college.
My stepfather and sister are proud and a little envious of me.

_____

_____

12. Working at a nutrition store has taught me a lot about working with the public.
Working at a nutrition store is demanding but interesting.

_____

_____

13. Lying has a snowball effect.
Lying creates ill feelings, distrust, and a sense of frustration.

_____

_____

14. Chrissy and Linda were beeping the horn.
They were my dates for the night.
The horn embarrassed me in front of the customers.

_____

_____

15. Each new baseball season reminds me of years ago when my dad took me to the city to see my first game.
Each new baseball season comes at my favorite time of year.
My dad now spends most of his time in a rocking chair.

_____

_____

_____

Practice in Composing

Now write five sentences of your own that include nonessential clauses describing *persons*. Each of these clauses will begin with *who* and must be separated from the rest of the sentence by commas.

1. _____

_____

2. _____

_____

3. _____

_____

4. _____

_____

5. _____

_____

Write five sentences that include nonessential clauses describing anything *other than a person*. Each of these clauses will begin with *which* and must be separated from the rest of the sentence by commas.

1. _____

_____

2. _____

_____

3. _____

_____

4. _____

_____

5. _____

_____

SENTENCE COMBINING REVIEW

Included in this sentence combining exercise are the various operations practiced in Lessons Two through Five, which, of course, include descriptive clauses (with the appropriate introductory words *who, which,* and *that*).

Once again, if you are unsure of a certain operation and the appropriate punctuation used with it, study the lesson in which the operation appears. Some signals have been provided in parentheses.

The following exercises were developed from student paragraphs. Combine the sentences, one after another, and reassemble the paragraphs. As a check to *hear* whether or not your sentences are good ones, *read aloud* as you are working through them.

Sentence 1

I have been trying to give up smoking.
Quite honestly, I hate it.

Sentence 2

I felt more relaxed.
I smoked.
I liked what I was doing better.

Sentence 3

A drive used to be heavenly.
The drive was in the car.
The drive was with music.
The music was soft.

(-ing) The music <u>filled</u> the air.
The drive was with the car gliding.
The gliding was over the road.
The road was open.
The drive was with a cigarette.

(-ing) The cigarette <u>glowed</u>.
It glowed dimly.

Sentence 4   Now having dinner is almost unbearable.
          Dinner is with a friend.
(who)   The friend is a smoker.

Sentence 5   In the past, what a relief it was to know I could create a screen.
          A situation came up.
          The situation was uncomfortable.
          The screen was of smoke.
(that)   I could disappear in the screen.

Sentence 6   It was sheer ecstasy.
          It was sheer ecstasy after a day.
          The day was long.
          It was sheer ecstasy to smoke.
          It was sheer ecstasy to listen to music.

Sentence 7   Smoking was an ending to a day.
(which) Smoking provided release.
          The release was for nervous tension.
          The ending was perfect.
          The day was horrible.

Sentence 8   I now realize that I am giving up a lot.
          I am giving up a lot by not smoking.

_____

_____

_____

_____

_____

_____

Sentence 1   Taking a test is something.
          (that)   I find taking a test incredibly difficult to do.

Sentence 2   I am tested on anything.
          I immediately become an idiot no matter how well I prepare myself by
              studying or practicing.
          The idiot is blithering.

Sentence 3   I always manage to forget everything.
          I know everything.
          The moment of truth arrives.
          (renaming)   The truth is the test.

Sentence 4   My mind draws a blank.
          I get a headache trying to remember what I've learned.
          My stomach becomes upset.
          My back starts to hurt.
          I am so tense that my muscles contract.

Sentence 5   I usually manage to run out of time.
          (-ing)   I change my answers.
          My stomach intensifies so much that I feel like I'm going to vomit.
          My stomach is upset.
          The vomiting is all over the place.

Sentence 6   I find tests so difficult.
          Maybe I will be fiendishly clever.
          I will vomit before my next test starts.
          The test is dreaded.
          I won't have to take it.

_____

_____

_____

_____

_____

_____

_____

_____

_____

_____

_____

_____

_____

_____

Sentence 1　　The most unpleasant experience was having surgery.
　　(that)　　I have had the experience.

Sentence 2　　I awoke to sounds.
　　　　　　　　The sounds were muffled.
　　　　　　　　They were from the P.A. system.
　　　　　　　　I awoke to objects rolling quickly past my room.

Sentence 3　　Soon an oaf of a woman barged in.
　　　　　　　　The oaf was fat.
　　　　　　　　The oaf was king-sized.

Sentence 4   In a voice she said, "Greg, it is time for your sedation."
The voice was semi-squeaky.
The voice was monotone.

Sentence 5   That very moment I knew what was in store for me.
I had been through too much surgery to think otherwise.

Sentence 6   I replied, "Sure, why not?"
I held my breath.

Sentence 7   I turned blue in the cheeks.
I literally turned blue.

Sentence 8   I felt the sedative's effect.
I felt it in less than five minutes.

Sentence 9   I felt listless.
I began to wiggle.
I began to shake.
(-ing)   I <u>tried</u> to keep myself active.
The blimp-nurse said, "Do not struggle. It'll only cause you to vomit after your surgery."

Sentence 10   Soon afterwards, I took my last fleeting glimpse of freedom.
(-ing)   I <u>looked</u> out toward the lovely Florida sunrise.
Two men hauled my body.
The men were tall.
The men were hairy.
(-ed)   They were dressed in hospital blue.
They hauled it carefully.
It was half-dead.
It was hauled onto the stretcher.

Sentence 11   All I could do was stare at the ceiling.
The ceiling was moving.
We rolled on down towards the operating room.

Sentence 12   I heard babies wailing.
I heard old people mumbling.
They were mumbling without any dentures.

Sentence 13

(-ing)

There I was.
I knew it.
I lay on the operating table.
I lay uncomfortably on the table.
The table was cold.
The table was sinister.

Sentence 14

(-ing)
(-ing)

Then I felt hands.
The hands were cold and clammy.
They stuck me with an i.v. needle in the wrong arm.
They shot me up with total blank-out sedatives.
I felt no pain.
My heart was racing the Indy 500 without the rest of me.

Sentence 15

I heard the doctors say, "Nighty-night."
Everything—sight, sounds—everything faded out.
It faded like a pair of Levis.
The Levis were in a washing machine for four hours.

Sentence 16

(that)

You would think that with all of the surgery I've been through, I should have been able to bravely face the ordeal.
I just recalled the ordeal.
The ordeal was monstrous.
The ordeal was terrifying.

Sentence 17

In all modesty, I can only say I am not about to go under the knife again.
I am too chicken.

_____

_____

_____

_____

_____

WRITING A PARAGRAPH

Here is what one student did with the general topic "A Self-Discovery" (or "Something I Learned About Myself"). As you read through the paragraph, notice the underlined descriptive clauses and the specific details.

A Self-Discovery

Finding out that I have the intelligence to learn is one very recent discovery that I've made about myself. Many people have always been aware that they are bright, but I've always felt I was a little on the dense side. What a surprise I had when, after extensive testing, I was told that I was a very bright lady with a higher than average intelligence! I felt they had to be wrong; after all wasn't it I who could never pass those history exams and only got average grades in each of my other subjects in high school, and wasn't it I who believed I couldn't learn and had decided it wasn't worth the effort? Now, thanks to some teachers, who continue to give me support, I'm learning that I can retain what I hear and read, applying it where it's needed. I'm gaining confidence in myself each day. It is a very pleasant and challenging feeling to find that I have the ability to learn.

Writing Assignment

Do as many freewritings as necessary to produce enough material for your paragraph on the topic "A Self-Discovery" (or "Something I Learned About Myself"). As you write your paragraph, try to work in a couple of examples of the two kinds of clauses practiced in this lesson and enough specific details so that your reader does not have to guess at your intended meaning.

Alternate topics:

1. "If I Could Choose to Live in the Past, Present, or Future"
2. "How My Family Feels About My Attending College"

3. "How My Family's Values Differ from My Own"
4. "A Meaningful Gift I Gave (or Received)"
5. "An Animal I Would Choose to Be"

IMPROVING A PARAGRAPH: ELIMINATING UNRELATED INFORMATION

Now carefully read through your paragraph and draw a line through any sentence that is not directly related to the opinion or reaction of your topic sentence. Any other information—no matter how interesting—will distract the reader from the one main idea you are communicating. *Remember, the purpose of a paragraph is to explain your opinion or reaction, not merely to discuss the topic.*

As you did with your paragraph in the previous writing assignment, you might get a second opinion by slowly reading your paper aloud to a partner who can help you determine what sentences, if any, need to be eliminated.

Lesson Six

Substituting Phrases and Clauses in the Whole Sentence

-ing SUBSTITUTE PHRASES (Verbal Noun Phrases)

In the following pair of sentences, the first sentence is changed somewhat and substituted for the word IT in the second sentence to form the rewritten sentence. You should not have too much trouble with this type of sentence because you are probably very familiar with it in your own speech.

(-*ing*) ~~I~~ <u>participate</u> in sports
IT helps me to relieve tension.

is rewritten as

<u>Participating in sports</u> helps me to relieve tension.

In the first sentence of the pair of sentences above, the first word is eliminated, and the underlined word is changed to its -*ing* form. The resulting phrase is substituted for the word IT.
Here is another example.

(-*ing*) ~~Some people~~ <u>kiss</u> on the first date.
IT is no longer considered inappropriate behavior.

is rewritten as

<u>Kissing on the first date</u> is no longer considered inappropriate behavior.

158

Practice in Combining

Combine the following sentences according to the examples above, using *-ing* SUBSTITUTE PHRASES for the word IT.

1. Children <u>play</u> with other children.
IT teaches self-discipline and communication.

_____

_____

2. I <u>watched</u> my father die.
IT changed my attitude about him.

_____

_____

3. I <u>said</u> the three words "I love you."
IT was hard for me.

_____

_____

4. I <u>understood</u> one problem.
IT did not insure my understanding the others.

_____

_____

5. I <u>soul-searched</u> and <u>faced</u> up to reality.
IT forced me to realize that I had been looking to someone else for answers that only I was capable of supplying.

_____

_____

6. I <u>heard</u> the sentence "the grass needs to be cut."
I͞T used to make me sweat before I even started that chore.

_____

_____

7. I <u>smoked</u> in the bathrooms, <u>skipped</u> classes, and <u>fought</u> with
    other girls about guys.
I͞T kept my life in turmoil.

_____

_____

8. I <u>drove</u> recklessly and <u>failed</u> to observe the caution light.
I <u>had</u> to appear in municipal court last spring for IT.

_____

_____

9. I <u>lay</u> in the sun with my eyes closed.
I <u>listened</u> to the loud roar of the waves at Myrtle Beach.
I͞T and I͞T put me in a strange mood by leading me into
    thoughts that I usually don't have.

_____

_____

_____

10. Someone <u>cuts</u> classes.
Someone <u>asks</u> for trouble.
I͞T is I͞T.

_____

_____

Practice in Composing

Now try writing ten sentences of your own that include substitute *-ing* phrases.

1. _____

_____

2. _____

_____

3. _____

_____

4. _____

_____

5. _____

_____

6. _____

_____

7. _____

_____

8. _____

_____

9. _____

_____

10. _____

_____

THAT SUBSTITUTE CLAUSES (Noun Clauses)

In the following pair of sentences, the entire first sentence is substituted for the word IT in the second sentence. The SUBSTITUTE CLAUSE (also called a *noun clause*) is always preceded by the connecting word *that*.

Man does not have the right to take another man's life.
I feel IT.

is rewritten as

I feel (that) man does not have the right to take another man's life.

Practice in Combining

Combine the following sentences according to the example above.

1. I will amount to something.
My mother believes IT.

_____

_____

2. I am not the mealy-mouthed, do-nothing person I thought I was.
I have proven IT.

_____

_____

3. They would never be able to sleep a wink all night long because they were so excited.
They both said IT.

_____

_____

_____

4. Old people should be able to make their own decisions about
   when they want to die.
   I think IT.

   _____

   _____

   _____

5. I was finished with my college education.
   I wish IT.

   _____

   _____

6. You have lied before.
   Because you have lied to me this time leads me to believe IT.

   _____

   _____

   _____

7. All of the students had made remarkable progress.
   At the end of the term the teacher announced IT.

   _____

   _____

   _____

8. Fine cars, a large bank account, or beautiful homes in themselves cannot bring happiness.
   I think IT.

   _____

   _____

9. A whole new outlook on life opened up to him.
   With hard work he reached his goal and found IT.

   _____

   _____

   _____

10. When traveling on the local transit system, I have noticed IT.
    People's behavior on the bus shows IT.
    They do not want their personal boundaries violated.

    _____

    _____

    _____

Practice in Composing

Now try writing ten sentences of your own that include ten *that* substitute clauses.

1. _____

   _____

2. _____

   _____

3. _____

_____

4. _____

_____

5. _____

_____

6. _____

_____

7. _____

_____

8. _____

_____

9. _____

_____

10. _____

_____

In the example below, the entire first sentence is once again substituted for the word IT in the second sentence. The substitute clause is always preceded by the word *that*.

You do not trust me.
IT is too bad.

is rewritten as

(That) you do not trust me is too bad.

Practice in Combining

Combine the following pairs of sentences according to the example above.

1. I couldn't see anything but a flashing red light.
   IT terrified me.

   _____

   _____

2. Everyone should have a choice about his life.
   IT is a belief of mine.

   _____

   _____

3. They really don't want to get involved and are afraid to do anything.
   IT puzzles me.

   _____

   _____

4. People are so quick to criticize others.
   IT makes me angry.

   _____

   _____

5. You like what I have written.
   IT makes me proud.

   _____

   _____

Practice in Composing

Write five sentences like the ones you have just completed.

1. _____

   _____

2. _____

   _____

3. _____

   _____

4. _____

   _____

5. _____

   _____

HOW, WHAT, WHEN, WHERE, AND WHY SUBSTITUTE CLAUSES (Noun Clauses)

There is another type of SUBSTITUTE CLAUSE that functions in the same manner as the "that" substitute clause. This clause, which is used in the place of the word IT in the second sentence, is introduced by the words *how, what, when, where,* and *why.*

Your choice of which of the five words to use will be determined by the underlined word or words in the first sentence of the pair. When you place the substitute clause in the second sentence, eliminate the underlined word(s) and place the introductory word at the beginning of the clause.

If the underlined word is *somehow,* use the word *how* to introduce the substitute clause.

Others see you <u>somehow</u>.
IT shapes your view of yourself.

is rewritten as

(How) others see you shapes your view of yourself.

If the underlined word is *something*, use *what* to introduce the substitute clause.

You do something with your life.
IT is up to you.

is rewritten as

(What) you do with your life is up to you.

If the underlined word is *sometime*, use *when* to introduce the substitute clause.

You arrive sometime.
I will know IT.

is rewritten as

I will known (when) you arrive.

If the underlined word is *somewhere*, use *where* to introduce the substitute clause.

You live somewhere.

IT is not important.

is rewritten as

(Where) you live is not important.

If the underlined words are *for some reason*, use *why* to introduce the substitute clause.

I don't understand IT.
Some people can't express their feelings for some reason.

is rewritten as

I don't understand (why) some people can't express their feelings.

Practice in Combining

Using the examples and instructions as your guide, combine the following ten sentences.

1. You eat <u>something</u>.
IT determines your health.

_____

_____

2. You say <u>something</u>.
I agree with IT.

_____

_____

3. You feel <u>something</u> about me.
<u>Something</u> is most important to me.
<u>IT is IT</u>.

_____

_____

4. I like <u>something</u> most about myself.
My persistence is IT.

_____

_____

5. You dress for an interview <u>somehow</u>.
IT is important.

_____

_____

6. Some professors do not treat college students as adults capable of
making their own choices <u>for some reason</u>.
IT is beyond me.

_____

_____

_____

7. We are <u>somewhere</u>.
We are headed <u>somewhere</u> as individuals.
IT and IT are <u>the subjects</u> of study in my Human Relations
course.

_____

_____

8. They bother to print such stuff <u>for some reason</u>.
Every time I pick up the daily newspaper, I wonder IT.

_____

_____

_____

9. An individual believes <u>something</u>.
He places his values <u>somewhere</u>.
He relates to others <u>somehow</u>.
IT, IT, and IT are <u>shaped</u> by a variety of influences early in life.

_____

_____

_____

10. I have had enough <u>sometime.</u>
    I know IT.

_____

_____

Practice in Composing   Write five sentences like the ones you have just completed, using a different introductory word in each sentence.

1. _____

_____

2. _____

_____

3. _____

_____

4. _____

_____

5. _____

_____

SENTENCE COMBINING REVIEW

Read aloud as you combine the sentences below and reassemble the student paragraph. Rely on your hearing to tell you whether or not your finished sentences are good ones.

Sentence 1   The first date was an experience of my life.
    The date was mine.
    The experience was the most embarrassing.

Sentence 2

I was the only girl.
The girl was from a family of four children.

Sentence 3

My family put that poor guy through <u>something</u>.
IT was traumatic.

Sentence 4

He came through the front door.
Everyone was there to greet him.

Sentence 5

This would have made anyone uncomfortable.
Then they started with fifty questions.

(-ing)   They <u>came</u> at him from all corners.
The corners were of the room.
They came at him with everything from who and what to where and
    how.

Sentence 6

Before he was even settled, I heard my father ask him IT, IT, IT, and
    IT.
He came from <u>somewhere</u>.
His father worked <u>somewhere</u>.
He happened to meet me <u>somehow</u>.
He wanted to do <u>something</u> for a lifetime.

Sentence 7

The guy was shy anyway.
The guy had a hard enough time just talking to me.
He must have felt uneasy.
I knew IT.

Sentence 8

Then I became frantic about the date.
I became nervous about the date.

Sentence 9

I would have to go through such torture.
I never expected IT.

Sentence 10

We escaped for the evening.
My poor date seemed totally defeated.
My date spent most of the "interview" staring at his shoes.
The shoes were new.
The shoes were for jogging.

(-ing)   He <u>muttered</u> words to himself.
The words sounded vaguely like "dummy" and "stupid."

Sentence 11   Those were the only words he spoke for the next forty-five minutes.
We drove to the movie.

(-ing)   Each of us <u>tried</u> desperately to think of something to say.

_____

_____

_____

_____

_____

_____

_____

_____

_____

_____

_____

_____

_____

_____

_____

_____

_____

_____

_____

_____

_____

_____

_____

_____

Sentence 1

(-ing)   I <u>watched</u> my father die.
IT changed my hatred to empathy.
My hatred was for him.

Sentence 2

My father was an alcoholic.
I can remember.

(-ing)   He <u>made</u> everyone in our house miserable.
He seemed bent on IT.

Sentence 3

(-ing)   I watched in fear and anger.
I can remember IT.
He turned his venom on my brothers.
He turned it on my mom.
He turned it on me.
He turned it over and over through the years.

Sentence 4   God, how I grew to hate him.

Sentence 5   Then on Father's Day, I took a card over to him.
Out of politeness, I took the card.
He was reaching seventy years of age.

Sentence 6   I walked into the living room.
I saw him slumping in the chair.
He was slumping with his head bent forward, saliva drooling down in front of him onto his shirt.

Sentence 7   I saw the abscessed hole in his leg.
The leg was resting on the stool.
I saw a huge black mark covering the top of his arm.

Sentence 8   I discovered IT.
This was where he had fallen.

(-ing)   He tried to walk back from the bar two nights before.

Sentence 9   I shook him slightly.
I woke him.
He looked up at me.
He looked up at me with an attempt to smile.
I was there for some reason.
I explained IT.

Sentence 10   I sat down on the arm of the chair.
I started to read the card.
He babbled happily about how nice it was of me to do this for him.
He reached to hold my hand.

Sentence 11

(-ing)   I read.

Tears were rolling down my cheeks.

I realized IT.

Sentence 12   I tried to finish reading.

I choked when I saw a glimpse of the man he really was inside.

I felt the pain he must have felt.

He had given up on life and was dying.

I realized IT.

Sentence 13   My hatred disappeared.

My fear disappeared.

My anger disappeared.

I looked at him as a human being.

I looked for the first time.

He was a human being with pain and problems.

I looked at him not as the person I thought he should be.

_____

_____

_____

_____

_____

_____

_____

_____

_____

_____

FINAL SENTENCE COMBINING REVIEW

If any of the operations called for here presents difficulties, rely on your own competence with language to determine just how you will work through the sentences.

Reassemble this student paragraph.

Sentence 1

The way to a man's heart is through his stomach.
I have been told IT.
I don't have a chance.
I would venture to say IT.

Sentence 2

(-ing)

I have bragged about being such a good cook.
I was put to the test by David.
I was finally put to the test.
David is a good friend of mine.

Sentence 3

One evening he invited me over.
He invited me over for a steak.
I was doing the cooking.
He neglected to tell me IT.

Sentence 4

I was looking forward to an evening.
The evening was relaxed.
I was looking forward to being waited on for a change.

Sentence 5

I arrived.
I was going to be "chief cook and bottle washer."
Much to my amazement, I discovered IT.

Sentence 6

I would have to do some work after all.
At first, I was dismayed to find IT.

Sentence 7   Then panic struck me.
                        I was on stage.
                        I had to put on a good show.
                        I realized IT.

Sentence 8   I observed the situation.
                        Broiling steaks was not too difficult.
                        I decided IT.

Sentence 9   I had overestimated my cooking abilities.
                        I was about to find out IT.

Sentence 10   I started cooking dinner.
       (-ing)   I felt very optimistic.

Sentence 11   I baked some potatoes.
                        I made a salad.
                        I put the steaks in the broiler.

Sentence 12   We drank some wine.
                        We talked for a while.

Sentence 13   Then I decided to check.
                        The checking was on the steaks.

Sentence 14   I went into the kitchen.
                        I opened the door.
                        The door was to the oven.
                        I pulled out the rack.
                        The rack was to the broiler.

Sentence 15   The steaks looked delicious.
                        I saw IT.

Sentence 16   I took a knife out of the kitchen drawer.
                        I cut.
                        The cutting was into one of the steaks.

Sentence 17   Suddenly, the floor was covered with the oven rack.
The floor was covered with the broiler pan.
The floor was covered with grease.
The floor was covered with steaks.
The steaks were mine.
The steaks were delicious.

Sentence 18   I screamed.
David ran.
His running was into the kitchen.
David stared.
His staring was with astonishment.
His staring was at our dinner lying on the floor.
The floor was of the kitchen.

Sentence 19   I was so crushed.
I was embarrassed.
I could have cried.

Sentence 20   The steaks were beyond repair.
My feelings were beyond repair.

Sentence 21   David tried desperately not to laugh.
David is a gentleman.
He was unsuccessful.

Sentence 22   He cleaned up the mess.
He took me out to dinner.
He took me out to dinner as a consolation.

Sentence 23   Needless to say, David prepared the next meal.
The meal was home cooked.

_____

_____

_____

_____

Writing Assignment

For this final writing assignment of Part One, you are being asked to write a paragraph on the general subject "A Time I Had to Cope with a Challenge." Since the reaction is given to you, you will need to free-write to discover your topic and, more importantly, to develop the supporting information for your reaction.

Alternate topics:

1. "A Time I Felt Successful"
2. "A Time I Felt Like a Failure"
3. "A Future Goal I Have"

WRITING A PARAGRAPH

The following paragraph shows what one student writer did with the subject "A Time I Had to Cope With a Challenge." As you read through the paragraph, notice the use of substitute phrases and clauses, which are underlined.

<u>Taking my English final</u> was a challenge I eventually dealt with. The class began with Mrs. Vaughn, our basic writing teacher, reading the choices of subjects for a paragraph. I drew a blank on every one of them. I had always been used to being able to take an assignment home, which meant <u>that I could spend the evening or whatever amount of time was necessary</u> to finish it properly. Now here I was, my whole grade depending on this one paragraph. All the efforts that I've put forth the last five weeks could be washed down the drain because of this one assignment. I had only ninety minutes to transform my thoughts about a particular subject into a well-structured, detailed paragraph. The challenge was immense. A stillness came over the room; all I could hear was the ticking of the clock, which seemed to become magnified as the period went on, banging click, click, click loudly inside my head. Everyone in the room except me seemed to be

having no problem, their pens moving quickly. Ten minutes had passed, and I hadn't a word on my paper. Then twelve, fifteen, and twenty minutes, still not a word. My mind continued to draw a blank. I wondered if there was any way I could overcome such a challenge. With what sounded like a loud bang, the hour hand clicked into the half-hour position. Since there was only an hour left, I knew that if I didn't begin writing at that moment, I would never finish. I proceeded blocking all sounds and thoughts out of my mind, concentrating only on the subject I was going to write about. At first I still drew a blank, but I kept searching deeper and deeper within myself until a thought arose. I quickly wrote that thought down before it was forgotten, and continued this process until two complete pages were filled. When I was finished, I still had ten minutes left to proofread and make revisions. Taking my English final was difficult, but being pressured to the point where I had no choice, I searched deep within myself and overcame the challenge. When I handed in my paper that day, I was confident in the quality of my work.

◆◆◆◆◆◆◆◆◆◆◆◆◆   **Writing Assignment**

Do as many freewritings as necessary to produce your paragraph on "A Time I Had to Cope with a Challenge."

◆◆◆◆◆◆◆◆◆◆◆◆◆

IMPROVING A PARAGRAPH: MAKING THE ORDER CLEAR FOR YOUR READER

There is only one more step you need to consider for improving a paragraph, and that is to make sure that all of your supporting sentences are put in an order that makes sense and is easy for your reader to follow.

Sometimes in freewriting or early drafts, a writer may record events as they occur to him or her rather than in the order in which they actually happened or in an order that appears natural for a reader. The following segment from a student rough draft about a time when the writer dived from a railroad trestle into the water below illustrates the confusion that is created for a reader when the natural sequence is broken.

I leaped from the bridge into space. As I flew down toward the stream in a blurry passing, I realized that I could not catch my breath. Another surprise greeted my senses when I discovered my stomach was somewhere back up on the bridge. I was also horribly surprised at how long it took me to fall and finally strike the surface of the water. I screamed my heart out all the way down. During those long, terrible seconds of my flight, I thought that it was surely the end for me. Before I knew what had happened, I was floating downstream on the current and looking back at the bridge.

In making his final copy, the student recognized the need to reorder the events as they happened so that the reader could more easily follow him. He rearranged the sentences and placed the material about his "flight" from the trestle before the information about striking the water.

I leaped from the bridge into space. As I flew down toward the stream in a blurry passing, I realized that I could not catch my breath. Another surprise greeted my senses when I discovered my stomach was somewhere back up on the bridge. During those long, terrible seconds of my flight, I thought it was surely the end for me. I screamed my heart out all the way down. I was also horribly surprised at how long it took me to fall and finally strike the surface of the water. Before I knew what happened, I was floating downstream on the current and looking back at the bridge.

The following segment from a student draft about an automobile accident also shows the confusion that is created for a reader when the natural sequence is broken. Can you see why?

As I came closer, I saw he was lying flat on his stomach but still breathing. I could tell he was an older man with gray hair. His hands came close to covering his head on the side facing down on the concrete. He began to moan, and I was overwhelmed by the smell of alcohol from his body. I realized that he had to have been drinking for days, for the smell was terrible. As he started out across the street, he was struck by a moving car, and I saw his body go limp like a scarecrow's tumbling through the air. I thought for sure he'd be dead.

Once you have completed your paragraph on "A Time I Had to Cope with a Challenge," check to make sure that all of your supporting sentences are in an order that makes sense and is easy for your reader to follow. One useful approach for doing this is to cover your paragraph with another piece of paper, then uncover one sentence at a time, from top to bottom, beginning with the topic sentence.

This strategy will allow you to determine whether or not your sentences are arranged in a sequence that is natural and makes sense to you and your reader. In other words, you might ask yourself, "Do my supporting statements follow a natural sequence, like one, two, three? Does every sentence follow naturally from the sentence before?"

It might be a good idea to do this with a partner.

Lesson Seven

Writing Beyond the Paragraph

Sometimes the writing you produce will be longer because a full discussion of the reasons for your opinion or reaction requires more than one paragraph. The way you produce this type of writing, however, will be much the same as it has been all along. You will still have a central idea that you support with reasons, details, and examples, but you will have more space to develop your topic into a more satisfying piece of writing.

Study the following multi-paragraph student paper. Notice that it contains a fuller discussion of the reasons for the writer's opinion or reaction than a single paragraph would allow.

REACTION   TOPIC

THESIS
STATEMENT:
First topic sentence
(first reason)

Supporting details
and examples

I disliked my first factory job immensely.
For one thing, it was extremely dirty work. Dry, brown dust floated constantly through the factory, and breathing the copper metal dust caused many problems. My lungs felt like burning blisters that needed a soothing ointment to heal them, and my nose bled constantly, for the dust was compounded from copper and acid. Once the dust began to settle on my skin and clothes, I turned into a lovely shade of avocado green from the acidity.

Second topic sentence (second reason)

Supporting details and examples

> <u>Another reason this job was so unpleasant was the intense heat that radiated from the furnaces</u>. I had to learn to bake my finished product, a clutch plate, onto steel that was inserted into furnaces of intense heat so the metal powder would melt onto the steel. While working in this area, it was not unusual for me to lose ten or fifteen pounds in a nine-hour shift, for the heat was so intense that it felt the way the Bible describes Hell, HOT. Working in the furnace area did have one good point. I could bring frozen dinners and prepare them on the furnaces for my lunch, which was more appetizing than warm peanut butter sandwiches.

Third topic sentence (third reason)

Supporting details and examples

> <u>Not only was the job hot, but it was monotonous as well</u>, for there was never any change in duties assigned to me. The hours I worked seemed slow and boring, and I felt a strong lack of motivation. Producing 3,000 clutch plates a day, I began counting them in my sleep after the first month of work. I hated anything that resembled a clutch plate; consequently, I knew the job at the copper metal power plant was not my line of work.

THE THESIS STATEMENT

The first sentence in this multi-paragraph paper, "I disliked my first factory job immensely," is similar to a topic sentence because it has a topic and an opinion about or reaction to the topic. This sentence stating the central idea in a multi-paragraph writing is called a *thesis statement*. In other words, the thesis statement is to the entire multi-paragraph paper what the topic sentence is to the paragraph.

Supporting the Thesis Statement

As you can see in the student example, the thesis statement of a multi-paragraph paper is supported by individual paragraphs, each of which has a topic sentence of its own. These topic sentences directly support the thesis statement because they are the reasons for the opinion or reaction. Further, each topic sentence, or reason, is itself supported by details and examples to prove that it is true. Note in the previous example that the first topic sentence and its supporting details are placed immediately after the thesis statement. The remainder of the topic sentences and supporting details form paragraphs of their own.

Here is another student example on a different topic.

TOPIC

THESIS
STATEMENT: A summer spent living in the country when I was

                                                        REACTION

                eighteen years old was one of the most satisfying
First topic sentence   times of my life. I fell in love with the beauty and
(first reason)   tranquility of nature. I lived on a small, fifteen-
                       acre farm in Copley, Ohio. At the time I was as wild
Supporting details   as any kid just out of high school. However, I loved
and examples   the fresh, pure smell of the country air. Out there
                       in God's paradise I got a special feeling, a form of
                       energy that sometimes overwhelmed me. The land was
                       still unchanged, not mutilated and destroyed by
                       what man calls progress. I have great respect for
                       nature and its wonders; therefore, I altered the
                       landscape as little as possible. However, I still
                       worked that small piece of country just like the
                       larger farms, except on a smaller scale.

Second topic   The hard physical labor of the outdoors was also
sentence (second   very satisfying to me. With the help of my close
reason)   friend Rocky, I raised different kinds of animals
                       and grew a wide variety of garden-fresh vegetables.
                       We raised chickens, pigs, rabbits, and also we kept
                       red worms, for they were easy to breed and there was
Supporting details   no expense of feeding them. Between the animals and
and examaples   the garden, there was always work to be done. The
                       animals had to be fed twice a day, once early in the
                       morning and again before the sun went down. The
                       garden, which was close to two acres in size, had to
                       be weeded every other day to keep it under control.
                       The worms were easiest of all to take care of, for
                       all that had to be done was to spread a thin layer of
                       shredded organic material over their beds, and the
                       wiggling little devils would take care of the rest.

Third topic
sentence (third
reason)

Supporting details
and examples

> Then after an exhausting day's work, I looked
forward to relaxing with friends. Dinner time was
the part of the day when everyone got together and,
as Rocky put it, ''Got all our talk out.'' My
girlfriend Pam and Rocky's wife Mary would make us a
fine meal, and we needed it, for our bodies were
exhausted and hungry after a hard day's work. All of
us would sit down and start telling each other what
exciting or disappointing events happened to us.
One of us would pop off with a few corny jokes and
crack everyone up, which helped us unwind. When we
all were done eating, we would grab a couple of
beers out of the refrigerator and go outside. Our
favorite place to sit and rap was under a huge oak
tree, where I had placed a long picnic table. This
would go on until around ten o'clock or a little
after; then everyone would turn in and get ready for
the next day. That was the way things went, with
very few exceptions. Though this may seem to some
like a boring way to live, I felt at peace with
myself and happier than at any time in the city.
I've lived in the ''fast lane'' before, and compared
to life in the country, the city doesn't stand a
chance.

Writing Assignment

In this writing assignment you are being asked to produce your own multi-paragraph paper. The following might suggest some general topics, which you will develop through the process of freewriting for ideas, writing, and rewriting:

1. One of your favorite earlier paragraphs that you would like to expand into a fuller paper, or one of the suggested alternate topics from Part One

2. One of the many topics suggested by the readings in Part Three

3. One of the following topics:
   "The Teacher I Liked the Least"
   "The Teacher I Liked the Most"
   "My Experience With English Classes"

"Something Important I Have Learned"

"An Experience That Contributed to My Self-Image"

"A Significant Experience That Changed the Way I Felt or Thought"

Once you have decided on a general topic to write on, begin your own multi-paragraph paper.

1. Freewrite as much as you need to discover the raw material for your first draft. This entails, as you will recall, finding a worthwhile topic and your opinion about or reaction to that topic. Once you have formulated what for the time being may be an approximate thesis statement, you may need to do more freewriting to arrive at the reasons for your reaction.

2. One way to arrive at your topic sentences or reasons is to question your thesis statement. The most useful questions to ask are "why" and "how." Write the answers as they come to you. Your answers may be the topic sentences for your paragraphs. Then check to make sure that these are directly related to your thesis statement. Also remember that you must supply enough reasons to convince your reader that the thesis statement is true.

3. For developing paragraphs for your individual topic sentences, once again, use your freewriting to generate specific details and examples, or question the topic sentence just as you questioned the thesis statement.

4. You might want to use the student multi-paragraph papers to guide you as you assemble the first draft of your paper.

5. When you have finished your draft, put it aside for a while. As you later reread it, you may find that you can improve it by asking yourself the following questions:

Does my paper contain a clear thesis statement?

Do my topic sentences, or reasons, directly support my thesis statement?

Is each topic sentence adequately supported?

Can my sentences be improved by applying what I've learned from sentence combining? Is the punctuation correct?

Are all of my sentences complete and free of any distracting errors that I've been working on?

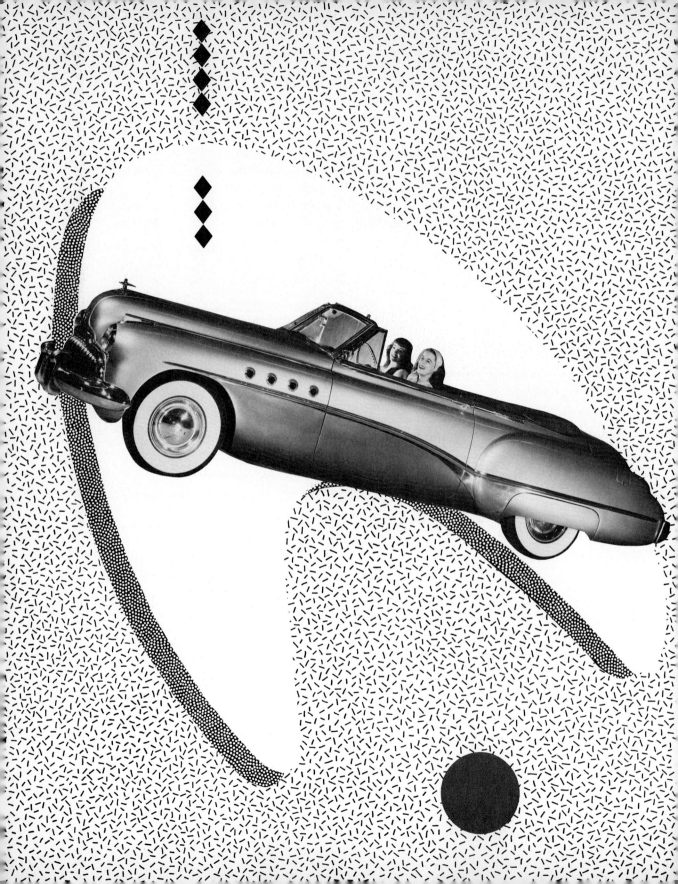

Part Two

Writing About Reading

INTRODUCTION

So much of the pleasure we experience with reading comes from the identification we have with characters, their thoughts or feelings, and particular situations. You know this to be true from your own life, from identifying with characters or situations in movies, television, and sports events, for example.

Here is an excerpt from *Growing Up*, the autobiography of Russell Baker, a well-known newspaper columnist.

From *Growing Up*
Russell Baker

[My mother] was a magician at stretching a dollar. That December, with Christmas approaching, she was out at work and [my sister] Doris was in the kitchen when I barged into [my mother's] bedroom one afternoon in search of a safety pin. Since her bedroom opened onto a community hallway, she kept the door locked, but needing the pin, I took the key from its hiding place, unlocked the door, and stepped in. Standing against the wall was a big, black bicycle with balloon tires. I recognized it instantly. It

---

From *Growing Up* by Russell Baker. Copyright © 1982 by Russell Baker. Reprinted by permission of Congdon & Weed, Inc.

was the same secondhand bike I'd been admiring in a Baltimore Street shop window. I'd even asked about the price. It was horrendous. Something like $15. Somehow my mother had scraped together enough for a down payment and meant to surprise me with the bicycle on Christmas morning.

I was overwhelmed by the discovery that she had squandered such money on me and sickened by the knowledge that, bursting into her room like this, I had robbed her of the pleasure of seeing me astonished and delighted on Christmas day. I hadn't wanted to know her lovely secret; still, stumbling upon it like this made me feel as though I'd struck a blow against her happiness. I backed out, put the key back in its hiding place, and brooded privately.

I resolved that between now and Christmas I must do nothing, absolutely nothing, to reveal the slightest hint of my terrible knowledge. I must avoid the least word, the faintest intonation, the weakest gesture that might reveal my possession of her secret. Nothing must deny her the happiness of seeing me stunned with amazement on Christmas day.

In the privacy of my bedroom I began composing and testing exclamations of delight: "Wow!" "A bike with ballon tires! I don't believe it!" "I'm the luckiest boy alive!" And so on. They all owed a lot to movies in which boys like Mickey Rooney had seen their wildest dreams come true, and I realized that, with my lack of acting talent, all of them were going to sound false at the critical moment when I wanted to cry out my love spontaneously from the heart. Maybe it would be better to say nothing but appear to be shocked into such deep pleasure that speech had escaped me. I wasn't sure, though. I'd seen speechless gratitude in the movies too, and it never really worked until the actors managed to cry a few quiet tears. I doubted I could cry on cue, so I began thinking about other expressions of speechless amazement. In front of a hand-held mirror in my bedroom I tried the whole range of expressions: mouth agape and eyes wide; hands slapped firmly against both cheeks to keep the jaw from falling off; ear-to-ear grin with all teeth fully exposed while hugging the torso with both arms. These and more I practiced for several days without acquiring confidence in any of them. I decided to wait until Christmas morning and see if anything came naturally.

Christmas was the one occasion on which my mother surrendered to unabashed sentimentality. . . . She took girlish delight in keeping her brightly wrapped gifts hidden in closets. . . .

She did not place her gifts under the tree . . . until Doris and I had gone to bed. We were far beyond believing in Santa Claus, but she insisted on preserving the forms of the childhood myth that these were presents from some divine philanthropist. She planned all year for this annual orgy of spending and girded for it by putting small deposits month after month into her Christmas Club account at the bank.

That Christmas morning she roused us early, "to see what Santa Claus brought," she said with just the right tone of irony to indicate we were all old enough to know who Santa Claus was. I came out of my bedroom with my presents for her and Doris, and Doris came with hers. My mother's had been placed under the tree during the night. There were a few small glittering packages, a big doll for Doris, but no bicycle. I must have looked disappointed.

"It looks like Santa Claus didn't do too well by you this year, Buddy," she said, as I opened packages. A shirt. A necktie. I said something halfhearted like, "It's the thought that counts," but what I felt was bitter disappointment. I supposed she'd found the bike intolerably expensive and sent it back.

"Wait a minute!" she cried, snapping her fingers. "There's something in my bedroom I forgot all about."

She beckoned to Doris, the two of them went out, and a moment later came back wheeling between them the big black two-wheeler with balloon tires. I didn't have to fake my delight, after all. The three of us—Doris, my mother, and I—were people bred to repress the emotional expressions of love, but I did something that startled both my mother and me. I threw my arms around her spontaneously and kissed her.

"All right now, don't carry on about it. It's only a bicycle," she said.

Still, I knew that she was as happy as I was to see her so happy.

When asked to write a response to Russell Baker's piece, one student clearly felt, as you can see from the writing that follows, that he had something in common with Russell Baker and took pleasure in the identification.

I found all of my Christmas gifts as Russell Baker did in the part of the book I read called Growing Up. I had fun finding all of my Christmas

gifts a week early, but it was also disappointing
and took all of the fun out of Christmas.

When I was ten years old, I couldn't wait for
Christmas to come. It was the week before, but I
wanted to know what I got. So I went on a Christmas
gift hunt. I waited until everyone in my family had
left the house and began to look. The first place I
started was in the basement. I checked behind the
bar to see if any gifts were back there and there
was. Right in front of me was a Star Wars pinball
machine. I was so excited and overjoyed because my
mom bought a pinball machine for me. I had a smile
on my face from ear to ear. All I wanted to do from
that moment on was play with that pinball machine. I
walked over and touched it to make sure that I
wasn't seeing things. Once I touched it, I couldn't
help but to start playing with it. After I found
this gift, I knew there had to be more. I went
upstairs and checked the living room. There was
nothing hidden in that room. I went upstairs to the
bedroom and began to look. I looked in my room, no
gifts there. I looked in my sister's room and found
my racing track behind her floor model color TV.
This made me even more excited because she had got
me the racing track I wanted for Christmas.

I thought to myself, my mom must really love me
to buy all these expensive gifts. I looked under her
bed and checked her closet to be sure there were no
more gifts in that room. Next I went to my mother's
room. I looked under her bed, nothing there. I
checked her closet and hit the jackpot. On the
floor, in her closet, under her shoe rack were a few
games like Pac Man, Life, and checkers. On the shelf
in her closet were a couple of dress shirts and
pants. In the back of the closet was a little
portable black and white TV. Finding all of these
gifts really made me feel wanted and cared for. My
mother had to spend a lot of money on all these
gifts, so I couldn't let her know that I found them.

The next day I began thinking about what I had
done. I said to myself, ''Boy, I would have been
really surprised on Christmas day, but now since I

know everything I am getting, that day won't be so
exciting.'' On Christmas morning my mother woke us
up bright and early. I didn't feel like getting up
because there were no surprises for me. The next
thing I knew, they all were looking at me, asking me
why I hadn't opened my gifts. So I started opening
them. As I opened each gift, I was acting very
excited, but inside, I just couldn't face the fact
that I had taken the fun out of Christmas. I felt
like the world had come to an end.

Christmas didn't seem so joyful this time even
though I had a lot of good gifts. I found that the
joy of Christmas wasn't playing with your gifts. The
joy was waking up in the moring going down stairs to
open your gifts not knowing what you were going to
get. This was the best part of the day, and I took it
away. The day after Christmas I was glad to have all
of my new toys, but that feeling was still there.

Because we are all different, though, and have had different experiences in life, we relate to a reading differently. A piece of reading may
mean different things to different people. You can see this for yourself in
another student's written response to the same piece by Russell Baker.

Russell Baker's Christmas story, about his
receiving his bike he wanted, brings back many
thoughts of my father and his ability to provide.
Looking back at my childhood, I have nothing but
love for my father. My father was a hell of a man! He
raised eleven children to be adults without any
financial help from anywhere and without much of an
education. He did it with a sixth grade education
and the grace of God, making him the type of man to
believe in taking care of his own. He worked,
taught, and loved us to the best of his ability. I
love him dearly for it. I love him for the knowledge
he gave me from the heart and not the book. He
taught me to have self-pride and to be responsible
for my actions. He also taught me that family is
basically all you have in the world. My father had
many long, hard and frustrating days but was proud

to do it, and I love him for it.

I learned a lot about survival from him. He taught me how to hunt, fish, and clean my catch for a meal. He taught me to always hold on to some money. I think of the many Christmases he made sure we had all we needed and half of what we wanted. By this I mean food, clothing, and a warm home were always there. When there were things we wanted, he would let us pick one or two things, and the rest, such as a few family games, he would have my mom pick out. I cherish the thoughts of those days. I think of the times he made us do without, to teach us about being wasteful. For example, he let us wear torn up shoes a while before he'd buy a new pair. When we were throwing out too much food, he'd put off going to the store and make us eat whatever was in the house. I look back on how he raised us working hard and how he taught us to respect our pay. I hope he rests in peace and realizes the love and respect I have for him. I also thank him.

The point is that even though readers respond differently to the same reading, every reader identifies with *something*. Some may identify with the entire piece; others, however, will relate to particular sentences, paragraphs, or segments.

Reading an excerpt about Christmas from Growing Up by Russell Baker reminded me of Christmas in my family, which has not changed all that much from when I was a child to now, and I get a lot of enjoyment out of carrying on a family tradition. Christmas, in my family, has always been a time of giving more than receiving. During the depression, when my parents couldn't afford to buy presents, they started making them. Their specialty was baked goods; however, they also made furniture, clothing, and even tatting, handmade lace items. Times have gotten steadily better in the fifty plus years since my parents started giving homemade gifts, but I've carried on the tradition. I still give homemade gifts for Christmas. I'm a fine furniture maker, from a simple stool to a dry sink that's really a

bar and just about everything in between. I'm a
terrific tailor, from a child's christening dress
to a man's three-piece suit. You name it, I've made
it. I'm also a dynamite doughnut maker, but I don't
tat, so I make wooden toys instead. I make toy
trains, wood puzzles, pull toys, and even hobby
horses. I get a great deal of enjoyment in both
making and giving the things I do, for they are more
than merely gifts from the shop, the sewing machine,
and the oven. They are gifts from the heart.

As the next student response demonstrates, "identifyng" with something in a reading does not mean a reader has to have had a similar
experience. It can mean just the opposite.

After reading an excerpt about Christmas from
Russell Baker's autobiography, Growing Up, my
thoughts slowly drifted back to childhood memories
of growing up in a family of five children with very
little money for Christmas presents. I remember
asking my mother for a racetrack, and she said, ''I
don't think Santa can afford that.'' This totally
destroyed my illusions of Santa Claus. I started to
wonder how he could afford all the gifts for
children on TV and not have the money to buy mine. I
felt extremely hurt and confused. I was shocked and
very sad when I came to the conclusion my mother was
paying for all these gifts. Coldly turning my
thoughts away from the joys of Christmas, I was soon
filled with greed and distrust. I hated to think
that toys for Christmas gifts had to be paid for. I
guess I was under the impression that Santa could
produce any gift I desired. When I found he couldn't
deliver what everyone was telling me he could, I
knew he wasn't real. That's when I started to
realize the truth about Christmas and the
surprising fact that it all had to be paid for.

All of the student writings that you have just read were produced
through the process that follows, a process very similar to the one you
have been using all along.

WRITING ABOUT READING

1. First read, and as you read, indicate (✔) points of identification or association.
   At this point it might be helpful to freewrite a brief summary of the reading in order to make some additional connections or associations that didn't come to mind as you read.
2. After you have discussed the various associations or points of identification, then write a focused freewriting for a couple of them.
3. After discussing the links between the reading and the associations, develop a sentence that links the reading with one of your associations. This sentence should become, or at least lead to, a topic sentence.
4. Now produce a rough draft, with focus and detail.
5. After rereading and discussing the rough draft, make whatever changes are necessary to improve it, drawing on what you have learned in the Improving a Paragraph sections in Part One.

What follows is one student's response to the Russell Baker article shown below. As you can see, the response begins with the student's checked points of identification or association, then progresses from freewriting to final copy.

From *Growing Up*
Russell Baker

1. I'd been bored by everything associated with English courses. I found English grammar dull and baffling. I hated the assignments to turn out "compositions," and went at them like heavy labor, turning out leaden, lackluster paragraphs that were agonies for teachers to read and for me to write. The classics thrust on me to read seemed as deadening as chloroform.

From *Growing Up* by Russell Baker. Copyright © 1982 by Russell Baker. Reprinted by permission of Congdon & Weed, Inc.

When our class was assigned to Mr. Fleagle for third-year English I anticipated another grim year in that dreariest of subjects. Mr. Fleagle was notorious among City students for dullness and inability to inspire. He was said to be stuffy, dull, and hopelessly out of date. . . .

Late in the year we tackled the informal essay. "The essay, don't you see, is the . . ." My mind went numb. Of all forms of writing, none seemed so boring as the essay. Naturally we would have to write informal essays. Mr. Fleagle distributed a homework sheet offering us a choice of topics. None was quite so simpleminded as "What I Did on My Summer Vacation," but most seemed to be almost as dull. I took the list home and dawdled until the night before the essay was due. Sprawled on the sofa, I finally faced up to the grim task, took the list out of my notebook, and scanned it. The topic on which my eye stopped was "The Art of Eating Spaghetti."

This title produced an extraordinary sequence of mental images. Surging up out of the depths of memory came a vivid recollection of a night in Belleville when all of us were seated around the supper table—Uncle Allen, my mother, Uncle Charlie, Doris, Uncle Hal—and Aunt Pat served spaghetti for supper. Spaghetti was an exotic treat in those days. Neither [my sister] Doris nor I had ever eaten spaghetti, and none of the adults had enough experience to be good at it. All the good humor of Uncle Allen's house reawoke in my mind as I recalled the laughing arguments we had that night about the socially respectable method for moving spaghetti from plate to mouth.

Suddenly I wanted to write about that, about the warmth and good feeling of it, but I wanted to put it down simply for my own joy, not for Mr. Fleagle. It was a moment I wanted to recapture and hold for myself. I wanted to relive the pleasure of an evening at New Street. To write it as I wanted, however, would violate all the rules of formal composition I'd learned in school, and Mr. Fleagle would surely give it a failing grade. Never mind. I would write something else for Mr. Fleagle after I had written this thing for myself.

When I finished it the night was half gone and there was no time left to compose a proper, respectable essay for Mr. Fleagle. There was no choice next morning but to turn in my private reminiscence of Belleville. Two days passed before Mr. Fleagle returned the graded papers, and he returned everyone's but mine.

I was bracing myself for a command to report to Mr. Fleagle immediately after school for discipline when I saw him lift my paper from his desk and rap for the class's attention.

"Now, boys," he said, "I want to read you an essay. This is titled 'The Art of Eating Spaghetti.'"

And he started to read. My words! He was reading *my words* out loud to the entire class. What's more, the entire class was listening. Listening attentively. Then somebody laughed, then the entire class was laughing, and not in contempt and ridicule, but with openhearted enjoyment. Even Mr. Fleagle stopped two or three times to repress a small prim smile.

I did my best to avoid showing pleasure, but what I was feeling was pure ecstasy at this startling demonstration that my words had the power to make people laugh. In the eleventh grade, at the eleventh hour as it were, I had discovered a calling. It was the happiest moment of my entire school career.

Summary Freewriting

Russell's struggle with English classes were constant always putting things off never doing ahead of time or even enjoying it was a prison sentence. Finally he came to a day in the English class instructor Mr. Fleagle who was known for being dull and not very motivating this Mr. Fleagle 11th grade English teacher gave an essay assignment and Russell's mind went totally blank. He waited till the night before it was due so he went through the topics selected for him by Mr. Fleagle and found one that caught his eye The Art of Eating Spaghetti. And all the mishaps, messes and different methods used to eat pasta. This put a sparkle in his eye and made him pick up the pen to write about it but just for himself and write later for his teacher. But by the time he finished it was later with no time to write the second essay so he had to hand this one in. He was expecting death by hanging instead his work was read aloud by Mr. Fleagle and brought lots of laughter which startled young Russell he

couldn't believe it was his essay that made people
laugh from that point he realized what he wanted to
do.

2. *Associations in Freewriting*

On writing for myself I think I understand young
Russell's feeling of writing one paper for himself
and one to turn in especially regarding family
events things that happen that are quite personal
and not easily shared they're private things that
make you happy not so much the food but the people
in Russell's case the food the people describing how
to eat pasta using different methods maybe some of
the messes caused by this pasta and one of the most
important factors is spaghetti was a novelty
meaning not eaten a lot and very few people in his
family knew how to eat it. I would have liked to
have been there with his family slurping spaghetti.
The closeness showed here was for family only not
for Mr. Fleagle.

Another thing I can identify with is turing in
papers and expect to be punished for not doing them
correctly. Mr. Baker believed no matter what he did
it would be terrible so why work? I can relate this
attitude to some subject they are difficult, trying
time consuming and you can't remember all the
factors involved. I've got to pass type of attitude.

◆

English is not my favorite subject when it came
to this subject especially grammar no matter what
you do it's dull like American history but mythology
was a blast that was one of the best courses
offered. It was the only English class offered I
made out on two B's and one C: <u>C</u> Grammar. English
composition I took and one year of it because thats

all I needed in a three year English requirement one
composition, one grammar, one mythology no English
Lit. I'm not a fan of that either I read Robert A.
Heinlein who was very popular at that time. I always
wondered why English couldn't be more like science
fiction what an imagination, descriptions were out
of this world, places were out of this world. I
probably would be a science fiction writer if they
would have offered it instead of grammar. But they
didn't and now I have to write about something
different I can relate to.

◆

Writing about things you know nothing about or
very little leaving you open to criticism and attack
topics selected for you must have facts, conclusion
and in them you have to find facts, opinions.

◆

The truly last thing I like are his comparisons
for instance deadening chloroform. I like using
statements like that and I will try to put more
creativity in my writing it puts the color back in
papers keeps the readers attention and clearly
states his feelings.

3. *Link and Topic Sentence*
A paragraph in Russell Baker's book Growing Up
dealt with writing an essay on personal
experiences. This composition was written for his
own pleasure and not for anyone else's, and this
mirrors my own thoughts that some of my scripts are
only meant to please myself.

4. *Rough Draft*
A paragraph in Russell Baker's book Growing Up
dealt with writing an essay on personal
experiences. This composition was written for his

own pleasure and not for anyone else's, and this mirrors my own thoughts that some of my scripts are only meant to please myself.

Just thinking about the passage when young Russell writes about his family getting together to eat pasta and how he enjoyed the warmth, the closeness and good feelings showed makes me think about the first time I missed all the holidays at home due to the Army, and that next year I would make sure I was home for at least Christmas. I remember the plane ride took forever, but when I saw my father and two older brothers waiting for me my anticipation left and all I felt was happy.

When I got home my brothers and sisters hugged and kissed me as if I had been away for a year, I had missed all of them a great deal too. That same evening we talked, laughed and shared all the events throughout the years and then we all went to Midnight Mass. This same special feeling Russell felt with his family sharing the dinner meal, and its not so much the food but the family sharing their affection for each other. Russell and I feel that same way, that some manuscripts are too private to share, and are only meant for us (Russell and I) to capture that moment of family togetherness.

These private and intimate emotions expressed at family functions were written only to please the writer. I write for myself because it helps me to remember the good occasions in my life and the times I overcame my personal struggles. These are my victories, my moments shared with my family and these will always be written to please myself.

5. *Final Copy*

A paragraph in Russell Baker's book Growing Up, dealt with writing an essay on personal experiences. This composition was written for his own pleasure and not for anyone else, and this mirrors my own thoughts that some of my scripts are only meant to please myself. Just thinking about the

passage when young Russell writes about his family
getting together to eat pasta and how he enjoyed the
warmth, the closeness, and good feelings shared
makes me remember the first Christmas in the Army
that I managed to go home to celebrate with my
family. When I got home, my brothers and sisters
hugged and kissed me as if I had been away for
years. I had missed all of them a great deal. That
same evening we talked, laughed, and shared the past
year's events, and then all ten of us went to
midnight mass. This was the same special feeling
Russell felt with his family sharing the dinner
meal, and it's not so much the food but the family
sharing their affection for each other. These
private and intimate emotions expressed at family
functions were written only to please the writer. I
write for myself because it helps me to remember the
good occasions in my life and the times I overcame
my personal struggles.

These are my victories, my moments shared with my
family, and they will always be written to please
myself. Russell and I feel the same way, that some
of our manuscripts are too private to share and are
only meant for us, to capture that moment of family
togetherness.

The following two student pieces, both final copies, were written in
response to the same Russell Baker article. As can be expected, each
response is individual, personal, and therefore different.

After I read a paragraph in Russell Baker's book,
Growing Up, which dealt with Russell writing an
essay on eating spaghetti, it reminded me of the two
different ways to eat pasta. Eating spaghetti is
truly an art, even for perfected Italians like me
who had to learn the hard way, the correct method of
eating pasta. My old way of eating spaghetti was
with only one utensil, which was a fork. I would
take this fork and proceed to push it towards my
heaping plate of spaghetti. When I got hold of a few
strands, I would lift my fork, and the long stringy

noodles hung there helplessly while the sauce
dripped off. My mouth would start to water, for I
couldn't wait to taste that first bite.

My older cousin, Mike, happened to spot me eating
my spaghetti at one of our family feasts. He
immediately started criticizing and correcting me.
He told me that if I were raised properly, I would
eat pasta with two utensils, a fork and a spoon. He
said that after my fork met with the long noodles, I
should bring my spoon into the picture by holding it
in place, and using it as a base while I wrapped the
spaghetti strands around my fork. Then when I placed
it in my mouth, I wouldn't have anything hanging
out. Every time I eat spaghetti, I think of my
cousin and the lesson he taught me. Eating spaghetti
is truly an art that I have finally perfected.

◆

I can identify with Russell Baker's concern over
his teacher's expectations of him. Many individuals
think that children who come from large public
school systems are illiterate and slow when it comes
to higher education. Therefore, I feel that I'm
being prejudged due to my past education. I feel
that people need to stop stereotyping youths that
graduate from public schools. A few weeks before
starting college, I started believing the statement
about students of public schools. After being in
college for a while, I no longer feel that way, for
in some classes I'm doing better than some private
high graduates. Nevertheless, I still have
butterflies in my stomach when I receive graded
papers. I feel as if my stomach is about to explode.
That same little voice in my head says ''I know I
failed, so I shouldn't look surprised.'' My knees
start shaking when the professor calls my name to
come receive my graded paper. I start praying under
my breath, saying ''God, don't let me receive a
failing letter grade, for I gave it my best.'' I now
know that some students, not just the ones from

public schools, suffer the same anxieties that I
have. Keeping this in mind, I have fewer
butterflies, and my confidence in my ability to
write has increased. I haven't reached complete
confidence, but I feel through helpful and
understanding professors that I am well on my way.

You will find that applying your developing writing skills to the readings that follow in Part Two, "Writing About Reading," is good practice because reading and writing are such closely related skills. By doing one, you build the other. It is also good practice since so often you will be asked in many of your college classes to write about reading.

The readings in this section might be used for discussion only, or maybe as opportunities for freewriting, or for additional practice in paragraph or multi-paragraph writing—in which case, you may choose to use the entire five-stage process provided in this section. Either way, you will be using the same skills you practiced in Part One, the only difference being that in Part One your ideas came from freewriting and here they come from reading or associations made from reading.

A number of readings are included so that you can choose to read the ones that seem most interesting to you. Some were written by basic writers and freshman composition students, others by professionals. For your convenience the readings are arranged according to subject.

Reading and Writing

The four readings in this group deal with personal experiences with reading and writing, some pleasurable, some painful. "Open Admissions," written by—it is interesting to note—a former basic writing student, and "A Remembrance" are both professional pieces. The other two were written by college students, Debbie Twigg's for basic writing and Vinh Le's for freshman composition.

Open Admissions and the Inward "I"

Peter J. Rondinone

The fact is, I didn't learn much in high school. I spent my time on the front steps of the building smoking grass with the dudes from the dean's squad. For kicks we'd grab a freshman, tell him we were undercover cops, handcuff him to a banister, and take away his money. Then we'd go to the back of the building, cop some "downs," and nod away the day behind the steps in the lobby. The classrooms were overcrowded anyhow, and the teachers knew it. They also knew where to find me when they wanted to make weird deals: If I agreed to read a book and do an oral report, they'd pass me. So I did it and graduated with a "general" diploma. I was a New York City public school kid.

I hung out on a Bronx streetcorner with a group of guys who called themselves "The Davidson Boys" and sang songs like "Daddy-lo-lo." Everything we did could be summed up with the word "snap." That's a "snap." She's a "snap." We had a "snap." Friday nights we'd paint ourselves green and run through the streets swinging baseball bats. Or we'd get into a little rape in the park. It was all very perilous. Even though I'd seen a friend stabbed for wearing the wrong colors and another blown away with a shotgun for "messin" with some dude's woman, I was too young

"Open Admissions and the Inward 'I' " by Peter J. Rondinone from *Change Magazine*, Volume 9, Number 5, May 1977, pages 43–47. Copyright © 1977 by Heldref Publications, Inc. Reprinted with permission of the Helen Dwight Reed Educational Foundation. Published by Heldref Publications, 4000 Abemarle St., N.W., Washington, D.C. 20016. Copyright © 1977.

to realize that my life too might be headed toward a violent end.

Then one night I swallowed a dozen Tuminols and downed two quarts of beer at a bar in Manhattan. I passed out in the gutter. I puked and rolled under a parked car. Two girlfriends found me and carried me home. My overprotective brother answered the door. When he saw me—eyes rolling toward the back of my skull like rubber—he pushed me down a flight of stairs. My skull hit the edge of a marble step with a thud. The girls screamed. My parents came to the door and there I was: a high school graduate, a failure, curled in a ball in a pool of blood.

The next day I woke up with dried blood on my face. I had no idea what had happened. My sister told me. I couldn't believe it. Crying, my mother confirmed the story. I had almost died! That scared hell out of me. I knew I had to do something. I didn't know what. But pills and violence didn't promise much of a future.

I went back to a high school counselor for advice. He suggested I go to college.

I wasn't aware of it, but it seems that in May 1969 a group of dissident students from the black and Puerto Rican communities took over the south campus of the City College of New York (CCNY). They demanded that the Board of Higher Education and the City of New York adopt an open-admission policy that would make it possible for anybody to go to CCNY without the existing requirements: SATs and a high school average of 85. This demand was justified on the premise that college had always been for the privileged few and excluded minorities. As it turned out, in the fall of 1970 the City University's 18 campuses admitted massive numbers of students—15,000—with high school averages below 85. By 1972, I was one of them.

On the day I received my letter of acceptance, I waited until dinner to tell my folks. I was proud.

"Check out where I'm going," I said. I passed the letter to my father. He looked at it.

"You jerk!" he said. "You wanna sell ties?" My mother grabbed the letter.

"God," she said. "Why don't you go to work already? Like other people."

"Fuck that," I said. "You should be proud."

At the time, of course, I didn't understand where my parents were coming from. They were immigrants. They believed college was for rich kids, not the ones who dropped downs and sang songs on streetcorners.

My mother had emigrated from Russia after World War II. She came to the United States with a bundle of clothes, her mother and father, a few dollars, and a baby from a failed marriage. Her first job was on an assembly line in a pen factory where she met my father, the production manager.

My father, a second-generation Italian, was brought up on the Lower East Side of Manhattan. He never completed high school. And when he wasn't working in a factory, he peddled Christmas lights door to door or sold frankfurters in Times Square.

My family grew up in the south Bronx. There were six children, and we slept in one room on cots. We ate spaghetti three times a week and were on welfare because for a number of years my father was sick, in and out of the hospital.

Anyhow, I wasn't about to listen to my parents and go to work; for a dude like me, this was a big deal. So I left the dinner table and went to tell my friends about my decision.

The Davidson Boys hung out in a rented storefront. They were sitting around the pool table on milk boxes and broken pinball machines, spare tires and dead batteries. I made my announcement. They stood up and circled me like I was the star of a cockfight. Sucio stepped to the table with a can of beer in one hand and a pool stick in the other.

"Wha' you think you gonna get out of college?" he said.

"I don't know, but I bet it beats this," I said. I shoved one of the pool balls across the table. That was a mistake. The others banged their sticks on the wood floor and chanted, "Oooh-ooh—snap, snap." Sucio put his beer on the table.

"Bullshit!" he yelled. "I wash dishes with college dudes. You're like us—nuttin', man." He pointed the stick at my nose.

Silence.

I couldn't respond. If I let the crowd know I thought their gig was uncool, that I wanted out of the club, they would have taken it personally. And they would have taken me outside and kicked my ass. So I lowered my head. "Aw, hell, gimme a hit of beer," I said, as if it were all a joke. But I left the corner and didn't go back.

I spent that summer alone, reading books like *How to Succeed in College* and *30 Days to a More Powerful Vocabulary*. My vocabulary was limited to a few choice phrases like, "Move over, Rover, and let Petey take over." When my friends did call for me I hid behind the curtains. I knew that if I was going to make it, I'd have to push these guys out of my consciousness as if I were doing the breaststroke in a sea of logs. I had work to do, and people were time consuming. As it happened, all my heavy preparations didn't amount to much.

On the day of the placement exams I went paranoid. Somehow I got the idea that my admission to college was some ugly practical joke that I wasn't prepared for. So I copped some downs and took the test nodding. The words floated on the page like flies on a crock of cream.

That made freshman year difficult. The administration had placed me in all three remedial programs: basic writing, college skills, and math. I was shocked. I had always thought of myself as smart. I was the only one in the neighborhood who read books. So I gave up the pills and pushed aside another log.

The night before the first day of school, my brother walked into my room and threw a briefcase on my desk. "Good luck, Joe College," he said. He smacked me in the back of the head. Surprised, I went to bed early.

I arrived on campus ahead of time with a map in my pocket. I wanted enough time, in case I got lost, to get to my first class. But after wandering around the corridors of one building for what seemed like a long time and hearing the sounds of classes in session, the scrape of chalk and muted discussions, I suddenly wondered if I was in the right place. So I stopped a student and pointed to a dot on my map.

"Look." He pointed to the dot. "Now look." He pointed to an inscription on the front of the building. I was in the right place. "Can't you read?" he said. Then he joined some friends. As he walked off I heard someone say, "What do you expect from open admissions?"

I had no idea that there were a lot of students who resented people like me, who felt I was jeopardizing standards, destroying their institution. I had no idea. I just wanted to go to class.

In Basic Writing I the instructor, Regina Sackmary, chalked her name in bold letters on the blackboard. I sat in the front row and reviewed my *How to Succeed* lessons: Sit in front/don't let eyes wander to cracks on ceilings/take notes on a legal pad/make note of all unfamiliar words and books/listen for key phrases like "remember this," they are a professor's signals. The other students held pens over pads in anticipation. Like me, they didn't know what to expect. We were public school kids from lousy neighborhoods and we knew that some of us didn't have a chance; but we were ready to work hard.

Before class we had rapped about our reasons for going to college. Some said they wanted to be the first in the history of their families to have a college education—they said their parents never went to college because they couldn't afford it, or because their parents' parents were too poor—and they said open admissions and free tuition ($65 per semester) was a chance to be educated so they could return to their neighborhoods to help "the people"; they were the idealists. Some foreigners said they wanted to return to their own countries and start schools. And I said I wanted to escape the boredom and the pain I had known as a kid on the streets. But none of them said they expected a job. Or if they did they were reminded that there were no jobs.

Ms. Sackmary told us that Basic Writing I was part of a three-part program. Part one would instruct us in the fundamentals of composition: sentence structure, grammar, and paragraphing; part two, the outline and essay; and part three, the term paper. She also explained that we weren't in basic writing because there was something wrong with us—we just needed to learn the basics, she said. Somehow I didn't believe her. After class I went to her office. She gave me a quick test. I couldn't write a coherent sentence or construct a paragraph. So we made an agreement: I'd write an essay a day in addition to my regular classwork. Also, I'd do a few term papers. She had this idea that learning to write was like learning to play a musical instrument—it takes practice, everyday practice. . . .

To deal with the heavy workload from all my classes, I needed a study schedule, so I referred to my *How to Succeed* book. I gave myself an hour for lunch and reserved the rest of the time between classes and evenings for homework and research. All this left me very little time for friendships. But I stuck to my schedule and by the middle of that first year I was getting straight A's. Nothing else mattered. Not even my family.

One night my sister pulled me from my desk by the collar. She sat me on the edge of the bed. "Mom and Dad bust their ass to keep you in school. They feed you. Give you a roof. And this is how you pay them back?" She was referring to my habit of locking myself in my room.

"What am I supposed to do?" I said.

"Little things. Like take down the garbage."

"Come on. Mom and Dad need me for that?"

"You know Dad has arthritis. His feet hurt. You want *him* to take it down?" My sister can be melodramatic.

"Let Mom do it," I said. "Or do her feet hurt too?"

"You bastard," she said. "You selfish bastard. The only thing you care about is your books."

She was right. I was selfish. But she couldn't understand that in many ways college had become a substitute for my family because what I needed I couldn't get at home. Nobody's fault. She cried.

When I entered my second year my family began to ask, "What do you want to do?" And I got one of those cards from the registrar that has to be filled out in a week or you're dropped from classes. It asked me to declare my major. I had to make a quick decision. So I checked off BS degree, dentistry, though I didn't enroll in a single science course.

One course I did take that semester was The Writer and the City. The professor, Ross Alexander, asked the class to keep a daily journal. He said it should be as creative as possible and reflect some aspect of city life. So I wrote about different experiences I had with my friends. For example, I wrote "Miracle on 183rd Street" about the night "Raunchy" Rick jumped a guy in the park and took his portable radio. When the guy tried to fight back Rick slapped him in the face with the radio; then, using the batteries that spilled out, he pounded this guy in the head until the blood began to puddle on the ground. Those of us on the sidelines dragged Rick away. Ross attached notes to my papers that said things like: "You really have a great hit of talent and ought to take courses in creative writing and sharpen your craft! Hang on to it all for dear life."

In my junior year I forgot dentistry and registered as a creative writing major. I also joined the college newspaper, *The Campus*. Though I knew nothing about journalism, I was advised that writing news was a good way to learn the business. And as Ross once pointed out to me, "As a writer you will need an audience."

I was given my first assignment. I collected piles of quotes and facts and scattered the mess on a desk. I remember typing the story under deadline pressure with one finger while the editors watched me struggle, probably thinking back to their own first stories. When I finished, they passed the copy around. The editor-in-chief looked at it last and said, "This isn't even English." Yet, they turned it over to a rewrite man and the story appeared with my by-line. Seeing my name in print was like seeing it in lights—flashbulbs popped in my head and I walked into the school cafeteria that day expecting to be recognized by everyone. My mother informed the relatives: "My son is a writer!"

Six months later I quit *The Campus.* A course in New Journalism had made me realize that reporting can be creative. For the first time I read writers like Tom Wolfe and Hunter S. Thompson, and my own news stories began to turn into first-person accounts that read like short stories. *The Campus* refused to publish my stuff, so I joined *The Observation Post*, the only paper on campus that printed first-person material. I wanted to get published.

My first *Post* feature article (a first-person news story on a proposed beer hall at CCNY) was published on the front page. The staff was impressed enough to elect me assistant features editor. However, what they didn't know was that the article had been completely rewritten by the features editor. And the features editor had faith in me, so he never told. He did my share of the work and I kept the title. As he put it: "You'll learn by hanging around and watching. You show talent. You might even get published professionally in 25 years!" Another thing they didn't know—I still hadn't passed my basic English proficiency exam.

Get into this: When people hear me tell this story about how I struggled without friends and closed myself off from most things, they often wonder: "Well, what did you do for . . . uh, you know, GIRLS!" And so I tell them: The only girlfriend I had, in my junior year, left me after 10 months. She got tired of watching television every weekend while I occupied myself with reading and studying; and she got tired of my pulling English usage books from under the pillow after we'd made love. But I did pass the English proficiency exam at the end of my junior year.

God, those early days were painful. Professors would tear up my papers the day they were due and tell me to start over again, with a piece of advice—"Try to say what you really mean." Papers I had spent weeks writing. And I knew I lacked the basic college skills; I was a man reporting to work without his tools. So I smiled when I didn't understand. But sometimes it showed and I paid the price: A professor once told me the only reason I'd pass his course was that I had a nice smile. Yes, those were painful days.

And there were nights I was alone with piles of notebooks and textbooks. I wanted to throw the whole mess out the window; I wanted to give up. Nights the sounds of my friends singing on the corner drifted into my room like a fog over a graveyard and I was afraid I would be swept away. And nights I was filled with questions but the answers were like moon shadows on my curtains: I could see them but I could not grasp them.

Yet I had learned a vital lesson from these countless hours of work in isolation: My whole experience from the day I received my letter of acceptance enabled me to understand how in high school my sense of self-importance came from being one of the boys, a member of the pack, while in college the opposite was true. In order to survive, I had to curb my herd instinct.

That Morning Sun

Debbie J. Twigg

As a child I hated to read and write. I couldn't sit still long enough to even know what the first paragraph said. I would simply stare at whatever I was reading as if in a world all of my own, dreaming of the many things I could and wanted to do, which was anything but what I was supposed to be enjoying at the time.

One of the reasons I feel that I couldn't concentrate might have been due to the fact that I was only four years old when I started school, although I did turn five the next month which was in October. I was just simply too young and immature and should have been kept out of school another year or two. I could never finish any school work fast enough; I was more interested in receiving the attention of my peers. I'd parade up and down the narrow aisles, flaunting my long blonde hair that touched the bottom of my dress, moving my petite frame, and flashing my big brown sensuous eyes as though I was a famous movie star or a beautiful princess waiting to capture my knight in shining armor. However, as I grew older, I realized I had to make some goals if I were to survive. Little did I realize it would take a traumatic shock to motivate me into what was to become one of the greatest decisions of my entire life. When I was in high school, I was married and had two daughters. My husband, who was three and a half years my senior was drafted to the Army and was sent to Viet Nam. The day he left, I sat down and cried all day and all night. I mean, rivers overflowed. How was I to ever be both parents, get a

220

job, cook, clean, and wash and change diapers. I know now that those had to flow and as I looked through my red, swollen, blood-shot eyes at the sun as it met the horizon, I realized the sun had dried the rivers up. I couldn't continue school if I couldn't concentrate and study, and that meant reading, and that meant writing, and so I couldn't imagine ever enjoying either. I was feeling depressed and very angry as I walked in to look at my beautiful, tiny, and innocent babies whose lives were now so dependent upon me and yet they lay there sleeping so peacefully, unaware of my pain. I suddenly knew I could never let them down. So I decided I'd start by opening kids story books, and I would read to them, and we'd all learn together. Well, I decided I'd try for one minute the first day; I even set the timer for sixty seconds. Believe me, that was one of the longest sixty seconds I ever waited for. Soon I could read for five, ten, and even thirty minutes, and now for hours. I truly do love to read and regret all the times I could have read of the many things that as a small child I'd only dreamed of. Now when I'm upset or just need to relax, I find a great book and escape with the story. You would never believe all the places I've visited and the things I've done. It's been twenty-two and a half years now since that river dried up with the morning sun, and it's only now that I've been able to come back to school to get an education for myself. That sounds so great—"myself."

Writing: The Pleasure and The Pain

Vinh Le

In a world where only hard work and perseverance can bring fruitful and satisfying results, pleasures usually come at the expense of pains. Like most people, I seek pleasures, but at the same time I can't avoid the pains. Writing gives me one kind of pleasure. But it can also bring frustration, disappointment or discouragement—all of which come from not being able to write well. Some writers might call it "the writing block." I call it pain.

When I am enjoying a dose of writing pleasure, I am in perfect solitude. The music is pouring out of my stereo, but I don't listen to it, I only feel the rhythm that keeps my creative juice flowing and from which the rhythm of my own story forms. Like an artist playing with paints on the canvas to create just the right touch, I am juggling words hoping to make the right connection. And when the magic combination clicks, I feel pleasure. Seeing my words coming alive and integrating into meaningful ideas and vivid pictures is the climactic moment of my writing process. It supplies the energy that keeps me going. What I have on paper is a work of art where words are the medium and where thoughts, ideas, and feelings are not merely communicated but create a beauty that sends shivers through my body. The knowledge that *I create it* gives me a mixed feeling of pride, egoism, and uncompared satisfaction. It's here that illusion plays its tricks. My environment is no longer what it is; rather, it is what I want it to become. Banana peels turn into beautiful flowers; the coffee stain on the table doesn't look ugly anymore, and the untidy room suddenly acquires a "my-mother-just-cleaned-it" look. What's more, at this moment I realize that I am inside *me*. Here is a rediscovery of a knowledge that has been buried by the fast flow of life. I've been too busy thinking about my future, the countless problems that are a part of life, about other people and what they think that I forget "me." In the reflection of my own words, I see what it is like being myself; I feel what I am capable of feeling. In a sense I discover something new which was there all along, and quite often I am pleasantly surprised by what I find. It also dawns on me that I am an artist. This is part of the pleasure because, you see, to have thoughts and feelings is one thing, but to be able to put them on paper and make them into art is something else. There is, in this extraordinary state of pleasure, a perfect joy and a sense of fulfillment that I find nowhere else. The pleasure only increases when the task is finished. Rereading my work, I grin at the funny parts; with a smile I stare into space and thoroughly enjoy myself. It's also hard to go to sleep after I've written well. I keep thinking about it for a long time, and as a result, can't sleep. Sometimes, I jump out of bed to read it one more time, to have one more giggle and to feel the beauty of my own words once more. The pleasure of writing, I think, is worse than coffee, it keeps me awake all night long.

But the pains can keep me up all night, too, especially when I just can't create, and the ugly deadline is dangerously approaching with its equally unfriendly comrade, Time, which keeps ticking on and pulling with it discouraged me. Sometimes the thoughts and feelings are inside my head; I know what I have to say, but I can't put them into words. The sentences, being forced together, come out awkward with no feeling; this depresses me. Or occasionally I write an exceptional piece whose only problem is that I've overdone it; this is no different from putting a mustache on the face of a beautiful woman. Therefore, revising or shaving off the mustache is necessary. Revising, to me, represents another pain. It means the cruel cuttings of my favorite expressions, "choice" phrases whose meanings don't quite fit in the essay. And on many occasions, revising also becomes a futile attempt to liven a dead paper. The result is a chopped up, unconnected piece of work that is worse than it initially was. All this adds up to the frustration and discouragement that are behind my avoiding writing. But that is not all. Sometimes, in the fever of creativity, I write something down without realizing its meaning. It sounds so good at the time, and then after I've turned it in, I begin to see how hypocritical and stupid it is. By then, I can't do a thing but kick myself, which I find very hard to do. One time, I wrote an essay on a personal experience in which there were real and honest feelings, but the essay turned preachy at the end; I almost sounded like a member of the Moral Majority. The principal of my high school, who happened to be a very religious man, liked it so much that he read it during the annual National Honors Society dinner. I never thought I could sound so stupid and hypocritical. Everyone was there, too! I almost wished that the ground would crack and swallow me off the face of the earth, or Superwoman would fly in, dressed in her bikini, to take me away. But since Superwoman didn't come and the earth didn't crack, that night I sat burning in embarrassment, suffering the pain and learning my lesson.

But there are other things in writing that you can't learn to do or not to do. The psychology of writing is a very complicated one. There is no sure way to create. Occasionally with no warning, I am stuck in the middle of an essay. This is like when I am half way through a jigsaw puzzle and just can't find the crucial piece that connects the rest. But once I am going smoothly, the pleasure outweighs the pain. I do like writing overall; yet like most writers, I also avoid doing it. This, at first glance, may not make any sense. But in a world where pleasure never exists in the absence of pain, the idea of liking something and at the same time avoiding it is very logical one.

A Remembrance of Letter Writing

Anthony Prete

At age nine, my daughter Kristin has undertaken the rather formidable task of covering every available piece of paper in the house with words and pictures. If Trish or I reach for a scrap to jot down a phone number, we wind up with a story about kittens, or a sketch of a horse, or a single word embellished with curlicues; should we flip through an apparently blank notebook, we quickly come upon evidence of the secret scribbler.

Careful explanations of "these are *your* papers, and these are *ours*" yield inevitably to childhood enthusiasm. Like the one or two cookies that masquerade on the cupboard shelf as a full box, like the single swallow of milk at the bottom of a gallon jug in the refrigerator, our paper supply is quickly becoming but a shadow of its apparent self. Threats of dire consequences are useless because they are only half-heartedly uttered. Secretly, I take parental pleasure in my daughter's compulsion to write.

I, too, was a childhood scribbler. But only when I left home at fourteen to attend school did my writing take form and direction. The reason was my mother, who insisted that one or two letters a week were hardly an unreasonable expectation. Multiply that number by the years I was away (high school, college, grad

"A Remembrance of Letter Writing" by Anthony Prete from *Media & Methods*, December 1979, Copyright © 1979 by North American Publishing Company. Reprinted with permission from *Media & Methods*.

school, a job in a distant city), add the occasional notes to other relatives and friends, and my letters must have numbered in the thousands. It's hard not to learn *something* about writing with all that practice.

The experience came in handy while Trish and I were dating. Though separated for a half year by ninety miles—she teaching in Chicago, I a student in Milwaukee, neither with money for frequent phone calls or train tickets—our courtship blossomed through the letters we exchanged. After we were married, I'd still write her letters: sometimes from a distant motel where I was away on a trip; sometimes from the kitchen table where I sat alone after we'd had a painful disagreement.

When tragedy struck someone close to me, a letter carried my sympathy and encouragement, talked of happier times and the things that endure beyond death. Later they'd say how much it meant to them, and I was glad I hadn't simply mailed a melancholy card.

Through the years I've written silly letters, serious letters, thoughtful letters, bland letters, poetic letters, chatty letters. When I think about it, this multiplicity of letters was probably the single most formative influence on whatever abilities I may have as a writer.

I don't write personal letters much anymore, not since my mother died two and a half years ago. Life gets hectic, the phone is easier, other people don't write—the reasons are legion. In fact, the last long letter I wrote was to my mother, just before she died. There were so many things I wanted to tell her, little things that just the two of us had shared. A letter seemed the most fitting way. It went on for pages, recalling the joys and sorrows we'd shared, the sacrifices she'd made for me, how as an adult I'd grown to appreciate her unselfishness and to recognize the pain that dogged her life. It was my testimonial to her.

She never got to read that letter. I carried it with me for three weeks, waiting for the proper moment, not wanting to intrude though daily she was slipping farther away. Finally, on a Sunday afternoon in late May, I sat beside her bed in the living room and read to her, through tears, the words I'd written. I held her hand for a squeeze of acknowledgement. There was none. The drug that fended off her pain closed her senses as well.

Late that night my mother died. At the funeral parlor the next day, before the friends and relatives came in, I placed the letter in her coffin. It seemed an appropriate gesture.

Self-Awareness

Most of the readings that follow recount experiences in which the writers came to learn something about themselves that they had not already been aware of. One piece, "Mental Labels and Tattoos," is related to these because it is about self-image. The pieces on peer pressure and anorexia nervosa were written by college freshmen Wendy Wiseman and Lori Henderson.

From Second Wind: The Memoirs of an Opinionated Man

Bill Russell

During my junior year in high school, in 1950, I had a mystical revelation. One day while I was walking down the hall from one class to another, by myself as usual, it suddenly dawned on me that it was all right to be who I was. The thought just came to me: "Hey, you're all right. Everything is all right." The idea was hardly earthshaking, but I was a different person by the time I reached the end of the hall. Had I been methodical I would have immediately written down my thoughts. Over and over again I received the idea that everything was all right about me—so vividly that the thought seemed to have colors on it. I remember looking around in class to make sure the other kids didn't think I was acting strange.

Those moments in the hall are the closest I've come to a religious experience. For all I know, it may have actually been one. A warm feeling fell on me out of nowhere. I wondered why the idea hadn't occurred to me before; everything seemed to fall into place, the way it does for a kid when he first understands simple multiplication.

Everybody remembers the "Aha!" sensation when a good idea hits you. I remember sitting in a logic class at the University of San Francisco, puzzling over something the priest had been explaining to us for the previous few days. Then it came to me. Bells went off; the mental pleasure was so great that I jumped as if someone had pinched me and yelled "Hey!"

The priest said, "Congratulations, Mr. Russell. You have just had your first real and complete thought. How does it feel?" He was patronizing me, but I didn't care because he had just given me a new way of seeing things.

What I saw in the hallway at high school that day was more than just an idea; it was a way out of self-rejection. In the four years since my mother had died, everybody I encountererd felt that there was something wrong with me. Worse, I *agreed* with them. I was clumsy at everything. When I opened a soup can, it felt as if I was trying to take apart a watch with a sledgehammer. I was insulted at the time. At my first and only football practice the coach lined up players to run over me all afternoon, and then complained to the team that he'd gotten the "bum of the family" instead of my brother, who was a star football player at a rival high school. I dropped football, swallowed my pride and went out for the cheerleading team. I didn't even make that. I was the classic ninety-pound weakling—except that nobody would have dreamed of using my picture in an advertisement.

The white cops in Oakland stopped me on the streets all the time, grilled me and routinely called me "nigger." Whenever they said it, it put me in such a state that I would shrivel up inside and think, "Oh, God. They're right." I gave everybody the benefit of the doubt—friends who ignored me, strangers who were mean— because I thought they were probably justified.

All this changed after that trip down the hall. I finished classes that day and went home feeling as if some golden bird had landed on my shoulder. Every time I checked to see if it was still there, I had expected it to be gone. Maybe it would leave just as mysteriously as it had come, and then I'd turn back into my old self. I remember going to bed that night thinking that sleep would be the real test. If I still had the warm feeling the next morning, I told myself, I'd accept that change as permanent; otherwise it would be just another of life's mysteries. I was so eager to find out whether I could keep this new gift that it took me hours to doze off.

I woke up the next morning and checked my mind to see what thoughts were in it. "Hey, you're all right," my mind told me, and I realized the feeling was still there. I jumped out of bed so happy that I embarrassed myself; you could have made moonbeams out of my smile. I decided I was a man.

From that day on, whenever I've felt hostility from someone, I've assumed that it was their problem rather than mine. It was just the opposite from the way I had been before. The teachers at McClymonds High School seemed different to me, for example. I knew that nearly all the teachers did not like their students, and since I had always looked up to these teachers as adults and authority figures, I'd assumed they must be right; there must be something wrong with all of us. But after my revelation I decided that there was nothing wrong with me, or with most of the other kids, so it must be the teachers.

There *was* something wrong with them. They were stuck in a ghetto school at low pay, trapped there just as firmly as their pupils. None of the kids really expected to go to college, and very few of the faculty expected to go anywhere either. It was not a school that inspired high hopes for anybody, and most of the teachers were bitter about it. They ran kids through "job-training" classes that consisted mainly of personal errands. They prepared kids for the harsh realities of the outside world by deflating their dreams with cynical comments. Once I almost told a teacher that I wanted to be an architect, but I stoppped myself; I knew what she would say.

Hostility and failure were still all around me, but I no longer accepted responsibility for them. Now people had a hard time making me feel guilty, and those who called me "nigger" saw me raise my hackles instead of tucking in my tail. I kept telling myself that it was all right to be who I was, and if I was all right, then anybody who insulted me when I was minding my own business deserved to be pushed back into his own territory. That's what I tried to do. I had a lot of fights in my late teens, and I was big enough to win most of them. My cowering look turned into a glowering one. The adults in my neighborhood, who seemed to notice every inch I grew as I pushed up past them, said I was growing up.

The process of growing up was anything but routine. In fact, I don't think I even *would* have if it hadn't been for that revelation which shook me out of self-hatred. It gave me a sense of confidence. At that time, no reasonable person could have looked at me or the circumstances of my life and predicted that I would accomplish anything. I was trapped and basically untalented; I had a way of gnawing on my failures as if they were leftovers from yesterday's lunch; and even after that day in the hall, I had no great sense of purpose. There were no thoughts of being a president or a star. I was still aimless, but one crucial factor had changed: whatever happened to me, I realized, I would still know that I was not fundamentally flawed. And if *I* knew that, what other people thought didn't matter. Most of them were probably attacking me because of some failing that they saw in themselves. I was basically sound, everything looked brighter to me, and I had a new sense of wonder. It was like waking up.

I knew at the time that this was a significant event in my life, but I didn't realize just how important it was. I was only sixteen, after all, and so every little change would look big. I kept waiting for something to come along and top the experience, something just as startling but more mature that I couldn't even imagine. But many experiences have come and gone in the decades since, and I'm still waiting for something to have a greater impact on me. Kids think that their really important life will begin when they're an adult, but many adults realize later that the important things in their lives happened when they were kids.

Fighting Back

Stanton L. Wormley, Jr.

In the spring of 1970, I was an 18-year-old army private at Fort Jackson, South Carolina. I had been in the Army for less than six months and was still making the difficult transition from life as an only child in an upper-middle-class black family. One rite of passage was particularly intense: on a cool April night, a drunken white soldier whom I barely knew attacked me as I lay sleeping.

My recollection of the incident is, in some details, still hazy. Like the seven other men in the squad bay, I was asleep in my bunk. I half-remember some vigorous off-key singing, the ceiling light going on and someone roughly shaking my foot. I sat up, drowsily irritated at being disturbed. Everything happened very quickly then: a voice began shouting, an arm tightened around my neck and a fist pounded the top of my head. I was still somewhat asleep and confused. Why was this happening to me? It didn't occur to me to fight. I simply covered my head as best I could. There was a hubbub, arms reaching in to separate us and then the sight of the man above me, struggling against the others holding him back, his face red with fury. By then I was fully awake, and I saw the strained tendons in the man's neck, the wormlike vein pulsing at his temple, the spittle that sprayed as he screamed obscenities at me. I wasn't hurt, at least not physically, and all I could do was stare, bewildered. I never did discover what had provoked him.

Afterward, I was angrily confronted by a young black streetwise soldier named Morris. He eyed me with unconcealed contempt. "What the hell's wrong with you, man?" he demanded. "Why didn't you fight back? I would've killed that mother." I had no answer for him. How could I have made him understand the sheltered world of my childhood, in which violence was deplored and careful deliberation encouraged. I was brought up to *think*, not just react.

Nevertheless, that question—*Why didn't I fight back?*—haunted me long after the incident had been forgotten by everyone else. Was I less of a man for not having beaten my attacker to a bloody pulp? Morris—and undoubtedly others—certainly thought so. And so, perhaps, would the majority of American men. The ability and the will to fight back are integral parts of our society's conception of manhood. It goes beyond mere self-defense, I think, for there is a subtle but significant difference between self-defense and fighting back. Self-defense is essentially passive; it involves no rancor, pride or ego. Running away from danger is what martial-arts instructors sometimes recommend as the appropriate reponse, the best self-defense strategy. Fighting back, on the other hand, is active and defiant. It involves the adoption of an attitude that one's retribution is morally justified—or even, at times, morally obligatory.

And we American men buy that attitude—especially those of us who are members of minority groups. For us, largely disenfranchised and often victimized by discrimination and poverty, fighting back is a statement of individual potency and self-determination. It is the very antithesis of victimization: it is a sign of empowerment. The symbolic consequences of fighting back—or failing to do so—reflect upon the group as a whole. To Morris, I had disgraced the entire black American population.

I suppose that there are still situations in which immediate, violent retaliation is necessaary. Sometimes it seems that fighting back is the only way to command respect in the world. Women are now learning that unfortunate lesson, as did blacks and other minorities in recent decades. I can't help feeling, however, that when one gains the ability to fight back one loses something as well. What that something is, I can't easily define: a degree of compassion, perhaps, or tolerance or empathy. It is a quality I hope is possessed by the men in Washington and Moscow who have the power to dispense the ultimate retribution.

Once in a great while, past events are repeated, granting people a chance either to redeem themselves or to relive their mistakes. Two years ago, in a small roadside diner in Virginia, a man—again white, again drunk—chanced to make a derogatory remark to me. I was sitting with my back to him and ignored it. Thinking I had not heard him, he drew close to repeat his taunt, grabbing my shoulder. I suppose I could have moved away, shaken his hand off or complained to the manager. But the accumulated frustrations of years of ignoring such remarks—plus the memory of the incident at Fort Jackson, dictated otherwise. Before I knew what was happening, I was up out of my chair. I hit the man hard in the stomach and he sank to one knee with a moan. Grasping his collar, I almost hit again, but it was obvious that he had had enough. He looked up at me, gasping, his face contorted with pain and fear. The man was perhaps 50, of average size, with a fleshy, florid face surmounted by close-cropped gray bristle. I noted that he had bad teeth, a fact that gave me a moment of spiteful satisfaction. Suddenly sober, he stammered something unintelligible—it might have been an apology—and I let him go.

As I walked away, I was filled with a feeling of exultation. I had not stopped to wonder why; I had not been checked by compassion or sympathy. I had retaliated and it had felt good. But later, my exhilaration passed, leaving a strange sensation of hollowness. I felt vaguely embarrassed, even ashamed. In my mind I was still confident I had acted rightly, but my heart was no longer sure. I remembered my fury, and the quiet way the people in the diner had watched me stalk angrily away. I remembered, too, the abject grimace on the man's face, partly from the pain of the blow and partly in anticipation of a second; and I realized that there was a trace of sadness in the knowledge that I, too, had learned to fight back.

From Being A Man

Donald H. Bell

The traditional reluctance of fathers to share in the sweat and difficulty of child care had many negative results. It helped to estrange us from our fathers (even while we might also identify with them), and it put an undue burden upon women as mothers and nurturers. Yet, for me and for many of the men with whom I have spoken, our relationship with our fathers—what we learned and did not learn from them, how we consciously and unconsciously modelled ourselves after them (and of course, how our fathers, themselves, got their own models and sense of masculinity)—has been of central importance in our lives. Indeed, even a father's death does not reduce his centrality, as many of the men with whom I have spoken have noted. "My father might now be dead," one of them told me, "but he's sure not forgotten. I carry him around with me, always."

Our feelings about our fathers' examples have also been confronted by a recent reality: the expectations which we now meet in the world are of a different sort than those of the past. In addition to being tough and competent males, we are now expected to be nurturers and comforters, as well. No past models now suffice, neither that of the strong and "supermasculine" father, nor even that of a father who might have displayed his

From *Being a Man* by Donald H. Bell, Copyright © 1982 by the Lewis Publishing Company. Reprinted by permission of Harcourt Brace Jovanovich, Inc.

softer side and whom we and the world might have considered weak. Many of the men I have spoken with note that they are suspended between the lessons they learned from their fathers and what they have had to learn for themselves. They have not completely traded one model for another but have attempted with varying success to find the way between contradictory messages about what it means to be man. This is especially true—as we shall see—when they speak about some of the major sources of their self-definition as men: about a sense of male competence, about how we show our feelings and emotions, and, of course, about sex.

"I still have lots of stereotypes from my father," Sam Doucet, a psychotherapist in his mid-thirties, tells me. Sam is a huge, imposing man but is also amazingly gentle and softspoken, and he has many insights about his relationship with his father:

> I still very much hold on to some of his ideas about being strong and potent, and these feelings used to scare me when I was younger, because I felt that I could never fill those images of masculinity. In some ways I still feel that I want to be king of my castle, just like him, and my wife and I joke about that a lot. It's also been important to me to earn more money than she does, even though she's a professional, too, and I feel sometimes that I still want to hold on to stereotypes about women that I got from my father, that basically women are emotional and are nincompoops. . . . You know, I try to filter out these attitudes or make light of them, but they're still buried deep inside.

My Race for Friends

Wendy Wiseman

The first word I learned in junior high school was not from a dictionary in English class; it was *popularity*, and I put it to use in order to survive through five days a week of pure hell, with people I never knew before in my life, people I was going to have to learn to get along with whether I liked it or not. Suddenly going to classes with three hundred new people (in my grade alone) was a drastic change from the six years before of having only a hundred other classmates. Not only were many of the people taller, but the halls seemed narrower, too, and it was easy to get swallowed up in the crowd. Every class I went to that first day seemed to have the same recorded message coming from the teacher's mouth. Besides the basic fire drill rhetoric (which seemed absolutely silly because there was no way I was going to get out in time with 999 other people screaming and running too, and I had a hard enough time fighting my way into class!), every teacher seemed to be saying, "The beginning of junior high is the biggest and most important step of your life since kindergarten. You'll make more friends and have more fun in these three years if you get involved and meet people." Well, that quaint little coaxing to action from the administration didn't seem to help me too much because it seemed certain people had their share of friends and fun, and they made it quite clear that they weren't in the market for any more. After all, how many people can surround a person within a two-foot radius at one time?

237

I had just learned my second vocabulary word in junior high, and that was *clique*. I don't know why, but I never seemed to have a running inventory of friends. I was behind, and I had to make up ground fast if I wanted to make it through school each day. It sounds terrible, but those who are not fortunate enough to be in the select group have to "pick and choose" through what's left. Left and left out was exactly how I felt, but I wasn't alone. Well, I was no dinner party hostess, but I managed to make a fair amount of acquaintances in a relatively short period of time. I worked fast enough to have someone to eat lunch with, anyway.

The rest of the day went all right, and each day after became a little easier. My third word that junior high taught me was *cool*, and that's how you act after you've made your friends. This is when junior high starts to have its advantages. New friends meant no one had to know I carried a "Raggedy Ann and Andy" lunchbox to school all the way through sixth grade, or that I didn't own a single pair of jeans until two weeks before seventh grade started. I didn't have to have a notorious history anymore, as long as I could keep quiet the people who went all the way through grade school with me. I could be someone else, provided that other person acted the way I thought my friends wanted me to. This is not to say that I developed an entirely new personality in front of my friends. I was careful about what I said and what they found out about me. I still kept friends from grade school, too. I just was not sure I would be liked or be good enough for a friend if people knew what I was really like. And I felt this way through grade school, too. I was insecure about myself and insecure around others. How could I be childish enough to play with dolls until I was twelve and give them up reluctantly even then. I was going into junior high. I had to grow up. I had to forget what I was like as a "child" and become a "young adult." I never believed that anyone I looked up to in school had played with Barbie dolls or Lincoln Logs for as long as I had. They were grown-up, and I had to act like them if I wanted them to like me.

Vocabulary word number four comes into play here, and that's *conform*. I wanted to look like everyone else and be like everyone else, so that I wouldn't be ridiculed because I was different, but I still wanted to get attention. I thanked God for those Levis because everyone wore them, and nobody even had to know that my mother used to buy me ugly polyester pants to wear, or that I actually wore them. I could be cool because Levis were cool; I could be in because anything other than jeans was out, and if I played my cards right, I might even be able to become popular.

It might seem that with all this time spent on learning the social aspects of junior high, I never had time to open a book. It was true that to have a lot of friends around you and act like you didn't really care about school was in, but to act like you really wanted to do your homework was not. But I had gotten A's all through grade school, and I wasn't about to give up that solid base for a chance to stand on the unsteady and ever-shifting ground of popularity. It didn't take me long to find a viable compromise, though.

Profanity worked well for me in many ways. No one ever expected a "straight A" student (and I was still getting A's) to use such words, much less know what half of them meant. I got attention from people who otherwise seemed not to know who I was, so I earned more friends and became more popular. I learned these words (several of them, anyway) from a girl whom I admired and wanted to be friends with, and it worked. And I wasn't a troublemaker, so teachers never lowered my grades for swearing in class. I was still the innocent, industrious student in their eyes, and in my parents'. They never had to know a thing.

This race for friends continued strongly all through junior high, and on into high school, but it began to lose ground as I got older. High school was a waking up period for me because I finally realized that the person I had become in the eyes of my friends wasn't me. It took two years of high school to figure this out and to believe in myself enough to show the real side of my personality, but by the time senior year came around, I was glad I did.

The first day of my senior year was a shock because everyone had really changed, and I would, too. Homeroom became a contest to see who got drunk the most the weekend before or who "scored" with the best-looking girls. Well, I didn't drink, nor was I in the running for a date with a football player, and I think that for a time I became the ultra-conservative in defense to this. I guess I was really scared of what would happen to me if I tried all the things everyone else was doing, or that I wouldn't be able to quit. It seemed everyone either wanted to get drunk or get to second base on a first date, and I was losing friends to their ongoing desire to be popular. They were willing to do things to keep friends that I wasn't, and I lost a lot of respect for many of my friends in that final year. I was no longer that popular, but I was beginning to be myself, and that meant forgetting what other people think. It meant remembering that lunch box and those clothes and not caring that I didn't grow up as everyone thought I should. The final word I learned in school was what it means to be *me,* and that means trying to please myself instead of always trying to please others.

What Is Obsession?

Lori Henderson

What does it mean to be obsessed? How does a person become obsessed? Obsession is not uncommon in today's society. People have obsessions with everything from religion to sports to food. What drives people to go to such extremes? Obsession is not easy to understand, but I am going to try and make some sense of it.

As a freshman in high school I became obsessed with food and calories in a fight for some area of control in my life. My problem started innocently enough, but before I knew it, my fight for control had gotten out of control. I continued blindly even though I was scaring my parents, my friends, and even myself.

It began with a decision to lose a little weight. My mom suggested I eat sensibly, but count calories and cut out junk food. When I started, I was completely ignorant as to how many calories were in an ounce of meat, or how many grams of fat were in a serving of french fries. I started reading magazine articles and figuring out how many calories I consumed each day. I became very conscious of how many calories I consumed in each of the three necessary meals, and then I refused to eat any desserts or anything between meals. My parents made me eat a sizable, well-balanced meal each evening, but I tried to cut calories wherever possible. If we had hamburgers, I didn't eat a bun, or I didn't eat any chips with my pizza, or by not buttering my bread, or by not using salad dressing on my salad or eating crackers with my soup. Anything to cut calories and still get by.

I also told everyone I was on a diet. It's easier to do anything with encouragement from others. When I went to my grandma's house, she started suggesting fruit instead of the usual ice cream or cookies. My family and friends knew I was making a conscious effort to watch my weight, so I was very conscious of what I ate in front of them. Since I didn't eat in between those mealtimes with them, I was always very conscious of my declared goal to be "careful."

This is where I think guilt comes into play with obsession. (At least mt personal obsession.) I felt so much guilt when I did slip up—even just a little bit. It wasn't worth it to "cheat." It was all mental, but I just felt like I was really cheating myself. I felt like—I may have the pleasure of this piece of pie for about ten minutes while it's going down—but it will probably affect the way my jeans fit, or the way the scale reads in the morning. I remember waking up terrified of the scale because I had eaten a piece of chocolate pie the night before at dinner. We had been invited to a friend's house for dinner, and the pie was what our host had prepared for dessert. I was obligated to eat it, and I felt terrible the next day.

So, I began concentrating on never having to feel guilty. I was always careful. That's where pride came in. I was really proud of myself for not giving in at times. Not having a dish of ice cream after dinner, or not having a cookie at a school sports banquet reception. I remember one day after school I was just bored, and I was just wandering around the house. I went to the refrigerator, and I saw a bag of miniature Snicker bars. I thought for a moment about eating one, but I read on the package that each little candy bar had 100 calories, and I just thought "Wow! What a waste of calories." I was so conditioned that I just walked away from the "calories." I didn't even once think that, hey, I was hungry, or that candy bar might taste good. I guess I just thought I would immediately blimp out or something.

Those feelings of pride over my "control" were tested and strengthened through a good friend. She decided to go on a diet at the same time as I did. We were good friends, but before we knew it we were both competing with one another. Every time we talked, we talked "diet." She was always bragging that she had only eaten a piece of fish or a salad for dinner, and I would feel guilty because I had eaten pancakes and sausage with my family, or something "less diety" like that. I thought if I didn't match her efforts she would lose and I would gain, so I cut the calorie corners even closer. We were constantly discussing how much differently our clothes fit this particular week, or how much our moms made us eat over the weekend. It was a vicious circle for both of us. One particular time we went on an all-night sports jamboree where we swam, bowled, and played tennis all night, and then went for breakfast in the morning. I was really hungry all night, but my friend kept saying she wasn't at all hungry. So, I thought it was just my "weakness," and I was determined not to each much at breakfast. We went to a pancake house, and I ordered a plate of pancakes. My friend ordered a plate of waffles, and while we were eating she proceeded to tell me her waffles were less fattening than my pancakes because of the little holes in the batter.

At this point, I had been dieting about two months. I had lost about twenty pounds, and I was very thin, and very happy with my weight. I was happy, but my friends and parents were getting worried. I was so thin my clothes were just hanging on my body, and it was very obvious I had become obsessed. People were commenting, "Lori, you're *so* thin!" That encouraged me even more. I felt that pride in what I thought was correct, and I felt good that my "efforts" were being noticed. I kept counting calories and kept cutting corners. I remember once I went to the roller skating rink with some friends, and I skated around and around the rink for about two hours. I didn't think about it being fun, I didn't think about being tired, I just thought about burning calories.

By the third month I was totally our of control. I believed, however, that I was totally *in* control because I had beaten every desire to "cheat" on myself. I now ate only when and what I *had* to. I weighed 92 pounds, and I knew deep down that that was very wrong. You just don't drop that much weight in such a short time period. My mom forced me to get on the scale every day, and I had discovered that by stationing my weight on the back of the scale I could make it read ten pounds more, 102 pounds. I passed inspection, for the most part, with my mom, but I knew deep down that I was too thin. I remember one Sunday morning in church when I was worried sick about what I was going to wear to school all week because I only had one pair of jeans that fit well. Also, I was becoming very weak, and I remember having difficulty walking to my third-floor classes at school.

If I realized all these things deep down, then why was I so repulsed by food every time I sat down to eat? I guess my conscious thoughts against food just outweighed my subsconscious thoughts that what I was doing was harmful. Whatever the reason, I counted calories right up until the 3:00 appointment at the hospital my mom felt forced to make. I still had one more controlling thought—count your calories; that thought was more important than anything else in my life. I guess that's what an obsession is—the most important and controlling factor in a person's life. Before my obsession ended I did serious damage to my system. I am still trying to understand why and how I let one thing completely control and change my life.

Mental Labels and Tattoos

I. Ralph Hyatt

The words "weird," "crazy," "oddball," and "kookie" are part of our everyday vocabulary. The term "neurotic," once reserved for a specific professional diagnosis, is bandied about across backgammon sets, dinner tables, and adolescent conversations. A problem is that we are often the objects of such descriptions, not only as adults, but as children. Did your mother ever say, "You act so strange sometimes"? (Many of us have heard this complaint at three a.m., when mother and father assumed we were fast asleep.) How about, "You're a stupid kid," or "Why don't you behave like your sister?," or "You never do anything right," or "Rather than have you mess it up, I'll do it myself"? There are hundreds of ways to communicate the message, which becomes subjectively interpreted as "There is something wrong with me!" The label is printed very easily. Depending on personal and life circumstances, the gum on back of the label either does not stick, having no holding power, or, like a tattoo, stays with us forever—and it is not hard for negative tattoos to become imprinted in our systems.

Maintaining Negative Mental Tattoos

There are six basic axioms for maintaining negative mental tattoos and labels:

1. The younger the person receiving the initial tattoo, the stronger the imprint.

2. The more intense the initial imprint, the greater the holding power.

3. The greater the frequency of the imprint, the better the holding power.

4. Parents have the most powerful imprint potential on their children.

5. The larger the number of people making a similar or equivalent imprint, the greater the holding power.

6. Personal and life stresses generate very sticky holding power.

These basic truths match the findings of clinical and developmental psychology. The dependent human baby, requiring another person to survive, becomes extremely attached to the "mothering" individual. Feelings of trust, security, and love—or their opposites—become quickly tattooed. The rejecting alcoholic mother, for example, communicates the intense message, "You are not worthwhile caring for." The father who attends business meetings almost nightly while his wife chairs favorable charitable organizations with continual telephone calls delivers a similar message. Wrong information about raising children ("They only respond to the back of your hand") or low tolerance for frustration, which leads to physical abuse, intensifies the impact. It starts to numb the child with an "I don't care" attitude because the clear message is "Nobody cares anyway." When language is available to the receiver, the imprint from an angry parent is loud and clear. Parental love frequently becomes closely associated with being "good" or "bad" and, unfortunately, the concept of being "bad" is easily inculcated. Since character traits run deep and do not change quickly, the chances are excellent that early messages will be repeated over and over again. Remember, the greater the frequency, the better the holding power. Imagine the poor kid who gets the same negative message from mom and pop—over and over again. Rival siblings will lunge to the vulnerable area and pour salt on the raw negative tattoo. Now and then, friends contribute their "zingers," so that the holding power of the label becomes stickier and stickier. Incidentally, it does not require a constant stream of bombardment—a little here and a little there goes a long way in creating cement-like qualities in the gummy label.

Physical characteristics such as lack of attractiveness, handicaps, and anomalies contribute heavily to believing the validity of early labels. "You clumsy ox" is obviously verified in a person with cerebral palsy, but almost as easily proven to a person with limited skills in skiing or playing tennis. "You're a disappointment to me" is conveyed with no problem to a child of limited intelligence, but also blares out sharply to a student bringing home a grade of "B" ("good") to a parent who accepts nothing less than "A" ("excellent"). Our compensations work most of the time, but, since life always manages to have its dips, the supporting structures we build for ourselves also sag. The young man who proves to his parents, friends, and family that he can be successful by working day and night (compensation) can become depressive when his business venture turns sour. The failure is tremendous. Marital difficulties, poor health, general fatigue, reactions to medication, and unemployment exemplify a few life stresses which can serve to validate early labels such as "You'll never amount to anything," "He's just like his cousin Joe," or "What can you expect from her?" As adults under prolonged stress, [we often play] mind games . . . self-destructively. We say to ourselves, one way or the other, "I guess they were right after all." We viciously attack ourselves with self-descriptions of stupidity, unattractiveness, self-blame, and guilt. Irrationally, we agree with some or all of the irrational statements made about us—especially those in our early history. It is similar to an individual who finally overcomes a paralyzing fear of flying—by flying, although not necessarily loving the experience—who regresses severely after a shaky, turbulent flight. Progress dissolves with one strong negative experience which "proves" the original irrationality. Actually, only two things were proven: life, by definition, has ups and downs (success and failures); and early and intense irrationalities are not easily erased.

Social Issues

$\mathcal{E}$ach of these readings focuses on current concerns and questions about the society in which we live. All were published in magazines and newspapers except for the piece by Laurel Harris, a college freshman.

Making Babies

Anne Taylor Fleming

Four years ago, when I was 21 and newly school-sprung, many of the women I knew—myself included—were agonizing about whether to marry. Most of us finally did. Now a lot of my friends and other women of my generation are agonizing about whether to get pregnant. Many of us haven't so far. And the troubling thought has crept into our souls or our wombs (presuming they are separate places, and sometimes I'm not so sure they are) that we just might never make babies, that we might enter middle age alone—perhaps divorced or widowed—childless, womb-tight and woebegone. Why, if women face this almost certain aloneness later on, are so many of us so strangely steeled against pregnancy?

Some non-baby-making women will explain it by saying something like "The world's in a hell of a mess and I don't want to bring a baby into it"; or "There are too many babies around already." I myself give lip service to answers like those; but I don't really buy them. After all, the world has always seemed a treacherous place to a prospective mother. As for over-population, it is a serious concern to serious-minded young women but I just don't believe it ever stopped one specific woman from having one specific baby.

The other most oft-given answer, and one I give more credence to, is "Well, I have a career to pursue and I can't risk dividing my energies and loyalties between work and a baby." How stern and unloving and downright corny that sounds. Yet I myself have said it many a time and will undoubtedly say it many more. I believe it. I believe that I am not put together enough right now to cope with dishes and diapers and postpartum depressions while trying to carry on what I imagine to be a life's work.

A baby was never going to fill my me-need, my what-am-I-going-to-do-when-I-grow-up-need. I always knew that. And then the women's movement came along and firmed up my resolve to work and the resolves of women like me. Also, many of us had watched our mothers try, at 40, to pick up the pieces of some long-abandoned life and work when our fathers had left them. Their example was not lost on us. I have many times said to myself and heard other women say, "That won't happen to me. I'll always have my work. Nobody—but nobody—can take that away from me."

And so, rather fiercely, we cling to our work as to a life raft, hoping that it will keep us afloat in good times and bad. Though we might in private moments yearn sometimes to trade back in our full heads and empty wombs for empty heads and full wombs, we cannot now. Having committed ourselves so early and so firmly to our so-called careers, we are afraid to commit also to a baby. We're afraid to risk failing twice. It is, in fact, precisely because we take motherhood so seriously—as, God help us, we seem to take everything these days—that we're staying away from it, at least for the moment.

There is something, though, deeper than our work that is keeping many of us from making babies, something to do with sex. What has happened to many young women, I think, is that effective contraceptives—which we have used faithfully for a decade—are now so much a part of our bodies, and of our consciousnesses, that we are scared to set them aside, scared to get pregnant, not physically scared, some other kind of scared, a bigger kind. Before the recent arrival of fail-safe contraceptives, lovemaking for women was always baby-making, pure and simple. But these new contraceptives put women on an equal footing—rather, on equal bedding—with men, so that for us, sexual pleasure is now no longer an accidental by-product of procreation, just as a baby is now no longer the by-product of accidental afternoon lust. The very urges themselves, the lovemaking urge and the baby-making urge, have become separated in women. Now we can, like men, bed at will, without being physically or psychologically penalized, without having the moment complicated, or dignified, by the possibility of procreation. What a relief! What a joy!

So we are very reluctant to set aside the contraceptives, and are unwilling to have sex become so serious again so soon, and are afraid to have one moment of pleasure become something so tangible and so permanent as a baby. We are ready to be true sex objects at last!

But—and the irony is obvious—many men I listen to these days don't seem quite ready for women's newly liberated libidos. They are already greatly scared and greatly weary of our fierce wakefulness. In the marriages I know, in fact, it is the men, not the women, who nowadays want to make babies, perhaps as a way of holding on to us, just as women were forever having babies to try to hold on to men. And when women refuse to get pregnant, men have in their eyes a hint of what for so long they saw in ours: that fear of being left or, worse, of being cuckolded.

This kind of fear is not pretty to me. Like many women, I have had too much of that kind of sexual fear myself all too recently. When the women's movement was in first bloom a few years ago, women, in their exhilaration, could not resist gloating a bit over male sexual insecurities. But now the movement is in its revisionist stage and men and women seem to want to be tender with one another again and to honor each other's needs, old and new. In that spirit, many of the women I know long to tumble easily and hopefully, into pregnancy, like their mothers and grandmothers before them, with no agony aforethought, long to pledge allegiance with their wombs to the men they love. But they can't. They're stuck in a holding pattern. So am I. I'm feeling willful and wobbly and—oh, why do we women feel the need to soft-pedal it?—I'm competitive and ambitious and confused a lot and I don't think any baby ought to be subjected to me right now. At least no baby of mine.

An Unusual Decision

Laurel Harris

It was a most unusual decision for such a young child to make. Of course, no one believed that I really meant it; even my mother thought it was just a passing fancy of an impressionable young mind. But I knew exactly what I was talking about, and at the age of four, I had made the most important decision of my life.

Growing up on the outskirts of North Canton, Ohio, afforded me a considerable amount of contact with nature, so I learned about animals long before I began school. With my mother beside me to answer the countless questions, I eagerly explored the woods behind our house and the pond down the street. Together we captured praying mantises, walking sticks, butterflies, caterpillars, and fireflies (which made excellent night-lights). I'd keep them for a while, then let them go because I knew they had their own lives to live and it wouldn't be fair to keep them in captivity.

Insects weren't the only animals with which I had hands-on experience. I used to come out of the woods with as many toads as I could hold and play with them in the sandbox. I even took some to school for show-and-tell once (the teacher was not pleased when they got loose). One year we had three mallard ducks that came up the street to our yard the same time every day, quacking as if to tell us they were on their way. We'd toss them stale bread, and I even got the female to eat out of my

252

hand. A year or so later, we found a nest of baby rabbits in our garden. We knew that the mother would abandon them, so we took them in and raised them on Cheerios. When they grew too big to keep, we released them in a wide-open field.

My first "regular" pets were three turtles, one of which I found under a violet in my grandmother's garden, and a parakeet. These were a lot of fun, but it was when we got our first dog—an Irish setter—that I realized what animals meant to me. One day my mother said she had to take Cinnamon to the veterinarian to get her shots. Veterinarian—that was a new word. And why would Cinnamon need shots if she wasn't sick? Mom explained that a veterinarian is a doctor for dogs and cats and all sorts of animals, and that pets had to have vaccinations just like I did. That moment, a year before I started school, I decided what I was going to do with the rest of my life, and not once did I change my mind.

Even while I was still little, my parents were very supportive of my idea of becoming a vet, but I know everyone thought it was just a phase I was going through and that I'd want to be a ballerina next week. When this "phase" went on year after year, my family realized I was serious. My mother filled me in on more of the details concerning vet medicine and reminded me from time to time that I would have to go to school for a long time, which didn't bother me a bit because I loved school. Mom never tried to discourage me or talk me into a more "traditional" career choice. She always said it was completely up to me—after all, it's my life—and whatever I decided to do, I would have all the emotional and financial support she could offer.

But where my family supported me, the rest of society did not. At the time, women were gaining their equality in the medical field, but not without a difficult struggle. When I would discuss my plans with adults outside my family (teachers, doctors, etc.), they were always careful not to say anything to hurt my feelings, but I knew what they would have liked to say, "Dream on, little girl; you're only here to cook and clean and have babies." At one point I completely stopped playing with baby dolls and swore that I would never get married or have children because if it came down to a choice, I would rather be a vet than a mother.

My junior year in high school, my guidance counselor actually tried to talk me out of my decision, completely on the basis of my being female. She told me that although I'd have a good chance of getting into vet school they would try harder to flunk me out. Then she went on to give me a handful of brochures, telling me how much better off I would be in veterinary *assisting*, because women were meant to be in assistant positions. I politely thanked her, walked out, and dropped the brochures in the trash. I have never been so insulted in my life, but I suppose she would never understand.

At this point, it may seem as if I've stuck to my choice merely to spite society. However, I only see this as an added challenge to a very special part of my life.

My mother had always told me that I'm too moody and impossible to get along with. Actually, I think I'm just less tolerant of my fellow *homo sapiens* than most people. When I get fed up with the human race, as I often do, I need a means of escape. Just being alone doesn't help much, so when I'm upset, I usually get my dog and go for a walk or just sit in the yard. And I talk to her, just as if she were another person. She looks at me with her big brown eyes, perking her ears up when she catches a familiar word or phrase. She'll sit down next to me and put her head on my shoulder as if to say, "I understand." That's all I need because I know that no matter what, she'll always be there with total love and devotion, which is more than I could ever hope to have from a human being.

Animals are not void of emotion, as many would like to think. I've worked with them enough to know when a macaw is having a bad day and spends it tearing plaster off the wall, or when a puppy viciously lashes out at everyone for being kept in a cage too long. My dog has days when she just can't spend enough time with me and others when she can't be bothered. Animals are also capable of reasoning to an extent. Especially when she was younger, we'd often catch my dog in the midst of a mischievous act. She'd stop for a moment, think about the consequences, and depending on her mood, she'd either stop doing it, or continue and cringe because she knew she would get hit. She was also housebroken in less than a day and was upset over the first mess she made, even though she had never been punished for that before. Maybe this is why animals mean so much to me. They deserve a lot more credit than we, the "superior" creatures, give them.

When I'm working with animals, I feel a sense of fulfillment that I get nowhere else. When I hold a trembling puppy or tame a bird that no one else can handle, I get the greatest feeling of satisfaction, even more so than when I hold a baby and get it to stop crying. I don't think I'm insensitive to people, but I'm just *more* sensitive to the rest of the animal kingdom. I've never thought of any career other than vet medicine because I feel like it's the *only* thing for me to do. I could never imagine what life would be like without animals. They say Heaven is a beautiful place, so I guess there must be animals there, too. If there aren't, I don't care where I go when I die.

The Dying Girl That No One Helped

Loudon Wainwright

The story is simple and brutal. As she arrived home in the early morning darkness, Kitty Genovese, a decent, pretty young woman of 28, was stalked through the streets close to her Kew Gardens apartment and stabbed again and again by a man who had followed her home and took almost a half hour to kill her. During that bloody little eternity, according to an extraordinary account published in the New York *Times*, Kitty screamed and cried repeatedly for help. Her entreaties were unequivocal. "Oh, my God!" she cried out at one point, "He stabbed me! Please help me! Somebody help me!" Minutes later, before the murderer came back and attacked her for the final time, she screamed, "I'm dying! I'm dying!"

The reason the murderer's actions and his victims calls are so documented is that police were able to find 38 of Kitty's neighbors who admitted they witnessed the awful event. They heard the screams and most understood her cry for help. Peeking out their windows, many saw enough of the killer to provide a good description of his appearance and clothing. A few saw him strike Kitty, and more saw her staggering down the sidewalk after she had been stabbed twice and was looking for a place to hide. One especially sharp-eyed person was able to report that the murderer was sucking his finger as he left the scene; he had cut himself during the attack. Another witness has the awful distinction of being the only person Kitty Genovese recognized in the audience taking in her final moments. She looked at him and called to him by name. He did not reply.

No one really helped Kitty at all. Only one person shouted at the killer ("Let that girl alone!"), and the one phone call that was finally made to police was placed after the murderer had got in his car and driven off. For the most part the witnesses, crouching in darkened windows like watchers of a Late Show, looked on until the play had passed beyond their view. Then they went back to bed.

Not all of these people, it must be said, understood they were watching a murderer. Some thought they were looking on at a lovers' quarrel; others saw or heard so very little that they could not have reached any conclusion about the disturbance. Even if one of her neighbors had called the police promptly, it cannot be definitely stated that Kitty would have survived. But that is quite beside the point. The fact is that no one, even those who were sure something was terribly wrong, felt moved enough to act. There is, of course, no law against not being helpful.

"You know what this man told us after we caught him?" Police Lieutenant Bernard Jacobs asked. "He said he figured nobody would do anything to help. He heard the windows go up and saw the lights go on. He just retreated for a while and when things quieted down, he came back to finish the job."

Later, in one of the apartment houses, a witness to part of Kitty Genovese's murder talked. His comments—agonized, contradictory, guilt-ridden, self-excusing—indicate the price in bad conscience he and his neighbors are now paying. "I feel terrible about it," he said. "The thing keeps coming back in my mind. You just don't want to get involved. They might have picked me up as a suspect if I'd bounced right out there. I was getting ready, but my wife stopped me. She didn't want to be a hero's widow. I woke up about the third scream. I pulled the blind so hard it came off the window. The girl was on her knees struggling to get up. I didn't know if she was drunk or what. I never saw the man. She staggered a little when she walked, like she had a few drinks in her. I forgot the screen was there and I almost put my head through it trying to get a better look. I could see people with their heads out and hear windows going up and down all along the street."

The man walked to the window and looked down at the sidewalk. He was plainly depressed and disappointed at his own failure. "Every time I look out here now," he said, "it's like looking out at a nightmare. How could so many of us have had the same idea that we didn't need to do anything? But that's not all that's wrong." Now he sounded betrayed and he told what was really eating him. Those 38 witnesses had, at least, talked to the police after the murder. The man pointed to a nearby building. "There are people over there who saw everything," he said. "And there hasn't been a peep out of them yet. Not one peep."

On the scene a few days after the killer had been caught and had confessed, Jacobs discussed the investigation. "The word we kept hearing from the witnesses later was 'involved,'" Jacobs said. A dark-haired, thoughtful man, he was standing on the sidewalk next to two fist-sized, dark-grey blotches on the cement. These were Kitty's bloodstains and it was there that the killer first stabbed her. "People told us they just didn't want to get involved," Jacobs said to me. "They don't want to be questioned or have to go to court." He pointed to an apartment house directly across the quiet street. "They looked down at this thing," he went on, "from four different floors of that building." Jacobs indicated the long, two-story building immediately next to him. A row of stores took up the ground floor; there were apartments on the upper floor. "Kitty lived in one of them," Jacobs said. "People up there were sitting right on top of the crime." He moved his arm in a gesture that included all the buildings. "It's a nice neighborhood, isn't it?" he went on. "Doesn't look like a jungle. Good, solid people. We don't expect anybody to come out into the street and fight this kind of bum. All we want is a phone call. We don't even need to know who's making it."

Richard Cory, All Over Again

Roy Meador

The same as the rest of us, my friend wanted to be somebody. To make his mark in the world. To have his life count. At the end, he did make his mark in headlines: Deaths Called Murder-Suicide. *Son Finds Bodies.*

Carl L. Stinedurf was a good friend. We often lunched together, and our conversations ranged from politics to literature. Carl enjoyed ideas. He knew how to laugh. Face-to-face, most people used his middle name, Larry. But the waitress called him "Frank" because he preferred Sinatra's old records to new stuff. Carl often talked enthusiastically about his family, his son at the university, his daughter in high school. He mentioned his wife, Norma, with special pride. In her 30's, with his help she had finished college and begun teaching. Carl was delighted with his family's accomplishments. But underneath, well-masked, there must have been agonizing terror. Carl carried his pain in silence.

My friend worked as an estimator and customer representative for a large printing firm. He was gentle, always softspoken, exceptionally conscientious. When I gave him work to do for my company, I knew it would be finished with care.

Carl tended toward the liberal. He thought more of people than

259

of profits. He deplored cruelty. I considered him one of those who patiently keep what we call civilization humming along after its fashion.

There was just one anomaly I never understood. Carl's hobby was guns. He kept a loaded .38 in his bedroom. There were handguns and rifles throughout his home. Carl used them for target shooting and hunting. A fellow hunter said Carl was an expert marksman, that when he fired at game he made certain of his shot so the animal wouldn't suffer.

I couldn't appreciate the gun side of my friend's character. I guess I had seen too much of the gun religion in the Korean war. Carl and I disagreed about guns. He would vote for George McGovern and simultaneously support every argument of the National Rifle Association and the gun lobbies. Yet because he was a peaceful, compassionate man, I considered him one of those who could be trusted to own and use guns responsibly.

I saw Carl on that last Friday afternoon. We talked about a printing job. He was cheerful, and I think he was already on the other side of his decision. He finished his work that day like someone going on vacation. Like someone not expecting to return on Monday.

We had a relaxed talk. Later I learned of the misery he had concealed. "He saw customers and kept control," his employer told me. "When the customer left, he often went in the restroom and vomited. Family trouble."

The virus of restlessness. Norma, after 23 years, with a new career and new friends, wanted to leave. She needed to seek that popular, elusive goal, "more out of life." But Carl was an old-fashioned man captive in a time of new fashions. He couldn't handle this threat to the family. He sought medical advice, but every answer seemed to require letting Norma go, with the frail hope she might come back. Carl couldn't live with the uncertainty.

It rained that Friday night. Carl went home and in their bedroom he put two bullets through his wife's head, one through his own. He used a .357 magnum handgun. One of Carl's friends told me this proved it was carefully planned. The .357 magnum meant Carl didn't want Norma to suffer. That friend and others were reluctant to credit guns as factors in the event. "Guns are simply tidier than axes," said one. But Carl was a sensitive, orderly man. I doubt he could ever have done the job with less efficient, messier weapons. It had to be over in a moment. So he used the mercy weapon, the no-pain gun, the .357 magnum. It was handy in a house of guns.

Endless postmortems began among those who knew Carl and Norma. Why in his torment couldn't he wait? Why couldn't he give time a chance? Why?

No one I listened to blamed the guns, questioned their proximity, their easy availability. It will probably be a long time before Carl's small estate is settled for the son who found the bodies, for the daughter in high school. I suppose his guns eventually will be sold and redistributed, including the .357 magnum. Guns are made from enduring metal. They outlive their owners. They go on about their business.

News accounts carried the standard facts: Description of Carl's hobby. His age, 39. The comment of a neighbor that Carl and Norma were "very nice." Details of the funeral. There was no indication whether or not gun clubs and the National Rifle Association sent flowers, or assistance for the survivors.

The irony department: Carl learned enthusiasm for guns as an adult. His teacher later abandoned guns in favor of photography.

I'll miss Carl very much. His last day was Edwin Arlington Robinson's poem translated into tragic fact. "And Richard Cory, one calm summer night,/Went home and put a bullet through his head." Richard Cory wasn't the sort to use an icepick. The same with Carl. Only a gun.

Damn those guns.

Letter to the Editor

Time Magazine

I am 83 years old, living in an excellent nursing home, but with failing sight and hearing like Shakespeare's seventh age of man. I am in a position to say this: Shouldn't compassion, common sense and economics unite to decree that some old folks' lives be mercifully terminated? It hurts me to think of the good that could be done with the $20,000 spent on my yearly expenses.

Cornelia S. Love
High Point, NC

Coping with a Challenge

*T*his last group covers a number of topics, all related to coming to terms with, or facing up to, life's challenges. The student pieces by freshman composition students Kathy McHugh, Kathy Poole, Roxanne Raber, and basic writing students Bobette Goode and Harry Wheeler are about acceptance of difficulties. Related to these is the piece, originally an address to a college class, by popular writer Annie Dillard.

Letting Go

Kathy McHugh

I was just shy of six when White Cloud, a blue-eyed, white Persian cat was born in my mother's closet on February 5, 1966. From the beginning, White Cloud was my cat, and as we grew, he became my closest friend and confidant. He made life bearable. At night he would sleep with me, and I would feel safe. When I was ill, he was always by my side. Although White Cloud was deaf, we had a language that surpassed and did not need words. We spoke to each other through our actions, our eyes, and our hearts. Countless were the times I held his warm, furry body close to mine, and sobbed on his soft shoulder. Slowly, the exhaustion, and tension, and depression would ebb away, while he snuggled closer, purring, trying to comfort me.

During those years, I convinced myself he would live forever, and I truly couldn't envision life without him. Then suddenly, one evening toward the end of October in 1979, I noticed a change in his habits. Instead of lying in his usual places, he would go down to the dark basement and crawl into the storage shelf. Or, he would lie by his water dish with his head hanging over it for hours. His behavior was the same the next day. Knowing deep in my heart something was terribly wrong, I took him to the animal hospital. As I waited for the doctor to come and examine White Cloud, I held him close and looked into his glazed eyes, begging him to please be all right, pleading with him to live, because I couldn't live without him. After the doctor checked White Cloud, I

264

was advised to leave him overnight so they could run some tests, but it didn't look hopeful. Arriving home alone, I endured one of the longest nights of my life, sleepless, weeping into my pillow. I called the hospital the next day and was informed he suffered from diabetes, dehydration, and kidney failure, which were causing heart problems and blood poisoning. One possible option was surgery, but they stressed that even if successful, it would only extend his life by a few months. They just had no way to treat his diabetes. I told them I would make a decision later that night, and hung up. I spent the next few hours thinking about White Cloud, and what he meant to me. He had given me comfort and companionship. He had been gentle, kind, and loving. He had taught me how to love and what it was. When I thought of that, I realized I could not prolong his life and have him suffer because of my selfishness in wanting him around. Love also meant letting go. Arriving at the hospital later, I informed them I had decided to have him put to sleep. I had struggled with the euphemism, for in truth, wasn't I having him killed? I went back to be with him during his final moments, and even in the hospital cage, with tubes in his legs, he looked as regal as ever. A serenity flowed from him, and I felt him telling me that I was not killing, but loving. I was giving him peace and rest. On that drizzly evening, November 1, 1979, Big Chief White Thunder Cloud ceased living.

Housework

Bobette Goode

My household duties at home are demanding and never ending. I am constantly on the go from the time I force my eyes open and stagger out of bed in the mornings till I finally collapse from total exhaustion at night. It is very difficult running a household and trying to go to college at the same time. As an example, when I come home from school, I must cook dinner, do some light cleaning around the house, and also do my homework; furthermore, I must be able to spare equal time for each of my children so I can stay in touch with their individual needs. Sometimes I feel that if I had a twin, this job could be a little easier for me, yet with my luck it would just be twice as demanding. Maybe I should put myself in the category of being a super human being, a super mom, to be more exact. After all, Superman may be able to leap buildings in a single bound, but can he do it with two screaming kids under his arms, one pulling on his leg, while he is making out a grocery list—and all of this with never a hair out of place and playing the part of a loving spouse? Then there are those sweet, adorable kids of mine, and God knows I love them. Yet there are times when they do not understand Mommy needs to rest a little. It seems as soon as I sit down to relax, someone needs help with homework or to eat again, and then for the climax a fight breaks out over who will watch what on television. When I have a day like this, I feel like running through the house screaming and pulling my hair out by its roots. However, I can't pull my hair out yet, for there are too many other things to do around the house. I have to finally come to the realization that clothes do not wash and iron themselves, so I must do them. I also must clean the bathroom bowl and floor; however, that is the highlight of my day—cleaning the toilet bowl—for now I can take out all my frustration on the bowl and scrub the daylights out of it. In conclusion, I would like to say if there is anyone who might have the nerve to say housework is a breeze, he must be out of his mind.

The Monster and the Mind Games

Kathy Poole

When thinking of seizures, most picture some poor madman rolling on the floor and flipping, uncontrollably, like a fish. However, the way a seizure surfaces takes hundreds of forms. Some people have convulsions, and others are blessed with only headaches. Mine are very different and even more difficult to describe. I used to say things like "I wouldn't wish a seizure on anyone, not even if he were the murderer of my father." It's a grand speech but hardly a working description. What does a comparison like that do, save indicate some dramatic tendencies? I suppose the one physical feeling that is similar to a seizure is an electric shock. If one continuous shock treatment is imaginable, that's almost close. When having a seizure, I am completely conscious and keep control of my body. Then I just sit or lie quietly until my "monster" goes away. My folks sometimes wondered if I were unconscious because sometimes I'd close my eyes and refuse to talk. It's so frustrating because no one will ever really understand this unless they've gone through the same thing. "Close" doesn't count.

I had problems with seizures during a few summers when I was very young. I was too young to worry and understand there was something very wrong. So, who cared? Mom and Dad didn't treat it like a real problem either. Now, it seems absolutely incredible that nothing was done about it! The winter of seventh grade brought back the seizures. I was then old enough to be

268

scared. The doctor ran tests that found nothing out of the ordinary. In the meantime, I stopped going to school as at least one "incident" a day was becoming predictable.

Fear is incredibly strong, and the mind even more powerful. I've often wondered if the two in combination were perhaps more dangerous to me than my actual physical state. I hated it when Mom, not knowing what to do, would stare into my eyes so intensely, trying to read something, to see what was wrong. She didn't understand that, during a seizure, my whole perspective changes. Everything is terrifying and ugly. When someone has a nightmare, she/he awakens with a sick, cold fear, to an atmosphere of evil confusion. That's how I felt emotionally and physically; it's exhausting. Her eyes into mine seemed so piercing that they scared me. I hate my "condition" for turning intended love and concern into something mean. All the time I played these little mind games, telling myself over and over, "It's OK, Kathy, it's all right. I'm sorry. I'm sorry." I'm not sure just what I was apologizing for, or to whom. Sometimes I apologized to God for being bad, sometimes to Mom and Dad for being so sick, sometimes to the very seizure for not liking it. The seizures became an enemy, the kind you hate but pretend to tolerate, almost like, for fear that "it" would get angry and hurt you. Of course, I knew that a seizure wasn't out to get me. The doctors told me, my folks told me, and I told me. Truly convincing me, however, was impossible. I once overheard Dad say to Mom, "I just can't stand it when she lies so still." I never realized. My insides so busy, my mind a blur, I felt anything but still. Poor Dad, for once he couldn't do anything for me. But he always held my hand. That connection was so important to me because I think I needed his strength.

Once the seizure was over, I began the association game. Let's see, what was I eating when it started? It was close to two years before I tried bean soup again. I still sometimes pretend that I don't like hot chocolate. What was I wearing? Since it's too expensive to throw out half my clothes, I logically avoided the combinations I happened to be wearing on the lucky day. How was I sitting? What was on TV? Last week I impulsively reached out and almost broke the radio dial when an old Top Forty love song played. I hated it yet didn't know why. It sounded threatening. Then I remembered the seizure that accompanied it so long ago. My strongest association is snow. To tell sledding enthusiasts that snow looks sinister is asking for a room at Bellvue. Maybe if they'd sat in snow at the top of a sledding hill for over an hour with only a seizure to keep them company, they'd stop asking me to "come outside and play in the snow."

Finally, it was hospital time. I liked to call it the Gallery of Horrors. I was 5′3″ and weighed eighty pounds. It's tough to eat when you have no appetite. I made Mom promise, swear, that if she and Dad decided to take me to the hospital, I would be the last to know about it. I can't remember what my reasoning was; maybe I just wanted to spend as little time as possible worrying about it. What I do remember is that she actually did it that way, just as I asked. It was such a trivial request that I thought she would forget or just not bother with it. Yet Mom put up with hundreds of little requests and demands. She was always there and always patient.

A car ride and two seizures later, I was settled into a room. It was a private room, but the lady next door often wandered in. She was sad and lonely and not too bright. I always wished she would go away but never had the nerve to be rude. Some days were better than others, good days being the ones I wasn't scheduled for tests. They strapped me in chairs and turned me upside down with an air bubble in my back someplace. X rays, X rays, and more X rays, CAT scans, EEGs, blood tests, and even allergy tests—the list goes on, but it's rather nauseating. Three weeks went by, and the doctors found a medicine that worked. Believe me, I was ready to take it and very grateful to them. They finally gave my problem a name I could pronounce: a focal seizure in the left frontal temporal lobe. A nice neat name for five months of hell. It's a sad situation that I would be ashamed to be labeled epileptic. I constantly cling to my one consolation, I don't have epilepsy, I have a "focal seizure disorder." Maybe the hairline difference shouldn't be so important to me, yet it seems to be less intimidating, not only to others but to myself.

For Dad's birthday I walked the length of my hospital room to sit on his lap. He was really happy. He told me that I tottered just like a newborn calf. It wasn't easy since it was the first time I had walked in almost three months.

Stopping the story on Dad's birthday, me on his lap, and everybody smiling, would've been really nice, but the effects of those five months are still present. The whole episode is remembered every single day in some way or another, by my association games, the pills I take three times a day, or maybe a bad joke about epileptics on TV. I have a lot of trouble accepting myself as is. Because of medication, I'm "normal" and can drive. A few months ago, the Bureau of Motor Vehicles sent me a little card that says I have seizures and must keep the card with me at all times. My reaction to it has been unreasonable and immature. I threw a fit, my temper at an all time high. It was quite a show. Yet the fact remains I just can't accept that card. I won't have it. Accepting it is agreeing, in black and white, that I do have seizures. Maybe acceptance comes with age.

In spite of the tough parts, I've faced a lot about myself. At least I'm curious now. Where I once refused to even talk about it, I now want to know everything written on seizures. I especially need to know why they happen. I don't feel quite so uncomforable telling someone about my "deep, dark secret." I once thought it should be a secret or it should be public knowledge. It's almost a happy surprise that people just don't care. And they forget. It's always painful to dwell on the fact, even tougher to write about it. Yet anything in life is a series of steps; I thought I wouldn't tell anyone, so I made myself talk to someone. I really wouldn't face parts of my "seizure story," so I wrote it down and made myself read it. I even throw snowballs. It can only get easier.

Octopus—Why Eat It?

Harry A. Wheeler

The very thought of letting this disgusting-looking creature, dead or alive, get within one hundred yards of me causes my blood pressure to rise ten points. Yet one evening in Hong Kong at a very plush restaurant, I found myself confronted with the very thing that gives me nightmares. Sitting there in a beautiful white china bowl were octopus tentacles, baby ones. I caught sight of this dish while talking with my date, unaware that the waiter had placed them on the table. I then turned to confront the very thing I did not want to see.

As I, a combat veteran of Vietnam, jumped back from the table, a hush fell over the room, and then sudden laughter burst out. Feeling a bit silly at the time, I laughed myself and then at myself for not upholding the Marine Corps code of not running in the face of danger. There was really no danger, only my insecurity, my fear of the unknown.

Easing back to my table and trying to appear as if nothing had happened, I drew in a breath and sat down, careful not to look at the objects at the center of the table. My date suggested that I was not obligated to eat the octopus and if I wished, I could order a more traditional dish. I thought for a moment and then said, "What the heck. Just taste it. Maybe you'll like it."

The octopus tentacles that were before me were cut into two-inch-long pieces except for the sucker, which looked like the amputated finger of someone's hand. The color was that of something dead or dying, a brownish green mix that would gag a maggot.

Baby octopus was not my idea of a gourmet dish. To start, I was unsure how to begin eating it, and second how to stop the natural gag reaction.

I was told by my date that to properly eat octopus you cut a bite-sized piece and then dip it into the sauce—the nature of which is still unknown to me. Having done the preparatory work, I set out to eat octopus that day. I felt as though I were being watched, not by the others present, but by that thing on my fork. I stared back. "What could it be thinking? This is silly." What I had was just a small part of the arm and not the head.

I gathered my nerve and touched the meat with my fingertip and drew back quickly. Good, it did not move. Placing the small cut into my mouth, I began to gag. "If I let go now, the evening is over," I thought. I was barely able to suppress the reaction.

Now I was tasting the sauce, which was not bad, but there was no taste of meat. The moment of truth had arrived. Biting down easily into the meat so not to receive a sudden rush of some unsavory substance, I began to chew. Nothing unpleasant so far. I chewed again, nothing. I was half expecting a fishy saltwater taste, but I received nothing for my efforts.

Suddenly, my perceptive tongue signalled my brain that I was on to something, or was it on to me? The suckers. Gag! It is not nice to throw up on the table, which I was about to do. Again I was able to put these reflexes on hold, but for how long? I began to chew again but was making no progress.

I have teeth, maybe not all that were issued, but teeth nonetheless, and still I was not gaining any ground with this thing. "What is this _____?" I thought. If baby is this tough, mother must be made of steel! I've made better progress chewing on erasers and rubber bands. At least I could bite through them.

After chewing for what seemed like minutes, I swallowed. The octopus was going down, down inside of me to do only heaven knows what. Three quarters of the way down my throat and the meat began to rise like freshly rolled dough. A quick drink of water cured all the adverse reactions I was having at the table.

I can only liken this adventure to a hungry man on a desert with only a tire next to him. He is compelled to either eat the tire or starve. He chooses to eat the tire and is surprised that the only compensation he receives by eating the tire is a strong jaw.

No taste, no nothing was my reward for dining on this delicacy of the Orient.

Is There Really Such a Thing as Talent?

Annie Dillard

It's hard work, doing something with your life. The very thought of hard work makes me queasy. I'd rather die in peace. Here we are, all equal and alike and none of us much to write home about—and some people choose to make themselves into physicists or thinkers or major-league pitchers, knowing perfectly well that it will be nothing but hard work. But I want to tell you that it's not as bad as it sounds. Doing something does not require discipline; it creates its own discipline—with a little help from caffeine.

People often ask me if I discipline myself to write, if I work a certain number of hours a day on a schedule. They ask this question with envy in their voices and awe on their faces and a sense of alienation all over them, as if they were addressing an armored tank or a talking giraffe or Niagara Falls. We want to believe that other people are natural wonders; it gets us off the hook.

Now, it happens that when I wrote my first book of prose, I worked an hour or two a day for a while, and then in the last two months, I got excited and worked very hard, for many hours a day. People can lift cars when they want to. People can recite the

"Is there really such a thing as talent?" by Annie Dillard from *Seventeen*® Magazine, June 1979. Copyright © 1979 by Annie Dillard and Triangle Communications Inc. All rights reserved. Reprinted by permission of the author and her agent Blanche C. Gregory, Inc., and Triangle Communications, Inc.

Koran, too, and run in marathons. These things aren't ways of life; they are merely possibilities for everyone on certain occasions of life. You don't lift cars around the clock or write books every year. But when you do, it's not so hard. It's not superhuman. It's very human. You do it for love. You do it for love and respect for your own life; you do it for love and respect for the world; and you do it for love and respect for the task itself.

If I had a little baby, it would be hard for me to rise up and feed that little baby in the middle of the night. It would be hard, but certainly wouldn't be a discipline. It wouldn't be a regimen I imposed on myself out of masochism, nor would it be the flowering of some extraordinary internal impulse. I would do it, grumbling for love and because it has to be done.

Of course it has to be done. And something has to be done with your life too: something specific, something human. But don't wait around to be hit by love. Don't wait for anything. Learn something first. Then when you are getting to know it, you will get to love it, and that love will direct you in what to do. So many times when I was in college I used to say of a course like Seventeenth-Century Poetry or European History, "I didn't like it at first, but now I like it." All of life is like that—a sort of dreary course which gradually gets interesting if you work at it.

I used to live in perpetual dread that I would one day read all the books that I would ever be interested in and have nothing more to read. I always figured that when that time came I would force myself to learn wild flowers, just to keep awake. I dreaded it, because I was not very interested in wild flowers but thought I should be. But things kept cropping up and one book has led to another and I haven't had to learn wild flowers yet. I don't think there's much danger of coming to the end of the line. The line is endless. I urge you to get in it, to get in line. It's a long line—but it's the only show in town.

Learning a Lesson of Love

Roxanne Raber

One of the people in my English composition class wrote a paper which said something to the effect that you don't realize you love someone until they're gone. This made me think of something that I have pushed to the back of my mind and chosen not to face for four years now. That thing is the end of my grandmother's life and how I dealt with it.

My grandmother (my mother's mother) had been a diabetic for nearly all her life. This was a major factor in her death. Ever since I can remember, I never wanted to hug or kiss her, or even get very close to her for that matter. I guess I thought it was grotesque to have to give yourself a shot of insulin, and I didn't want any part of it. That seems so cruel now because she couldn't help being diabetic, but I was a child and was only aware of things on my own terms. I wasn't old enough to have enough compassion to accept her situation. I never was emotionally close to her either. She was a very social person and seemed to regard children as a lower form of life, not to be taken seriously except when it was time to come in for dinner. She never really talked to me even up until the last time I saw her in good health. She was always talking to other adults, and it seemed she couldn't relate to me or any other children. With these two factors in mind, there was always a distance between us.

When I was about thirteen, she became ill. I don't know if you would call it an illness, but she lost the will to live. I don't know if she did so because she was suffering or if she figured she was so old that she just didn't want the hassle of trying to live anymore. She became totally dependent on my mother in particular.

My grandmother was eventually put in a rest home. My mother wanted to bring her home and take care of her, but she had to be fed through a tube, and we didn't have the facilities for that. She was in the rest home a year and a half until she died, and not one time did I go to see her. All of my other cousins live out of state, and they came to see her. I lived in Akron, and I didn't see her once. I didn't even know what rest home she was in.

I can remember we got the phone call telling us she had died. I was talking on the phone to my boyfriend, and the operator cut in with an emergency call. I didn't know who the call was from, but I knew what they were going to say. I got off the phone and went upstairs to tell my mom there would be a call in a few minutes. I watched as the phone rang, she answered it, and she started to cry. She hung up and told me what I already knew. At that moment I wanted to cry for my grandmother, but I didn't; I cried for my mother. She had been so involved with my grandmother for the past two years and now grandmother was gone. Mom said she wanted to die herself and I could truly understand why she felt that way.

At the funeral in Tennessee I felt like a stranger. I didn't feel I had the right to mourn openly because I hadn't really known my grandmother that well.

When the time came to walk by the casket and I had to stand there and look at her for the last time, it was like a door opened inside of me and all these emotions and feelings that I hadn't let show before came flooding out. I really started to bawl, and I wanted to tell her that I didn't want her to die and that I was sorry I was angry with her and most of all, I wanted to touch her; I wanted to hold her hand. I didn't touch her though. There were so many people around. I think if it would have been just me there, I would have said everything I was feeling in hopes that she would hear me and possibly forgive me. Before we left Tennessee to come home, I was telling everyone goodbye, and I went over to my grandfather and hugged him and started to cry. I told him, for the first time that I loved him, which is something I never said to my grandmother.

The saying "You don't realize you love someone until they're gone" is true for me. I now make a point to be open with my other grandmother. I say what I feel most of the time, and I visit her as much as I can because she's not going to be around forever. This is the first time I have really thought about my grandmother's death and the first time I have attempted to organize my feelings about what happened. I think I learned from my mistake, and it has taught me to appreciate my grandparents.

Part Three

Proofreading

Part Three is made up of a number of separate lessons, each focusing on a different problem area. It is designed to meet individual needs and to be used in any of several ways. For example, some teachers may determine that you will benefit from working through only certain lessons. Other teachers may prefer to assign selected lessons to your entire class, while still others may ask all students to do all lessons in Part Three because the areas included are those with which student writers often encounter difficulty. Regardless of which method is employed, the exercises that follow give the opportunity for practice in specific areas that require strengthening and for developing your ability to become a good proofreader of your own writing.

Proofreading what you have written is an essential part of the entire writing process and therefore must be attended to as carefully as the act of writing itself. An excellent way to proofread your writing is to read it *aloud* to *hear* whether it is correct. Proofreading is essential and must be developed through practice.

Lesson One

Recognizing Incomplete Sentences

An incomplete sentence, that is, a sentence fragment, is often derived from the type of error shown in the following examples.

My first date was with a weird guy. <u>Who brought his sister along.</u>

<u>Because I was successful in football last year.</u> I reached my goal, The Most Valuable Player Award.

As I approached the side of the bus, it started to move. <u>Rolling away without me.</u>

In the examples above, the underlined groups of words are not complete sentences. *If you read them aloud, you can hear that they do not sound complete.* Usually, an incomplete sentence needs only to be attached to the whole sentence of which it is a part.

You can hear sentence completeness once the groups of words are attached as they are below.

My first date was with a weird guy <u>who brought his sister along.</u>

<u>Because I was successful in football last year,</u> I reached my goal, The Most Valuable Player Award.

As I approached the side of the bus, it started to move, <u>rolling away without me.</u>

Practice in Proofreading

Carefully read the student paragraphs below, which have been changed to include incomplete sentences (fragments). Your task here is to determine which sentences are *not* complete. A useful approach is to read the paragraph *from the bottom up;* that is, read the last sentence of the paragraph first, listening closely as you read *aloud*, making your way to the first sentence in the paragraph. Underline all incomplete sentences as you go. Once you have identified all the incomplete sentences, go back over the paragraph and attach these to the whole sentences to which they belong, as shown in the examples above. Then, read the new whole sentences aloud as a final check.

A. Crawling around in dark, dirty, and smelly basements as a termite inspector was not my idea of a good job. In late fall I was crawling under an old farmhouse in Medina County. That had half a basement and half a crawl space. The basement part was old and dark, and the smell of mold and mildew drifted in the air like fog floating over an abandoned shipyard at night. The only light in the room came from a bulb that looked as if old Tom Edison made it himself. I grabbed my trusty flashlight and screwdriver and started to tap on the ancient hand-cut rafters above my head. While finding spiders and ants. I didn't find any termites in the basement. My next goal was to check out the crawl space. When I looked into this miniature cave under the house. I saw the reflection of my flashlight on cobwebs and dust. I jumped in on my stomach. And started to crawl around and tap the rafters. While closing in on the far side of the house. I didn't notice that the ground in the crawl space was sloping up and the house still was level. Before I knew it, my body was wedged between the house and the ground like a cork in a wine bottle. I started to panic and yell. For I had never been stuck this bad in a place that looked this close to Hell before. The old, fat, and decrepit farmer came wobbling down the stairs and looked into the crawl space. I told him to help me out, but he said he couldn't reach me. I felt sweat run down my back, and I knew if I didn't get out of there quick, I was going to pee in my pants. After what felt like an eternity. I wiggled, pulled, and turned myself free. Luckily I still had time to make it to the bathroom. After a few more gloomy experiences not as bad as this time, I came up with the conclusion. That bugs were not my calling in life.

B. I thought I could make a million dollars quick and easy, as a young boy, working as a part-time salesman, but all I earned was a lesson by the cruel world of business. I felt very positive. When I started working for Metro Exterminating and Co. and thought that this was an easy way to make money. After a short training period. The salesmen sent me out to talk fast. And to make my fortune. Boy, I was surprised when I approached people with the most determined look in my eye and all they did was laugh at my sales pitch. Who would take an eighteen-year-old boy with a bad complexion and a peach fuzz mustache seriously. When he came up to you and tried to convince you to spend a lot of money on something you really didn't need. I felt very depressed and discouraged. Because I failed at my big chance to make a lot of money. I later laughed at myself. When I realized what a fool I looked like by begging these people to take me seriously and realized that I needed an education of marketing and sales to give me an excellent background. In the profession which I chose. I have since then given up the idea of trying to make a quick buck. And have decided to make a million just like everyone else does—by winning the lottery.

C. Cleaning the kitchen transforms a mild, young teenager into an old prune-looking, back-breaking, arthritis-suffering, and senile person. Doing the dishes is the first stage of my transformation. After running the hot water into the sink. It is time to place my beautiful hands into the water of aging. Now that the plates, glasses, and silverware are clean, the water is dirty, and all the soap suds are gone. The water has taken its toll on my hands. What were once young, healthy looking hands are now taking on the characteristics of a prune. They look as if fifty years have been added to them. I drain the dirty water. And replace it with clean water to finish the pots and pans. My arms become tired from scrubbing so much. That they start to become sore. Arthritis is starting to set in, and the second stage of my transformation is beginning. When the dishes are put away. I feel as if fifty-five years have passed by in just twenty minutes. When I'm done putting away food into all the cabinets. My legs start to wobble like rubber bands. I lose track of my thoughts. This comes from going back and forth to different cabinets. Which makes me dizzy. When everything is in its original place, the final stage occurs. I am sweeping and mopping the kitchen, and hall floors. My back starts to become stiff. I complain about my nasty-looking hands. My clothes are dirty, and my whole body feels dirty. This task has drained every ounce of my energy. I had left. But the kitchen is clean, and Mother is pleased. Now we have a dishwasher, and unfortunately my little sister will never have the pleasure of becoming old in just a few hours as I have.

D. Cleaning up my room can be a very gross job. First, I would like to tell you I have clothes scattered from one end of the room to the other. Chewing tobacco cans are all over my dressers and desk, and bird droppings are all over the room too. Cleaning up my room can be gross. Because when I move my bed to clean up underneath, there are always at least three spit cups of chew that have spilled onto the carpet and have turned it brown. This way I have to scrub the carpet on my hands and knees. To get out the stains. And I have to take the cups of chew that haven't spilled and empty them out. Then I go around in search of dirty clothes. Pick them up, and place them in the dirty clothes hamper to be washed, and some of the clothes that I have picked up have been aging in my room for weeks. I also have two birds. Which are cockatoos. They are green, white, and yellow. The birds fly around my room. Because I never lock them up in their cage because it smells too bad. The birds fly from one end of the room to the other. Letting their droppings fly mostly onto the curtains that hang in my room. To take the curtains down becomes very gross because the droppings fall on my head. Cleaning up my room is a very sick job.

E. I believe that some things happen for the best, but I don't believe that everything happens for the best. For example, if an athlete missed a road trip because of a broken leg and the plane carrying the team crashed. One could say that it was a good thing that the athlete broke his leg. But, if a family man was paralyzed in a car accident. How could one tell his wife and kids that it happened for the best? So I believe that while sometimes there is something good to say about a bad incident. Everything does not happen for the best.

F. ''Everything happens for the best'' is a fantasy, a beautiful daydream. But hardly a reality. Only the innocent, who have been sheltered from all evil, can possibly believe a statement such as that. Reality is when a young, eager soldier, with a promising future dies an untimely, gruesome death in a hellhole called Vietnam, or when you read about a falling bridge that has killed a loving mother and father. Leaving behind three, small, defenseless children to fend for themselves. I saw a small, fragile boy, wearing a protective helmet over his damaged skull. Being pushed in a wheelchair by his saddened grandmother. He had seen both of his parents and his sister killed in an automobile accident, and he would never walk again. How can a dehumanized act of raping and killing an eighty—

five year old woman be for the best? A person kills himself. Because of some terrible inner turmoil. A mother dies in agony from cancer, and a woman with leukemia and rheumatoid arthritis walks only because she has great courage and stamina. Tell me, if you can, how can any of these things be for the best?

G. I disagree that everything happens for the best. A lot of life involves coping with reality. As is the case of losing a loved one by premature death. Some good can come from the loss of a loved one. If family members, for instance, become extremely close at such a time. Nevertheless, the void of emotional emptiness can never be filled. During this crisis. The mind can become a mass of confusion and withdrawal. Someone once said, ''Nothing is forever.'' In my experience this statement holds true, especially in relationships where sincere emotional ties are involved, because the ties can be cut and lost forever. Therefore, if we were to remove our colored glasses. We would see that everything doesn't happen for the best.

H. I have been brought up to believe that everything does happen for the best. My grandmother was ninety-three. When she died. She spent her last seven years in a nursing home. She couldn't walk or move her arms and legs, and some days she would just lie in bed and cry. Not even recognizing members of the family. When Grandmother did die, the entire family was sad and mourned her death. But on the other hand, we felt a sense of joy. Because we knew that she was in peace. My grandmother was in a world. Where she would not have to put up with any more pain. To this day I can still hear my mother saying. ''Everything will work out for the best!''

I. One may think that everything happens for the best, but I disagree. For example, if my house burned to the ground. It would not be for the best. It would

be terrible. Some things may happen for the best,
but ''everything'' does not. Walking through life,
some people see only what they want to see. These
are people. Who live in a dream world, fearing
reality. Therefore, they believe that everything
turns out for the best. If everything turned out for
the best. There would be no sorrow or sadness in the
world, but there is sorrow and sadness occurring.
Even though some people feel that everything
happens for the best. I do not feel that it does.

Writing Assignment

Now try your hand, writing a paragraph on the topic "Everything Happens for the Best." In this writing assignment, focus primarily on sentence completeness. To ensure that all of your sentences are complete, read your finished paragraph *aloud, beginning with the last sentence first and working your way to the first sentence.*

Lesson Two

Recognizing Run-Together Sentences

A major sentence problem occurs when two whole sentences run together without any stopping or starting point between them. This error is called a run-on or a run-together sentence.

I feel this class will help me survive English Composition without it I would probably fail.

If you read this student sentence *aloud*, you can hear that one sentence ends with the word "Composition" and another begins with the word "without."

I feel this class will help me survive English Composition. Without it I would probably fail.

A period is used to indicate to your reader the end of a sentence, and a capital letter is used to show the beginning of the second sentence.

There are other options, of course, which you practiced in Lesson Two of Part One. As you recall, two complete sentences also can be joined by a comma and a short joining word or a semicolon and a long joining word.

I feel this class will help me survive English Composition, for without it I would probably fail.

I feel this class will help me survive English Composition; furthermore, without it I would probably fail.

289

Your choice depends on which sounds better to you when you read the sentences aloud.

> Now I'm really glad I made that decision going to college was probably the most important decision I've ever made.

Here again, if you read the student sentence *aloud*, you can *hear* that two complete and separate sentences have been written together as one. You can *hear* a clear break between the words "decision" and "going." By going back over the group of words beginning with "now" and ending with "decision," you can hear one complete sentence. The same is true of the group of words beginning with "going" and ending with "made." A period is used between the words "decision" and "going" to show two complete and separate sentences.

> Now I'm really glad I made that decision⊙ Going to college was probably the most important decision I've ever made⊙

You also, of course, can use a short or long joining word and the appropriate punctuation.

Sometimes student writers join two complete and separate sentences with a comma (,). This is also a major sentence problem.

> I had no idea what I was getting into, I did not really care.

The use of a comma *alone* between two complete and separate sentences is considered an error in writing because a comma is not used to mark the end of a sentence. The comma, in this case, attempts to splice the two complete sentences together, and this error is, thus, called a comma splice. To show two complete and separate sentences, the above student sentence can be rewritten as

> I had no idea what I was getting into⊙ I did not really care⊙

Practice in Proofreading

Carefully *read aloud* the student paragraphs below, which have been changed to include run-together sentences. Your task here is to identify those sentences and correctly separate them with a period and a capital letter (or, if you choose, a short or long joining word and the appropriate punctuation). Then, as a final check, read the new whole sentences *aloud*.

A. A demoralizing experience was having dinner at Ponderosa Steak House. The salad bar was well stacked that night, plus I was ravenous. Everything looked appealing, so I piled my salad platter high with lettuce, red juicy tomatoes, mushrooms, cheese, onions, pickles, carrots, and cucumbers and topped it off with spoonfuls of extra thick blue cheese dressing, it was a masterpiece of salad platters, and the anticipation of eating it was killing me. On the way back to the booth, I got caught in a crowd behind a booth where a couple was sitting when all of a sudden an elbow out of nowhere hit my own elbow pushing my arm forward, turning my piled high salad platter upside down on two unsuspecting people.

My first reaction was to hide by trying to blend in with the crowd, but this didn't work, I then tried to hide my platter, but that didn't work either. My wife, who saw this happen, turned around and walked quickly to the booth, leaving me there to face this humiliating accident myself. The couple had blue cheese dripping from their heads, lettuce, mushrooms, and cheese on their shirts, and the rest of the salad was on their pants and shoes to add to this, their mouths were wide open, and not a word was coming out. Instantly everybody at Ponderosa stopped eating, the crowds stopped pushing, and all eyes focused in on me and the couple for what seemed like an eternity. I quickly broke the stares and silence by apologizing, then I started cleaning blue cheese from the man's glasses. I grabbed some more napkins to clean off the rest of the salad and kept apologizing the whole time.

I then offered to pay half the cost of cleaning their clothes. The salad—covered people accepted my apology and offer to clean their clothes. Nowadays I go to Ponderosa after the dinner rush, and I stay away from crowds when carrying my salad platter.

B. My most embarrassing moment was at a high school football game. When the game started, all of my friends and I were really rowdy, and we started screaming at the opposing side. At one point, all of my friends and I stood up and started yelling before I knew what was going on, they sat down, and I was

the only one left standing up yelling my brains out.
When I realized this, I quickly sat down and hid my
face in my hands, I could feel my face getting hot,
and sweat began to form. I thought I would die of
embarrassment, I thought everyone saw me, so I
looked around, and a few people were grinning I
wanted to leave. But after a while I began to laugh
and enjoy myself again.

C. An embarrassing moment for me was when I walked
into and used the ladies' room by mistake I was
fourteen at the time and was up at Lake Erie to go
sailing with my uncle and brother. We were out on
the lake and not too far from our destination when I
realized that I had to go to the restroom and bad!
After what seemed to be years we reached the island,
this time I was in so much pain, I thought my eyes
were going to pop out. So I jumped off the boat, ran
up the hill, opened the door, and walked into the
restroom. When I walked back outside, there was a
group of women just standing there looking at me.
Wondering why, I turned and looked back at the two
doors one read ''his'' and one read ''hers.''
Realizing that I came out of the one that read
''hers,'' I turned red, politely said excuse me, and
ran back down the hill to the boat.

D. I had a really embarrassing moment just a few days
ago. A couple of friends and I were having a little
party after the football victory as the party died
down, I fell asleep in my room on the floor. Two of
my buddies decided to play a joke on me, so they got
a role of tape and taped me to the floor. Then they
woke me up and told me to go to bed, but to my
surprise I could not move. After they found out I
could not move, they invited the whole floor of my
dorm over to see me even the resident assistant
there. If you want to talk about feeling like an
imbecile, well I did. I think that was the most
awkward moment I have ever been in, I felt like a
simpleton. I could feel my face turn red and start

perspiring. The next day I was so self—conscious, I thought everybody was looking at me and laughing after I walked by. It just felt like everybody knew what happened the night before I hope I never have another situation as embarrassing as that again.

E. What I would do if the world ended on a Sunday is get together with all my family and spend a nice day we would have dinner at my parents' home, we would then relax and tell stories about each other I can even imagine what my mom would cook she would make our favorite dishes of baked beans, meat loaf, cheese cauliflower, and, last but not least, strawberry shortcake. Mmm mmm! After dinner, we would play ball, hit golf balls, and probably play tag in the large back yard. Since I couldn't tell anyone about the world ending, we would probably work on our cars too if it was really warm, we would walk to my uncle's lake to go swimming or fishing, all in all we would just spend a happy, relaxing, and special day <u>together</u>!

F. The world will end with people in a state of mass hysteria as the predestined end creeps up on them slowly people will realize that their time is coming soon. Widespread panic across the land will have young and old flocking to the altars to beg forgiveness while others frantically dash around like rabbits being sought by the hunter. All business and social events will suddenly cease, the only concern will be to fulfill dreams gathered since childhood. The freeways will be jammed with high speed vehicles, racing as if they could steer to an eternal homestead. Lovers everywhere will be clenched together in the heat of emotion, wondering why life is so finite. The truth, unspoken until now, will find its way to the lips of those burdened with a guilty conscience tension will be strung everywhere as the fear of the unknown dissolves people's sanity.

Writing Assignment

Write a paragraph telling how either you or others might react to the statement "The world will end in twenty-four hours." Once you have completed this writing assignment, read the finished paragraph *aloud*, sentence by sentence, making sure that it contains no run-together sentences.

Lesson Three

Recognizing and Using the -s Ending on Present Tense Verbs

Most standard dictionaries list four forms of each verb. A verb is always indicated by *v.* (or *vb.*, *vt.*, or *vi.*).

1. present:
(breathe *v.*)

2. past:
breathed

3. past with
have, has, had:
breathed

4. *-ing* form:
breathing

THE VERB USED WITH *HE, SHE, IT,* OR SUBSTITUTE WORDS

The first form, called the *present tense*, is the basic verb form used to indicate present time and actions, especially those actions that occur regularly, that is, as a matter of habit. Student writers rarely make mistakes with any of the various forms of the present tense, with the exception of the verb form used with *he, she,* or *it*, which ends in *s* or *es*.

I *breathe*.
You *breathe*.
He, She, It *breathes*.

We *breathe*.
You *breathe*.
They *breathe*.

Notice that the present tense verb ends in *-s* if it is used with *he, she,* or *it*.

The present tense verb also ends in *-s* when used with words that can substitute for *he, she,* or *it*.

295

I *breathe.*   We *breathe,*
You *breathe.*   You *breathe.*
(Joe) (Nancy) (The plant)
He,   She,   It *breathes.*   They *breathe.*

For each of the following sentences, circle the correct verb form. Notice that if a word or words can substitute for *he, she,* or *it* the verb form ends in *s.*

1. My <u>grandmother</u> drive/drives to church every Sunday.
2. The <u>students</u> usually walk/walks to the library on West Avenue.
3. My <u>aunt and uncle</u> always take/takes a vacation in June.
4. <u>Bill</u> often buy/buys a hamburger for lunch.
5. <u>Bob</u> like/likes his coffee steaming hot.
6. Our St. Bernard <u>dog</u> eat/eats twenty-five pounds of dog food every two weeks.
7. My <u>writing</u> continue/continues to improve each week.
8. <u>Practice</u> make/makes perfect.
9. Those <u>fans</u> seem/seems terribly rowdy tonight.
10. <u>Aging</u> bring/brings problems to many people.
11. <u>Understanding</u> grow/grows as a <u>person</u> mature/matures.
12. <u>Happiness</u> sometimes come/comes unexpectedly.

Write twenty sentences of your own that include present tense verbs that end in *-s.* Use a different verb in each sentence and also vary your use of *he, she, it* and words that can substitute for *he, she,* or *it.*

1. _____

2. _____

3. _____

4. _____

5. _____

6. _____

7. _____

8. _____

9. _____

10. _____

11. _____

12. _____

13. _____

14. _____

15. _____

16. _____

17. _____

18. _____

19. _____

20. _____

HAVE/HAS, DO/DOES

Two of the verbs that student writers often have trouble with are the verbs *have* and *do*. *Have* and *do*, however, follow the same rule in the present tense as the verb *breathe;* that is, all forms in the present tense look alike except the one that ends in *-s*.

I *have* feelings
You *have* feelings.

We *have* feelings.
You *have* feelings.

He, She, It *has* feelings.   They *have* feelings.
(or a substitute)   (or a substitute)

I *do* homework.   We *do* homework.
You *do* homework.   You *do* homework.
He, She, It *does* homework.   They *do* homework.
(or a substitute)   (or a substitute)

Write twenty sentences, some of which include *has* and some of which include *does*. Also, vary your use of *he, she, it* and words that can substitute for *he, she, it*.

1. _____

2. _____

3. _____

4. _____

5. _____

6. _____

7. _____

8. _____

9. _____

10. _____

11. _____

12. _____

13. _____

14. _____

15. _____

16. _____

17. _____

18. _____

19. _____

20. _____

AM/ARE/IS

The following present tense verb forms require attention because they have more variation than other present tense verb forms, as indicated by the circled words.

I (am) glad to be alive.   We *are* glad to be alive.
You *are* glad to be alive.   You *are* glad to be alive.
He, She, It (is) glad to be alive. They *are* glad to be alive.
(or a substitute)   (or a substitute)

Write twenty sentences of your own, using each of the forms of this present tense verb at least a couple of times. In most of your sentences, use the verb *is* with *he, she, it* (or words that can substitute for these).

1. _____

2. _____

3. _____

4. _____

5. _____

6. _____

7. _____

8. _____

9. _____

10. _____

11. _____

12. _____

13. _____

14. _____

15. _____

16. _____

17. _____

18. _____

19. _____

20. _____

Practice in Proofreading

Carefully read the following student paragraphs and place a circle around each present tense verb form that ends in -s (including *is*). There are other kinds of words that also end in -s. Do not circle any of these. Place a circle only around *verbs* that end in -s. If you are unsure of whether or not a word is a verb, look it up in your dictionary.

Train yourself so that you can learn to *hear* and *see* the final -s on this form of the present tense verb. While it takes time to accomplish this, it can be mastered with practice.

A. My father reminds me of Santa Claus. He is a five-foot eight-inch man with gray-black hair. The dark, rough, whiskered face goes well with his elongated nose. The green or hazel eyes he has are fierce looking. The Indian in his blood line causes him to be dark complexioned. His seventeen-and-a-half-inch neck blends right into his rounded and thick

shoulders. On his left arm there is a green homemade
tattoo with his name in it. His right hand is
smaller than his left, as he was born with a defect.
His belly is round, and when he laughs, it shakes
like a bowl of jelly. His legs are short and stocky.
As a child, my father was always picked on because
of his hand. The other children called him short
finger. His hand never limited him, and he was more
determined to do well. My father works really well
with children. He is always jolly and makes them
laugh at everything. I am really proud of him
because he succeeds with his defect. My father is
not like a parent to me but more like a friend. I
would like to be the same type of father as my
father.

B. An interesting person that teaches one of my
college classes could be called a comfortable
version of a college professor. He has short, curly,
brown, pepper-colored hair, and his neatly trimmed
mustache is a brown pepper color also. His other
facial features include thick brown pepper
eyebrows, long dark eyelashes, sparkling brown
eyes, a large nose, and a wide grinning mouth, all
contained in a light complexion. He wears a small,
bright diamond earring on his medium-sized left
ear. His normal bone structure and fair medium build
stand comfortably erect. He wears warm, thick top
garments like mellow flannel shirts, nicely
coordinated sweaters, and mellow-colored
turtlenecks. Soft Levi blue jeans and large leather
cream-colored boots complete his dress. He wears a
plastic Swatch-type watch, and he sometimes uses a
pair of reading glasses. Sometimes he has an aroma
of pipe tobacco smoke since he smokes a carved
English pipe. He carries a large, bulky, light-
colored leather saddlebag loaded with books,
papers, and other odds and ends. His deep, slightly
husky voice often makes a loud, chuckly laugh. I
feel comfortable and relaxed because of the casual
style of this professor.

In the following student paragraphs, which have been altered for this exercise, (1) supply the present tense -s endings where they have been omitted, and (2) where there is a choice to be made, choose the correct form as needed and circle it. It is good practice to get used to *hearing* the sound of a sentence in which the verb form is used correctly. You should, then, read the sentences *aloud* after you have completed them. If you are in doubt about a particular verb ending, check the models at the beginning of the lesson.

A. My biggest fear (is/are) that I will not succeed in life. I'm scared that life will pass me by before I know what I want to do with myself. I would like to see myself as an architect making good money, driving nice cars, and living a happy life with my gorgeous wife, who will wear luxurious clothing. We will live on the beautiful shores of the Atlantic ocean, and someday we will have a little girl and boy that will grow up to be proud of their successful father. I fear that instead of seeing this, I will see myself still working at a place only making nickels and dimes, living in a house that (is/are) falling down, with old torn up shingles, broken windows, and doors coming off the hinges. Instead of a nice car, it (is/are) an old, run-down, beat up, rusted old Ford. My wife (is/are) still beautiful, but instead of nice clothes, she (is/are) wearing blue-light specials. She still (has/have) to work and watch the children, just so the kids can have a decent meal and clothes on their backs. The children will later grow up and say, ''That (is/are) my father, still scooping ice cream at Baskin-Robbins. He (is/are) still trying to decide what he want to do with his life. Isn't he a pitiful sight with his grey beard. He still (has/have) not found a decent job to support Mom, so she still work at the I-77 truck stop.'' So you see, this (is/are) what I fear the most, not succeeding, not knowing what I want to do with my life, and most of all not getting a good job to support my beautiful wife and kids.

B. I believe the things that affect me most are the
methods a person use to achieve success and the
standards or values he go by. I cannot respect a
person who steps on others to get to the top, nor
can I respect a person who cheat. Success (is/are)
not being a business tycoon either. Success (is/
are) just achieving one's goals, whether winning a
race or becoming the President. I think if a person
set certain goals and achieve these goals in a
socially recognized manner, then he or she (is/are)
a success to me. Success just (do/does) not stop
when one get to the top either. I believe once an
individual achieve his goals, he (is/are) obligated
to help others along the way. These (is/are) the
things that for me determine a person's success.

C. A successful person (is/are) one who (is/are)
prosperous in his work. He accomplish certain tasks
that he set out to do. He thrive on the work he (do/
does); therefore, he (is/are) achieving. He (have/
has) a promising future and expect to be fruitful in
his earnings. Since he (is/are) happy and enjoy what
he (do/does), he (is/are) a hard worker. He
overwhelmingly strive to this peak, and because he
work to his maximum, success show in him.

D. The best aspect of Marine Corps life (is/are)
recruit training or boot camp. It (is/are) here that
each private go through an extensive physical and
mental training program. He drill and drill until he
(is/are) prepared to automatically respond to any
given situation. It (is/are) at this time that he
learn military customs, hand—to—hand combat, rifle
marksmanship, and how to be a well—rounded Marine.
By the time the recruit graduate, he (is/are) glad
the vigorous training (is/are) over. He (have/has)
earned the title ''Marine,'' a title that takes him
three months of discipline and hard work to get.

Writing Assignment

Write a paragraph in the *present tense* about someone you know who is old. Since you are writing about someone else, most of your *verb forms will end in -s* when used with *he, she, it,* or words that can substitute for these. Once you have completed this paragraph, *proofread it, paying special attention to present tense verb forms.*

Lesson Four

Recognizing and Using the Endings on Past Tense Verbs

The *past tense* verb form is always the second of the four forms listed in standard dictionaries. Remember, a verb is always indicated by *v.* (or *vb., vi.,* or *vt.*).

1. present: breathe *v.*

2. past: (breathed)

3. past with *have, has, had:* breathed

4. *-ing* form: breathing

-d AND -ed ENDINGS

The past tense form, indicating past time or action, is different from the present tense form. Most past tense forms differ from the present tense form because of the simple addition of a *-d* or *-ed* ending. (A few dictionaries list only the first verb form, for example, *breathe*, and the fourth form, *breathing*. If this is the case with your dictionary, the past tense verb form ends in either *-d* or *-ed*.)

I breath*ed*.
You breath*ed*.
He, She, It breath*ed*.

We breath*ed*.
You breath*ed*.
They breath*ed*.

IRREGULAR ENDINGS

Some verbs, however, form the *past tense* in an *irregular* way.

1. present: **2. past:**   **3.** form with   **4.** *-ing* form:
run *v.*   (ran)   *have, has, had:*   running
                                         run

I *ran.*   We *ran.*
You *ran.*   You *ran.*
He, She, It *ran.*   They *ran.*

Get used to checking in a dictionary to determine whether the past tense is formed in a regular way (*-d* or *-ed* ending) or in an irregular way, as is the past tense for the verb *run.*

Write twenty sentences that include past tense verbs. Use a different verb in each sentence and check the dictionary to see whether the past tense verbs you use are formed regularly or irregularly.

1. _____

2. _____

3. _____

4. _____

5. _____

6. _____

7. _____

8. _____

9. _____

10. _____

11. _____

12. _____

13. _____

14. _____

15. _____

16. _____

17. _____

18. _____

19. _____

20. _____

WAS/WERE

The past tense forms require attention because they have more variation than other past tense verb forms, as indicated by the circled words.

I (*was*) new to the college classroom.
You *were* new to the college classroom.
He, She, It (*was*) new to the college classroom.
(or a substitute)

We *were* new to the college classroom.
You *were* new to the college classroom.
They *were* new to the college classroom.

A substitute is a word that can take the place of *he*, *she*, or *it*.

(He)
Joe was new to the college classroom.
(She)
Nancy was new to the college classroom.
      (It)
The computer was new to the college classroom.

Write twenty sentences of your own, using each of the forms of this past tense verb.

1. _____

2. _____

3. _____

4. _____

5. _____

6. _____

7. _____

8. _____

9. _____

10. _____

11. _____

12. _____

13. _____

14. _____

15. _____

16. _____

17. _____

18. _____

19. _____

20. _____

**Practice in
Proofreading**

Carefully read the following student paragraphs and place a circle around each past tense verb form. If you are unsure of whether or not a word is a verb, check your dictionary. A verb is always indicated by *v.* (or *vb.*, *vi.*, or *vt.*).

A. My first date was one of the weirder experiences of my life. I was about thirteen years old, and it took me a long time to talk my mother into saying I could go. The guy was pretty young also, so we had to go with his sister. We were going to a movie. His sister had a little girl whom she took also. They came to pick me up, and as soon as I entered the car, the little girl hit me. I was steaming mad, but I couldn't hit a little girl. She continuously hit me all the way to the show, and no one asked her to stop! During the movie she insisted on sitting with us and spilled buttered popcorn all over me. I took a lot of abuse from that little girl that day. I also ended up with the guy for the next couple of years, and I believe I got her back for all the things she did to me.

B. My first sailing in the ocean was fun. I went with a couple of friends out of Miami, and if I have the chance, I'll do it again. It was like I was in a whole different world, being away from the hectic city life. I saw a small shark, a floating jellyfish, and a swimming dolphin. It was hard work trying to get the sails in their right position; however, the work paid off. I sat on the front of the twenty-seven-foot boat, letting the salty waves and the cool breeze bounce off of me. It was a quiet, enjoyable sound as the boat dipped in and out of the waves. When the sunshine of the day was coming to an end, I returned to port, ending a peaceful day away from the noisy city.

In the following student paragraphs, replace all the present tense verb forms, which are in parentheses, *with their correct past tense forms*. It would be a good idea to consult a dictionary if you are not sure how a particular present tense verb forms its past tense. Many will form their past tenses regularly, by the addition of *-d* or *-ed*. Others will have irregular past tense forms, like the verb *run*. The verb *was* is the past tense form for *am* and *is*, and the verb *were* is the past tense form for *are*. Study the models at the beginning of the lesson if you are in doubt about a particular verb form.

A. My best friendship (is) _____ almost destroyed because of the influence peer pressure (has) _____ over me in high school. I remember the first day of high school as if it (is) _____ yesterday. Sue (comes) _____ right up to me and (introduces) _____ herself. I (cannot) _____ believe someone as pretty and nice as she (is) _____ talking to me, the quiet little fat girl. I (remember) _____ the label all too well from junior high school. She (asks) _____ me if I (am) _____ going home for lunch. I (tell) _____ her that I (live) _____ too far away to make it back on time to school. Then she (asks) _____ me if I (want) _____ to go to her house. Thinking about being alone in the crowded cafeteria, I happily (accept) _____ her offer. From that day on, Sue and I (become) _____ inseparable. We (schedule) _____ all our classes together. We even (join) _____ the art club together. She (ends) _____ up being the president, I, the treasurer. Our relationship (seems) _____ so perfect until the middle of our senior year. I (start) _____ overhearing other people talking. They (call) _____ us the ''Bobbsey twins.'' Determined not to wear a label from my peers ever again, I (start) _____ to look for other friends. Since I (have) _____ lost a lot of weight my junior and senior year because of a tough gym teacher, I (know) _____ now that I (can)

_____ fit in with the ''in groups.''
It (is) _____ something that I (have)
_____ always wanted to experience.
Soon I (become) _____ friends with a
girl named Connie, who (is) _____ a
cheerleader. She (knows) _____ all the
football players and where all the parties (are)
_____ held.

   After a while, I (realize) _____
that all Connie and her friends (like)
_____ to do was party. I (try)
_____ to pretend to myself it (does
not) _____ matter that my grades (are)
_____ dropping and I (have)
_____ been dismissed as treasurer of
the art club, that I once (am) _____ so
proud of. I even (try) _____ to
pretend it (is) _____ no big deal that
my best friend (will) _____ not
associate with me. All the while in my heart I
(feel) _____ sick, as if I (have)
_____ made the biggest mistake of my
life. I (am not) _____ proud of being
me anymore. I (am) _____ now a
follower in a large popular group of idiots. It
really (gets) _____ to me. One day I
(go) _____ to Sue and (tell)
_____ her how I (feel)
_____ . Then I (apologize)
_____ for being such a jerk. Sue
(understands) _____ and (forgives)
_____ me. She even (says)
_____ she (is) _____ glad
we (are) _____ friends again.

B. My first experience in a storm on Lake Erie (is)
_____ quite frightening. There (are)
_____ four of my family members in our
boat and three other boats traveling with us. Every
summer vacation we (travel) _____ by
boat to Canada. Traveling across each Great Lake

(is) _____ a beautiful sight; however, on the way back, we (are) _____ caught in a gigantic, thundering mass of rain, hail, and wind. Because winds (are) _____ blowing sixty to seventy-five miles per hour, and the waves (are) _____ ten to fifteen feet high, all I (can) _____ see was water. Especially when the boat (goes) _____ down into a wave, all I (can) see (is) _____ a slick glass-like wall of green, cool water, which (comes) _____ crashing down on top of us. Furthermore, one of our engines (quits) _____ working, slowing us down to a crawling pace. We (are) _____ all very hungry, wet, and tired, wishing we (are) _____ on land eating hot soup and drinking coffee; however, we (settle) _____ for home-canned hot pepper sandwiches with mustard. We finally (see) _____ shore and (make) _____ it to the dock.

C. My first attempt to water ski (is) _____ a bad experience from start to finish. Rick, Tom, and I (are) _____ down at the dam near our house. Rick (owns) _____ the boat, and Tom (has) _____ just finished skiing, so it (is) _____ my turn to make a fool out of myself. It only (takes) _____ me two tries until I (get) _____ up, but I (learn) _____ that getting up (is) _____ only half the battle. My legs (will) _____ start to go from underneath me, and when I (see) _____ we (are) _____ about to turn, I (know) _____ it (is) _____ ''all over'' for me. The boat (turns) _____ left, but I (swing) _____ to the far right at about double the speed, then (fall) _____ on my face. But I (am)

_____ not about to give up. I (am)
_____ right back up, this time to fall
at the next turn and lose my high school class ring.
Needless to say, I (am) _____ getting
tired by this time, so I (get) _____
back into the boat with a nice red sunburn.

♦♦♦♦♦♦♦♦♦♦♦♦♦♦ **Writing Assignment**

Write a paragraph *in the past tense* about an experience you had.

    Once you have finished the paragraph, *proofread your writing*, paying special attention to past tense verb forms. If you are in doubt about any of the past tense forms, *use your dictionary.*

Lesson Five

Recognizing and Using the Form of the Verb Used with *Have, Has, Was, Were*

The *third* of the four verb forms listed in standard dictionaries is always used with a helper, such as *have, has, was,* or *were.* If your dictionary does not show a third form, it is because it is the same as the second form shown.

1. present:
breathe *v.*

2. past:
breathed

3. past with
have, has:
have breathed,
has breathed

4. *-ing* form:
breathing

(A few dictionaries list only the first verb form, for example, *breathe,* and the fourth form, *breathing.* If this is the case with your dictionary, the past tense verb form ends in either *-d* or *-ed.*)

HAVE AND HAS WITH VERBS THAT END IN *-d* OR *-ed*

I *have breathed* too much pollution.

You *have breathed* too much pollution.

He, She, It (or a substitute) *has breathed* too much pollution.

We *have breathed* too much pollution.

You *have breathed* too much pollution.

They *have breathed* too much pollution.

314

A substitute is a word that takes the place of *he, she, it,* or *they.*

(He)
Joe has breathed too much pollution.
(She)
Nancy has breathed too much pollution.
(It)
The plant has breathed too much pollution.
(They)
Joe and Nancy have breathed too much pollution.

HAVE AND *HAS* WITH IRREGULAR VERBS

With most verbs, the third form is identical to the second form. With the irregular verbs, however, such as the one below, the third form is not identical to the second form.

1. present:
run

2. past:
ran

3. form with *have, has:*

have run,
has run

Whatever the form of the third part, it must still be preceded by one of the helpers.

I *have run* a mile.
You *have run* a mile
He, She, It *has* run a mile.
(or a substitute)

We *have run* a mile.
You *have run* a mile.
They *have run* a mile.

If you are unsure of the third form of any verb, *check the dictionary.* If there is no listing in your dictionary for the third form, remember, it is the same as the second form.

Write twenty sentences that include the third form of the verb preceded by the helpers *have* or *has.* As the model illustrates, *has* is used only with *he, she, it,* or words you can substitute for *he, she,* or *it.* Try using a different verb in each sentence and vary your use of *I, you, he, she, it, we, they* or any words that can substitute for these.

1. _____

2. _____

3. _____

4. _____

5. _____

6. _____

7. _____

8. _____

9. _____

10. _____

11. _____

12. _____

13. _____

14. _____

15. _____

16. _____

17. _____

18. _____

19. _____

20. _____

WAS AND *WERE* WITH VERBS THAT END IN *-d* OR *-ed*

The third form of the verb is also used with *was* and *were*.

I *was* asked a question.
You *were asked* a question.
He, She, It *was* asked a question.
(or a substitute)

We *were asked a* question.
You *were asked* a question.
They *were asked* a question.

WAS AND *WERE* WITH IRREGULAR VERBS

I *was* *shown* how to write an effective sentence.
You *were shown* how to write an effective sentence.

He, She, It *was* *shown* how to write an effective sentence.
(or a substitute)

We *were shown* how to write an effective sentence.
You *were shown* how to write an effective sentence.
They *were shown* how to write an effective sentence.

Below write ten sentences of your own that include the third form of the verb with *was* or *were*. Use a different verb in each sentence.

1. _____

2. _____

3. _____

4. _____

5. _____

6. _____

7. _____

8. _____

9. _____

10. _____

**Practice in
Proofreading**

Carefully read the following student paragraphs and place a circle around all *third-form verbs and their helpers.*

A. Academically, this year has turned out well because it has brought me new kinds of experiences, a different kind of fulfillment, and responsibility for myself that I would never have dreamed of. I have encountered new experiences that have provided me with a sense of accomplishment. I am more or less out on my own, and the accomplishments that I have worked for are my own. I have come to feel good about myself. I feel this way because I have not given up even when times have been rough. Also I feel this way because I know that I am, and no one else is, the reason that I have received the grades that I have. I am responsible for acquiring the help I need, but I do my own work. Therefore, because of the respect that I have for myself and my qualities, I feel that this year has turned out well.

B. This past year has brought total chaos for me, although I would not have missed it for anything. For one, going back into ''single life'' again has become challenging, exciting, and terrifying. I have met a lot of interesting and good people. Unfortunately, I also have been disappointed in the quality of some people I have met. Also, I have struggled to adjust to being a single parent, and the discipline is left totally up to me. I constantly question whether or not I am making the right decisions. And when my nephew came to live with me, that really turned my home into an uproar. Nevertheless, as a result of that, I have learned to be more patient and understanding. In the future, I will probably recall this year with amusement, but now it seems almost impossible to bear.

In the following paragraph, write out the correct *third* form for the present tense form in parenthesis. Remember that each of the third forms must be accompanied by an appropriate helper, whether it be *have, has, was,* or *were.* Refer to the models at the beginning of the lesson if you need help.

A. I _____ (study) _____
and (sweat) _____ for nine months now,
and I'm ready for a long summer vacation. When we
began in this writing class, I had no idea that
things would end up as they have. I'm the most
surprised of all that my writing _____
(improves) _____ . I
_____ (tell) _____ at the
beginning of the year that there was more work ahead
than I could imagine. My teacher was so right! We
_____ (teach) _____ how
to find ideas on our own and how those ideas are
made into sentences and paragraphs. More important
than this, we _____ (learn)
_____ how important writing is for us
as individuals. Even though I _____
(find) _____ this year harder than
most, I _____ not (regret)
_____ the time that I
_____ (spend) _____

B. My girlfriend recently _____
(dumped) _____ me for another guy, and
I am so jealous that I _____ (change)
_____ a lot of important things in my
life and almost _____ (become)
_____ seriously ill. I had invested
all of my feelings and trust into the relationship I
had with Carrie, my girlfriend, before she dumped me
for John, her new boyfriend. The relationship
between us had been very serious, for we had even
discussed marriage on several occasions. It lasted
for about six months until she broke it off with me
to be with John. My shattered, upset, and confused
feelings _____ (turn)
_____ into a jealousy so intense that
it can almost be described as hateful. I would not
_____ (be) _____ so
terribly jealous about Carrie leaving me to be with
John; however, it is as though my whole life
_____ (be) _____ taken
away from me. All of my dreams and plans with Carrie

are gone, dashed away by John. It is really hard on
me because all three of us work at the same place, a
retail department store. I remember one depressing
Saturday afternoon at work after Carrie had broken
up with me. Working in one of the departments in the
back of the store, I was having a horrible day.
John, working right beside Carrie on the front
registers, was flirting and laughing with her.
Everytime I heard their flirtatious laughter on the
public address system, I became distraught and
bitter at the two of them and was painfully reminded
that Carrie had chosen to have John as a boyfriend
instead of me. These kinds of episodes
_____ (continue) _____
on and on until I can take no more. My jealousy
_____ (become) _____ so
great that I can find little satisfaction on the
job, so I _____ (decide)
_____ to quit. I _____
(become) _____ even more distressed
because John _____ (start)
_____ attending the church where
Carrie and I are members and sits with her where we
used to sit on the right side of the chapel in the
back. This really makes me hot under the collar, but
there is not much I can do about it, for John
_____ (take) _____ my
place in Carrie's life. They seem really happy, but
I am completely miserable. I do not feel good about
being at my church anymore, so I _____
(decide) _____ to leave and find
another to join. During all of these incidents, my
angry, aggressive, and hostile feelings have
literally been eating me up inside, for after a
visit to my doctor, I _____ (be)
_____ informed that I
_____ (begin) _____ to
develop a peptic ulcer. I am beginning to realize
that I _____ (be) _____

letting my rotten jealousy dissolve my happiness in
life; moreover, it is destroying my health. This
past year _____ (bring)
_____ about drastic changes in my life
and has almost ruined my health with an ulcer.

Writing Assignment

Write a paragraph about what this year has been like for you. Use the third form of the verb when appropriate. Once you have finished the paragraph, *proofread* your writing, paying special attention to *third form verbs and their helpers*. Consult a dictionary when necessary.

Lesson Six

Recognizing and Using Plural Noun Forms

-s AND -es

An -*s* (or in some cases -*es*) ending is added to nouns that are *plural*, that is, nouns that refer to *two or more*.

Singular (one)	*Plural* (two or more)
horse	horse(s)
idea	idea(s)
motor	motor(s)
class	classe(s)

All horse(s) eat grass.
Idea(s) stimulate me.
The boat motor(s) are in good condition.
Horse(s) stimulate me more than ideas do.
There are various class(es) of boat motors ranging in price from $200 to $1,000.
All the class(es) like that teacher.

Write twenty sentences of your own that include plural nouns that end in -*s* (or -*es*). As illustrated in the examples above, plurals may appear in a number of places in the sentence. In some of your sentences, try using at least two of these.

1. _____

2. _____

3. _____

4. _____

5. _____

6. _____

7. _____

8. _____

9. _____

10. _____

11. _____

12. _____

13. _____

14. _____

15. _____

16. _____

17. _____

18. _____

19. _____

20. _____

IRREGULAR PLURAL NOUNS

The plural forms of a few nouns are irregular. These plurals do not end in -*s* (or -*es*).

Singular (one)	*Plural* (two or more)
child	child(ren)
baby	bab(ies)
man	m(e)n
deer	deer
fish	fish
wolf	wol(ves)
half	hal(ves)

Many dictionaries do not list the plural form of regular nouns (ones that end in -*s* or -*es*); therefore, when the plural form is not listed, use -*s* (or -*es*) to form the plural. The dictionary does, however, list irregular plurals.

For each of the singular nouns listed below, find its irregular form in the dictionary and use it in a sentence of your own.

woman **1.** _____

lady **2.** _____

sheep **3.** _____

leaf **4.** _____

mouse **5.** _____

Practice in Proofreading

Carefully read the following student paragraphs and circle each plural noun.

A. I recall an experience that happened a little less than a year ago when I was playing drums in a pop-rock band. It turned my face a blushed red and made me feel totally incompetent. I usually started the songs we played; however, I would sometimes take

turns with the other players when beginning
different songs we performed. We had not been
playing together for a very long while, so our sets
weren't polished perfections. During one of our
shows on the second set I made a genuinely silly
blunder. We were preparing to play a Cars' tune. I
believe it was called ''Shake It Up.'' This was one
of the songs that I would initiate. I glanced at the
others in the band, checking to see if they were
ready. Mike and Scott, the band's guitar and bass
players respectfully, were trying to tell me how to
commence the song. This song had a fast rhythm, so I
decided to count off the beat and play the first
measure on the cow bell like the guys wanted me to
do. I crashed into the song and suddenly realized
that all I could hear was the bang of my drums.
Where was the rest of the band I wondered. I stopped
and looked at Scott. He was staring directly back at
me. A lump developed in my throat. I felt so
terribly dumb that I wanted to run off stage and
hide somewhere. In my eagerness to start the song
according to Mike and Scott's directions, I
committed the mistake of starting too fast and
losing the rest of the band. Not one single person
in the audience said a thing. They all just stared
at us and waited. Quite a few of our peers were in
the crowd that evening. This only increased my
awkwardness. I certainly felt like a stupid idiot.
It was time for me to get a grip on things. I quickly
regained my composure and counted the beat to start
the song. As we began playing, I kept thinking to
myself how I could have made such an ill—witted
mistake. I don't think anyone actually noticed it,
and the band didn't place too much importance on it,
but I still felt like a ridiculous fool because of
my cloddish error.

B. If I were allowed the choice of living my life in
either the past, present, or future, I would choose
the present. Living in the past would be a terrible
experience because health conditions were poor and

health care was even worse. Plagues and illnesses of
all kinds were killing off thousands of people.
Having a constant fear of living from one day to the
next is not my kind of life-style. Moreover, living
in the future would not be considered peaches and
cream. All of our present trivial worries will be
major catastrophes in a hundred years or so. Nuclear
advancement will be so great that fear will be a
national pastime. Living in the present isn't all
bad; gasoline might be a little scarce and prices a
little high, but I enjoy the time period I live in.
The present has everything that I want or need. So
what has passed and what the future holds in store
can do without me right now.

Carefully read the student paragraphs below, and change the nouns
that should be plural to their plural forms. Determine this by reading
the sentences aloud and letting your ear and your sentence sense be
your guides.

A. Experiencing parental separation was hell for me.
My parent separated when I was a senior in high
school. That year, which was supposed to be so
special, was ruined by their breakup. My mother was
gone for three long month, which was tormenting, for
out of those three month I only saw her twice. I
remember hating to talk to her over the phone, for
hearing her voice made me miss her more. I'd lock
myself in my room crying after these conversation.
Realizing as close as we'd been in the past, we
weren't a family anymore, I felt so alone. Out of my
parents' five children, there were only two at home,
my younger sister and I. As I anticipated leaving, I
couldn't because I knew my sister would have no one,
and we desperately needed each other. Because I
couldn't talk to anyone, I kept my feeling inside. I
wondered why they were putting us through this and
why this wretched event had to take place. I began
strongly disliking my parents' action. My parent
would talk to one another through me. My mother
didn't want my father to know where she was;

therefore, I had to be their mediator. My father
accused me daily of taking side with my mother,
lying about her whereabouts and not caring for him.
My grade fell drastically, for I could never keep my
mind on my school work. I felt tired, angry, lonely
and pressured. I yearned for my parents' madness to
cease, for hell is something I wouldn't want to put
any child through.

B. One of the most difficult experience I ever
encountered was leaving my parent and sister for
basic training. I can remember the day I left
distinctly. It was June 9th. They were taking me up
to Cleveland because I left the next day. The trip
was two hour long, but it felt like ten minute
because I did not want to leave. We had dinner at
the Holiday Inn that I was staying at for the night.
I had the hardest time eating, because all I could
think of is how hard it would be to say good-bye.
After dinner the time had come, and this is not what
I was waiting for. As my palm started perspiring, I
said good-bye to my grandmother. Then saying good-
bye to my parent was probably the most difficult
thing I did. I gave them a kiss and a big hug, as the
tear rolled up in my eye. All I could think of was
eight week without seeing anybody I loved. Watching
them pulling away, I knew that the most difficult
part was over.

C. If I could choose whether to live in the past,
present, or future, I think I would like to live in
the past about 1900. Although we did not have a lot
of the modern convenience then, time were much more
peaceful and fulfilling. That was a time when people
truly knew their neighbor and when they took the
time and concern to help each other. Also, the crime
rate was much lower, which was due to the fact that
people did protect and look out for one another.
There wasn't the constant hustle and bustle to do
everything and go everywhere at top speed. People
knew how to take life easy and enjoy the simple and

good thing of life. There was room to breathe, and they could take a deep breath without choking from the stench of pollution. We may not have had the advancement in medicine then, but, at the same time, we did not have modern technology constantly creating new health hazard. Although I have been spoiled by modern time, I would gladly do without appliance and do a little more work or take a little more time, as long as I knew my son could go for a walk in a fresh green park without the threat of danger.

Writing Assignment

Using as many plural nouns as possible, write a paragraph of your own, telling whether you would prefer to live in the past, present, or future—and why.

Once you have finished the paragraph, *proofread* aloud, paying special attention to plural forms. If you are in doubt about how to form any of the plurals, *use your dictionary.*

Lesson Seven

Recognizing and Using Possessive Forms

-'s AND -s'

Notice how the 's ending is used in the following examples.

OWNER   WHAT IS OWNED

The student('s) notebook shows that he has done a lot of work
The children('s) toys are scattered throughout the house.
The woman('s) long, black hair is strikingly beautiful.
The deer('s) hiding place is far from any human presence.
The class('s) teacher cares that each student learns.
The men('s) room is located at the end of the hall.
The collie('s) pups are cuddly balls of fur.

In order to show ownership, an 's is added to the *owner* word. This is true whether the owner is singular (student) or an irregular plural form (children) that does not end in -s. The only exception occurs when the owner is a plural form that already ends in -s (for example, *horses*). To a plural form that already ends in -s, add only the apostrophe (*horses' stables, boys' bedroom*).

Write twenty sentences of your own that include the possessive form. Use some singular forms and both regular and irregular plural forms.

329

1. _____

_____

2. _____

_____

3. _____

_____

4. _____

_____

5. _____

_____

6. _____

_____

7. _____

_____

8. _____

_____

9. _____

_____

10. _____

_____

11. _____

_____

12. _____

_____

13. _____

_____

14. _____

_____

15. _____

_____

16. _____

_____

17. _____

_____

18. _____

_____

19. _____

_____

20. _____

_____

**Practice in
Proofreading**

Carefully read the following student paragraph and circle each use of the possessive forms.

An unpleasant experience my family and I had was when a huge white rooster attacked us. I had bought fifty cute little chicks at a farmers' auction. The chicks' warm little bodies were all yellow and fuzzy; however, cute little animals grow into big adult ones. Out of the fifty chicks,I had one rooster that I thought would give me healthy, fertile eggs. Well, this rooster was very protective, which is good, for he kept the wild animals out of the hen house. However, he no longer looked like an ordinary rooster but rather like some kind of monster. One day as I went to feed the hens and collect eggs, I heard the rooster's familiar sound and spotted him walking beside me but at a distance; consequently, I didn't pay any attention to the mean brute, and he ran and bit my leg. I thought to myself, ''Why did he do that?'' and forgot about the whole thing happening. The next day he managed to get into the children's play area and bit one of my kids, and that went on for quite some time. I would throw my son's heavy coat over him just so I could collect eggs, for he could not get out from under the coat to attack anyone. Finally, one day he suddenly and violently jumped on my husband's back, claws digging in and pecking away. The whole family became terrified of this rooster; consequently, it was in the family's best interest to end the nasty bird's position of lord and master over the hen house. The rooster was destroyed, and we all lived in peace thereafter.

Carefully read the following paragraph and provide the correct possessive forms with correctly placed apostrophes where needed.

A. A pig life is not the easy, carefree life I thought it was. I discovered this shortly after I left my parents home to live in the country. Since I was far from the city and had plenty of land to raise animals on, I thought my neighbor idea to raise pigs was a good one. Just getting the pig was quite an initiation for me. The sow temper flared as the old farmer hands pulled her baby from her. But once home, I soon forgot about the sad separation and became quickly familiar with the little piglet grunting sounds. It was fun to see the children curiosity come alive with one look at the little pig. As the summer became fall, the old sow baby grew larger and ornerier, however. As the days went by, I knew she was getting too big and too dangerous to keep any longer, and so my neighbor call to the local slaughterhouse was inevitable. My pig life was short and her days to the slaughterhouse numbered. It was this difference between the pig life and mine that revealed to me how hard it is to be a pig.

B. I was never jealous of my boyfriend, until last summer when I met his ex—wife. I thought I would have nothing to worry about. How could someone with a name like Hilda be any competition; moreover, she lived over six hundred miles away in Texas. When I entered Hilda apartment, I was really disappointed to find she was a very beautiful woman. She had a cute face, wore fashionable clothing, and had a European accent that surely could melt any man heart. The minute I saw her I felt like putting a blindfold over my boyfriend eyes, as if he had never seen her before. To top it off, she had a sweet, outgoing personality. Sitting in her plush living room that made my apartment back home seem like a barn, made me discouraged. I sat quietly, annoyed as Jim, my boyfriend, and Hilda, laughed and talked about old friends and family. I was at a loss for words. What do you say to your boyfriend ex—wife? It was disturbing realizing she knew him better than I, for they were married for twelve years. She asked him how his business was going. I then was getting upset. It was none of her business, if you ask me. Luckily, Crisshawn, their daughter whom we had

originally came to visit walked in. We left shortly
thereafter. Knowing they had been divorced for six
years made me realize it was silly to be jealous;
nevertheless, I'm glad Hilda lives in Texas.

Writing Assignment

Write a paragrah on a topic of your own choosing in which you strive to
use as many possessive forms as are appropriate.

Once you have finished the paragraph, *proofread* your writing, paying special attention to possessive forms and the apostrophes.

Lesson Eight

Recognizing and Using Pronoun Forms

PRONOUNS USED BEFORE THE VERB

You are familiar with pronoun forms used before a verb: *I, you, he, she, it, we, they.*

(I) smoke cigars.
(You) smoke cigars.
(He,) (She,) (It) smokes cigars.

(We) smoke cigars.
(You) smoke cigars.
(They) smoke cigars.

PRONOUNS USED IN OTHER POSITIONS

Each of these pronouns also has another form that is used in other positions in the sentence: *me, him, her, us, them. You* and *it* always stay the same, regardless of the position in the sentence.

My sons gave (me) cigars for Father's Day.
Ethel loves (me.)
The fraternity invited (you) to the party.
The class nominated (him) to be the valedictorian.
The class nominated (her) to be the salutatorian.
Before buying (it,) we gave (it) a good looking over.

They wouldn't let (us) in the dance because we were too rowdy.
I would like to commend (you) for your efforts as students.
I saw (them) stealing Mr. Wilson's strawberries.

You usually know which form of the pronoun to use, whether it be *I* or *me*, *he* or *him*, *she* or *her*, *we* or *us*, *they* or *them*, when only one is used by itself in a particular position in a sentence. For example, in the sentence "I smoke cigars," you can hear that the pronoun *I* is the correct form to use in this position in the sentence.

Confusion sometimes occurs, however, when other words are used *with* the pronoun in that same position. Is "Bill and *I* smoke cigars" or "Bill and *me* smoke cigars" correct? If you mentally eliminate the words *Bill and*, you can hear that *"Me* smoke cigars" is incorrect. On the other hand, you can hear that *"I* smoke cigars" is correct. Therefore, the correct form for this sentence is "Bill and *I* smoke cigars."

To determine which form of the pronoun to use, simply read the sentence aloud, mentally eliminating the added word or words. *The pronoun form that is correct when used alone is also the correct form to use with the added word or words.*

The same applies with the pronoun in other positions. Is it correct to write "He gave Bill and *I* two cigars" or "He gave Bill and *me* two cigars"? Using the elimination rule, you can hear that "He gave Bill and *I* two cigars" is incorrect.

When using two pronouns in the same position in a sentence, you can check each one individually by mentally eliminating first one and then the other. If you mentally eliminate either the word *him* or *me* in the sentence "Him and me have tickets for the concert," you can hear that *"Me* have tickets for the concert" and *"Him* have tickets for the concert" are incorrect.

Write twenty sentences of your own that include all of the pronoun forms *I/me, you, he/him, she/her, it, we/us, they/them* with additional words in the same position in the sentence (as illustrated above).

1. _____

_____

2. _____

_____

3. _____

_____

4. _____

_____

5. _____

_____

6. _____

_____

7. _____

_____

8. _____

_____

9. _____

_____

10. _____

_____

11. _____

_____

12. _____

_____

13. _____

_____

14. _____

_____

15. _____

_____

16. _____

_____

17. _____

_____

18. _____

_____

19. _____

_____

20. _____

_____

POSSESSIVE FORMS

Pronouns also have a possessive form to show ownership.

Unlike other possessive forms, pronouns *do not* use any special punctuation mark to show ownership.

In some cases, depending on sentence position, some possessive pronouns can change form, as in the sentences beneath the table on the following page. Even then, however, *no punctuation mark is used*.

	Possessive Pronoun	What is owned	
	(My)	English class	gives me a chance to explore who I am.
	(Your)	writing	has improved immensely since you began the course.
He said	(his)	life	was empty and hopeless.
	(Her)	attitude	was holding her back from becoming a successful student.
	(Its)	carburetor	is just about 'shot.''
	(Our)	family reunion	ended up a disaster.
	(Your)	grades	will be posted on the outer door of my office.
Where were	(their)	parents	when they needed them?

The English book on the desk is *mine*.
The second seat from the left is *yours*.
The idea was really *hers*.
The cabin by the lake was *ours* for years.
The campsites on the ridge are *yours*.
The mangy dog with fleas is *theirs*.

Using the models above as guides, write twenty sentences of your own that include possessive pronoun forms, both regular *(my, your, his, her, its, our, your, their)* and ones that change form *(mine, yours, hers, ours, yours, theirs)*. Remember that *no punctuation mark* is used with possessive pronoun forms.

1. _____

_____

2. _____

_____

3. _____

_____

4. _____

_____

5. _____

_____

6. _____

_____

7. _____

_____

8. _____

_____

9. _____

_____

10. _____

_____

11. _____

_____

12. _____

_____

13. _____

14. _____

15. _____

16. _____

17. _____

18. _____

19. _____

20. _____

Practice in Proofreading

Carefully read the following student paragraphs and (1) place a circle around all pronoun forms shown and (2) supply the correct pronoun form where called for. Refer to the models at the beginning of the lesson when necessary.

A. Entering my bedroom, I glanced quickly at _____ little twin bed to make sure White Cloud was there. Seeing a furry white bundle sprawled on the bed, I closed the door quietly and turned on the overhead light. The bright light that

filled the room was much too bright for my liking,
so _____ dimmed it until a warm glow
was all that was left. The thick shag carpet seemed
to grow warm, and the colors mellowed to a
yellowish, red—orange. Sitting down in the only
chair there was, I removed _____ boots
and let the soothing warmth calm me. My ceramic
Indian, a Christmas present from _____
grandfather, stood a little to one side of the door,
as if he was guarding _____.''A big
job for one only three feet tall,'' I thought, until
I noticed the authority and wisdom in his weathered
face, and the strength in the fibers of
_____ body. My stereo was silent
across the room, but soon I had Simon and
Garfunkel's ''The Sounds of Silence'' playing. Just
above the stereo was my bird collection. I had birds
from England, Mexico, Germany, and Spain, made of
porcelain, china, glass, and wood. Some were hand
painted, hand blown, or carved. On the bed, White
Cloud had begun to snore quite loudly, and no
wonder, he had his paw over _____
nose. _____ tried not to disturb
_____ as I lay down on the bed, but he
awoke anyway. I scratched and petted him for a
while, and soon he was sound asleep. On the wall
next to my bed, I had many pictures hanging.
_____ favorites are the ones of my
father in his Air Force uniform, and his graduation
picture from Valley Forge, in which he also wore a
uniform. He looks so young and brave in those
pictures, and he must have been, for in the middle
of all the pictures hang his medals: the
Distinguished Flying Cross, two other flying
medals, and a good conduct medal.
_____ wings and bars—he was a second
lieutenant—are displayed with the medals. I
treasure them and dream of how great he was and how
it must have felt to receive those honors. Looking
away, I noticed my desk was cluttered with work,
reminding me that there was no time to waste on

dreams. _____ left White Cloud and my
little room sadly, but with a feeling of peace.

B. I just couldn't believe it when my mother called me
that morning and told me my father had passed away.
I couldn't understand why _____ had to
die so young, fifty-three years old. It seemed as if
we had only become friends a few years ago. Feeling
angry, I wondered how he could give up so soon.
_____ remember thinking to myself,
''Who is going to call me and tell me that I can do
anything I put _____ mind to? Who is
going to stand proudly at my college graduation and
sincerely say: I knew you could do it all along?''
When my mother and my sister came to the house that
day, _____ made everything all the
more difficult. The only thing they could think of
saying was, ''Who's going to pay for the funeral?
How will we bury him?'' I guess my dad never was
very good at saving money. I didn't want to be
alone, but they weren't being much of a comfort. I
sat there all day listening to them, hoping my
brothers would show up soon. My youngest brother had
gone to school that day. I guess he knew that's what
my father would have wanted. My oldest brother lived
in Arkansas. I knew it would take at least 28 hours
for _____ to arrive. Memories of my
father keep pouring through my mind. I remembered
the last time I had seen him and made him promise
that he would take _____ medications
like the doctors had told him and give up the foods
that he always loved to eat, as his diet was
prescribed for him. I remembered the last, brief,
conversation I had with him over the phone and how
he explained to me that he had to sleep standing up
or he couldn't breathe. I thought about how he used
to joke about dying, saying he wanted to be cremated
and put into sugar packets with his picture on them
and have them passed out to _____
friends. I also remembered how he used to tell
_____ he was going to haunt us when he

died. That night I didn't sleep at all, wondering if
he was going to show up and haunt me. In a way, I was
wishing he would, just so I could tell him one last
time how much I loved him. On the other hand, it
would be kind of unnatural, so I had mixed feelings.
When my brother arrived, he began to cry, and that
made me cry. My family and I went to make the
funeral arrangements the next day. I believe this
was the most difficult part because it felt as if I
was a part of putting an end to dad. Facing the
death of my father was very difficult, I guess,
because I never really believed he would be gone.

Writing Assignment

Write a paragraph about a favorite possession of yours, using as many
pronoun forms as is appropriate.

Once you have finished the paragraph, *proofread* your writing, paying special attention to *pronoun forms*.

Lesson Nine

Recognizing and Using Words That Sound Alike or Look Alike

Student writers often have difficulty distinguishing between words that sound somewhat alike or look somewhat alike. The difference between these words, however, must be learned because they cannot be used interchangeably. Concentration is required here to learn the differences.

AN/A/AND

An is used before words that begin with vowel sounds (a, e, i, o, u).

an apple
an elephant
an idea
an orange
an unpleasant experience

A is used before words that begin with any sound other than a vowel sound.

a baboon
a cocoon
a dragon
a writing assignment

345

And is a joining word.

    men <u>and</u> women
    Bill <u>and</u> I
    I ate, <u>and</u> she talked.

Write five sentences of your own that include the word *a* correctly used, five that include *an*, and five that include *and*.

1. _____

2. _____

3. _____

4. _____

5. _____

1. _____

2. _____

3. _____

4. _____

5. _____

1. _____

2. _____

3. _____

4. _____

5. _____

IT'S/ITS

It's is the shortened form of the words *it is* or *it has*.

It's fine with me if you turn your paper in late.
When you're a student, *it's* important that you take responsibility
for your learning.
It's been a beautiful day.

Its is the possessive form for the pronoun *it*.

The sun lost *its* golden luster when the clouds moved in.
The birch tree lost many of *its* branches in last winter's ice storm.

Write five sentences of your own that include *it's* and five that
include *its* correctly used.

1. _____

2. _____

3. _____

4. _____

5. _____

1. _____

2. _____

3. _____

4. _____

5. _____

PAST/PASSED

Past is a word that refers to a previous or earlier time.

Only by knowing what happened in the *past* can we prepare for the future.

Since I'm interested in the *past*, I decided to study history.

Passed is the past tense form of the verb *pass*, meaning to *go by* or to *successfully complete*.

I *passed* her on the street

I *passed* the course with flying colors.

Write five sentences of your own that include *past* and five that include *passed* correctly used.

1. _____

2. _____

3. _____

4. _____

5. _____

1. _____

2. _____

3. _____

4. _____

5. _____

QUITE/QUIET/QUIT

Quite is a word meaning *very*.

She was *quite* stunning in her long black evening gown.
The exam was *quite* difficult.

Quiet is a word meaning *silent* or indicating little or no sound.

In the *quiet* morning we set out for our favorite fishing hole.
It was very *quiet* when we stood under the stars last night.

Quit is a word meaning to *stop*.

I *quit!*
Regrettably, I *quit* school too young.

Write five sentences of your own that include *quite*, five that include *quiet*, and five that include *quit* correctly used.

1. _____

2. _____

3. _____

4. _____

5. _____

1. _____

2. _____

3. _____

4. _____

5. _____

1. _____

2. _____

3. _____

4. _____

5. _____

THAN/THEN

Than is a word used to show comparison between two persons or things.

She is taller *than* I.
It is hotter *than* yesterday.
My attitude toward writing is better *than* it was in the past.

Then is a word indicating time.

I think it would be best to postpone it until *then*.
Attend class first; *then* buy your books.

Write five sentences of your own that include the word *than* and five that include *then*.

1. _____

2. _____

3. _____

4. _____

5. _____

1. _____

2. _____

3. _____

4. _____

5. _____

THEIR/THERE/THEY'RE

Their is the possessive form of the pronoun *they*.

It is the parents' responsibility to make sure *their* children do *their* homework.
Their vacation was enjoyable.
We wish we were in *their* shoes.

There is a filler word that usually appears at the beginning of a sentence.

There are a number of reasons why I like you.
There is something I want to tell you.

There also is a word that is used to indicate a place.

You will sit over *there*.
There is where we would like to go.
Whether we stay here or go *there* doesn't matter to me.

They're is the shortened form of the words *they are*.

They're nice country folks.
Let me know when *they're* here.
They're the best student writers I have ever taught.

Write five sentences of your own that include the word *their*, five that include *there*, and five that include *they're* correctly used.

1. _____

2. _____

3. _____

4. _____

5. _____

1. _____

2. _____

3. _____

4. _____

5. _____

1. _____

2. _____

3. _____

4. _____

5. _____

THREW/THROUGH/THOUGH

Threw is the past tense of the verb *throw*.

Namath *threw* a sixty-yard pass for a touchdown.
I accidentally *threw* the baseball through the neighbor's window.
She *threw* me a kiss.

Through is a word that means *in one side and out the other*.

We drove *through* the desert under the blistering sun.
My walk *through* the woods was delightful.
The huge steamship barely made it *through* the canal.

Through also is a word that means *over and done with*.

I'm *through* with her for good.
When he was *through* with his exam, he went for a beer.

Though is a word meaning *in spite of the fact that.*

> *Though* the morning started out dreary and dismal, it soon became sunny and warm.
> *Though* I do not love you, I still like you.

Write five sentences of your own that include the word *threw*, five that include *through*, and five that include *though* used correctly.

1. _____

2. _____

3. _____

4. _____

5. _____

1. _____

2. _____

3. _____

4. _____

5. _____

1. _____

2. _____

3. _____

4. _____

5. _____

TO/TOO/TWO

To is a word that means *going or moving in a certain direction.*

Let's go *to* town and paint it red.
We went *to* Lovers' Lookout.

To also is used before a verb.

Even as a young child he wanted *to* grow up *to* be a doctor.
It took him years *to* learn how *to* love someone.
"*To* err is human; *to* forgive is divine."

Too is a word meaning *excessively* or *also.*

He is *too* old for you.
She was *too* frightened to move.
I want to go *too*.
You *too* can learn to dance.

Two is a word used for the numeral 2.

Two and *two* make four.
It takes *two* to tango.

Write five sentences of your own that include the word *to*, five that
include *too*, and five that include *two* used correctly.

1. _____

2. _____

3. _____

4. _____

5. _____

1. _____

2. _____

3. _____

4. _____

5. _____

1. _____

2. _____

3. _____

4. _____

5. _____

USED TO/SUPPOSED TO

Used to are words indicating a condition that no longer exists. Often this phrase is written incorrectly as "use to."

I *used to* be a pack-a-day smoker.
I *used to* be sad and lonely before I met you.

Supposed to are words that mean *must* or *should*. Often this phrase is written incorrectly as "suppose to."

You were *supposed to* be home by midnight.
I am *supposed to* behave myself in church and in school.

Write five sentences of your own that include the phrase *used to* and five that include the phrase *supposed to*.

1. _____

2. _____

3. _____

4. _____

5. _____

1. _____

2. _____

3. _____

4. _____

5. _____

WERE/WHERE/WE'RE

Were is the past tense form of the verb *are*.

The New York Yankees *were* world champions for many years.
They *were* surprised to learn that they *were* going to have twins.

Where is a word indicating place.

Where were you when we needed you?
They didn't tell us *where* to meet them.

We're is the shortened form of the words *we are*.

We're like two peas in a pod.
We're pleased that you can accept our invitation.

Write five sentences of your own that include the word *were*, five that include *where*, and five that include *we're* correctly used.

1. _____

2. _____

3. _____

4. _____

5. _____

1. _____

2. _____

3. _____

4. _____

5. _____

1. _____

2. _____

3. _____

4. _____

5. _____

WHOSE/WHO'S

Whose is the possessive form of the pronoun *who*.

He is someone *whose* opinion I value.
Whose right is it to take a life?

Who's is the shortened form of the words *who is*.

Who's coming to the party?
Who's the telephone call for?

Write five sentences of your own that include the word *whose* and five that include *who's* correctly written.

1. _____

2. _____

3. _____

4. _____

5. _____

1. _____

2. _____

3. _____

4. _____

5. _____

YOUR/YOU'RE

Your is the possessive form of the pronoun *you*.

Your breath is less than refreshing.
Your toupee is leaning a little too far to the right.

You're is the shortened form of the words *you are*.

You're the one I dream of.
You're a pain in the "you-know-what."

Write five sentences of your own that include the word *your* and five that include *you're* correctly used.

1. _____

2. _____

3. _____

4. _____

5. _____

1. _____

2. _____

3. _____

4. _____

5. _____

Practice in Proofreading

In the following student paragraphs, which have been altered for this exercise, choose the correct word in the parentheses and circle it.

A. I walk into the (quiet/quite/quit) basement of a church and (their/there/they're) I see (an/a/and) older man who looks like a broad-shouldered, weather-beaten derelict, aged beyond his years, drinking a cup of coffee. His grey scruffy hair catches my eyes because it looks as (threw/through/though) someone plopped a small dry mop on his head. I squint to get a better look at him. I notice the forbidding shadows over his eyes, (an/a/and) I construct various ideas about him. His right eye seems (to/too/two) be pointed inward, (an/a/and) his left eye is clouded over. Maybe he is blind. I raise my eyebrow and see he is looking over his cheek and giving me a smile of recognition and friendship. I see his rough weather-beaten skin which suggests that he has abused himself for many years. His tossed hair, hollow eyes, salt-and-pepper beard remind me of the bust of the Greek god Zeus. He is wearing blue denim overalls, a faded jean jacket, and a pair of scuffed brown work boots which are just like mine. I look into his sparkly eyes, shake his hand, and he smiles knowingly. Finally I realize that we have a lot more in common (than/then) just our clothes.

B. During my childhood, we (where/were) (a/an) very poor family. Mother, having had six children, had

(too/two/to) worry (where/were) the next meal was
coming from. Many a time (their/there/they're) was
only one can of soup to split among the six
children. It (use/used) to be that the days of
eating mush seemed endless. Since money was rare,
our utilities would be turned off occasionally.
Shoes (where/were) bought at the Goodwill Mission
House, (a/an/and) clothing (too/to/two) was
secondhand. (Where/Were) my mother got her spirit
(than/then) I'll never know. She kept up the whole
family's morale. She made the best of all
situations. When we had only soup to eat, she made
extra bread; clothes (where/were) altered (too/to/
two) fit another child. When the lights went out, we
sat around in candlelight telling ghost stories,
laughing and singing. Today whenever I tell the
story of my (past/passed), many wonder how I made it
(through/though/threw) those years. As far as I'm
concerned, because of my mother, we never knew real
poverty.

C. Angie Melas McTovish McMikell is a mouthful to say;
nevertheless, this pedigreed Scottish terrier was
little more than (a/an) handful when we first met.
Our early years together saw many memorable
experiences and lots of happy times (to/too). She
was (a/an) avid hunter, (a/an/and) I am (a/an/and)
ardent outdoorsman, so our times together usually
led us to the woods. Her crisp, clean, piercing bark
could be (quit/quiet/quite) easily distinguished
from those of other dogs, and she readily responded
to both her name and my whistle and would drop
whatever she was doing and come to my side as she
was (suppose/supposed) to. As obedient as she was,
she still had an independent streak in her a yard
wide. She wouldn't sit next to anyone but did like
to be in the same room. She's gone now, but she is
affectionately remembered always!

D. My (to/too/two) year-old nephew Antoine came over
my house (to/too/two) spend the day with me;
however, I didn't know at the time I agreed to keep

him that I would have to go to the mall;
nevertheless, I took him along. I don't know what
came over my nephew, but he started to cut up on me
really badly. When I say this, I mean he was overly
playful. He was shouting, screaming, and singing at
the top of his voice. He tried to jump in front of
(a/an/and) lady with (a/an/and) baby in a buggy (a/
an/and) held his hands on the rail when she (past/
passed) by. I grabbed him, and for no reason at all,
he fell on the floor in uncontrollable laughter. I
tried to calm him down with some carmel corn, but
that only lasted for a moment before he took the
popcorn and (through/though/threw) it across the
floor of the mall. People (where/were/we're)
staring at us, and my face suddenly became warm from
embarrassment. I got down on one knee to scoop up
the popcorn while Antoine was busy terrorizing
other children and (there/their/they're) parents. I
eventually made my purchase. The salesman expressed
a sign of relief as we (where/were/we're) leaving
the store, and this I understood perfectly. After
leaving the mall I sat Antoine in the car, (then/
than) proceeded home. As I pulled up in the
driveway, I looked over at the little terrorist, who
was now sound asleep and wondered how he could look
so sweet. I picked up his small, limp body and
carried him into the house. I told my sister about
the incident and asked her if she thought Antoine
should take some sort of medication to (quit/quiet/
quite) him down from time (to/too/two) time. She
just looked at me, smiled, and nodded her head
saying, ''Oh, he's always a little rambunctious
when he hasn't had his nap.'' I was speechless.

Lesson Ten

Recognizing and Using Capitalization

There are only a few instances in which words must begin with capital letters. These special cases are easily learned with concentration.

1. *The first word in a sentence*

(I)'s an easy matter to learn rules for capitalization.

2. *The pronoun I*

If (I) were you, (I) would think twice before withdrawing from college.

3. *Days of the week, months of the year, holidays*

On the third (T)uesday in (D)ecember, we begin our (C)hristmas vacation.

(N)ew (Y)ear's falls on the first (M)onday in (J)anuary.

Not seasons.

I love fall, but for some reason it always makes me feel sad; maybe it is because winter is coming.

4. *Streets, cities, states, parts of the country, countries, and other named locations.*

(M)ain (S)treet in (A)kron, (O)hio, is the major street, as it is in most cities.

The (H)awaiian (I)slands probably draw more tourists each year than any other islands.

362

A number of people that I know find the North preferable to the South, while there are also those who would rather live in the West.

Not directions

He headed west on Highway 66.

5. *Names and titles used with names, and names of products*

Zenobia Dwerp and Billy Joe Mangaroo are a "hot item" on campus this year.
Judge Roy Bean, for better or for worse, is part of the history of Texas.
Professor Asher is a dream.
The man who delivered my baby was Dr. Archibald.
Professional athletes often drink Gatorade during a game.

Not titles used without names

The judge sent him to the jail house.
My professor is a sincere, intelligent woman.
I am no longer surprised to see a woman doctor.

6. *Family relationships used with names*

Even though Uncle Horace and Aunt Tillie never speak to my parents, they are still my favorite relatives.
Grandmother Alice can still remember the Spanish American War.

Not family relationships used without names

All of my uncles and aunts and grandparents attended my brother's graduation.

7. *Languages and academic courses used with course numbers*

I have only a 10-minute break between English and Psychology 101.

Not academic courses without course numbers unless they are languages.

I prefer mathematics to philosophy.

8. *First and last and important words in titles of books, plays, poems, movies, and musical compositions*

I prefer the movie *Gone with the Wind* to the book by Margaret Mitchell.

Arthur Miller's play *Death of a Salesman* shows us a great deal about our American way of life.

Robert Frost's "Stopping by Woods on a Snowy Evening" is one of the most widely read American poems.

9. *Races, nationalities and religions*

It is unfortunate that the Protestants and Catholics of Northern Ireland, both of whom are Irish, cannot live peaceably with one another.

Most Indians of North America live not on the land on which they were reared, but on reservations set up by the government.

Using the models above as your guide, write twenty sentences of your own that include various examples of capitalization. In this exercise, be sure to use each kind of capitalization at least once.

1. _____

_____

2. _____

_____

3. _____

_____

4. _____

_____

5. _____

_____

6. _____

_____

7. _____

_____

8. _____

_____

9. _____

_____

10. _____

_____

11. _____

_____

12. _____

_____

13. _____

_____

14. _____

_____

15. _____

_____

16. _____

_____

17. _____

_____

18. _____

_____

19. _____

_____

20. _____

_____

**Practice in
Proofreading**

In the following exercise, using the models as your guide, capitalize where necessary.

A. i remember a place from my childhood, and i will share the memory with you. the place is demeter's general store, located in jenny lind, arkansas. demeter's no longer exists, but a lot of memories do. the building was at the intersection of old highway 71 and ft. chaffee road; it was the only business left in town besides jones' barbership and antique store. old and run–down looking in its day, it was magical in its appeal to me. the long, narrow store had high ceilings and windows, except for two narrow glass windows in the front. i suppose its curious appearance is what was most fascinating. it was like visiting any small town store in 1930. the ceiling was made of stamped metal, a floral design, painted white, but grayed with age. from the ceiling, a fan hung. it seemed to turn about once every two hours, and the electric light near it hummed loudly. over on the one wall were gray shelves, old, and pretty dusty. there, one could find canned goods, soap, tea bags and the like. opposite those shelves were the meat case, a small

ice cream freezer and a long display case filled
with candy, chewing tobacco, and cigarettes. it was
on this counter that mr. demeter kept the cash
register. the cash register was old enough to make
you wonder whether it might have been the first one
ever made; it was huge, painted a gold color, and
possessed an unmistakable ring whenever used. up
front, near the entrance, opposite a calendar with a
photograph of the dionne quintuplets, stood the
soda cooler. it was a coca cola cooler, filled with
water and ice, into which you could always reach for
the coldest soda imaginable. the water always
looked black because the store was dimly lit and
painted gray also. nehi, rc, and coke were all you
would ever find in the cooler. nobody knows why, but
my cousin did get a bottle of dr. pepper once. no
saturday afternoon was complete without a visit to
demeter's. just about all the young people came in
every saturday, looked around to see what was new,
and have a soda, arkansas-style. to do this, first,
you buy a bottle of rc, then a bag of planters'
salted peanuts, open them both, and go outside. once
you have sat down on mr. demeter's porch, you put
the peanuts into the bottle of soda. the soda fizzes
over the top, and then it's ready to be drunk. most
kids really enjoyed a soda this way. i forgot to
tell about the fly swatters in an old shell casing
by the door. the idea was to sit on the porch and
swat flies while enjoying a soda with peanuts.
informal ''contests'' often took place, with the
winner being treated to a soda ''on the house.'' the
contests were necessary because a lot of visitors to
the store came on horseback, bringing flies with
them, it seemed. mr. demeter is dead now; the store
closed on the day he died and never opened again.
life in jenny lind was never the same and probably
never will be again.

B. often when i hear someone play the piano well, one
event from my childhood comes to mind—my piano
recital. the date of the program, sunday, may 15,

seemed far in the future at first. however, as that
spring day drew nearer, i felt the first stirrings
of apprehension. would i be able to ''play it by
heart''? what if i made a mistake? this uneasiness
turned to real fear when i learned on the saturday
night before the recital that not only my parents
and two sisters, but both grandmothers, my favorite
aunt, aunt helen, and our neighbor, reverend
jenkins, would be on hand to applaud as i played
''waltz of the flowers.'' fear turned to absolute
panic on sunday morning when mrs. newton, my piano
teacher, called to say that i should do my very
best, for the top three performers would later be
televised live, playing in cleveland in a summer
talent show. i still remember the queasy feeling
that that news brought. suddenly i was on the monroe
high school stage, seated at the piano, hands
poised. a quick glance at aunt helen and grandma
mary reassured me, and i began to play. as i neared
the end of the first page of the memorized piece,
the last few notes began to fade from my mind. then
everything faded; i could't remember any of the notes on
pages two, three, four, or five. my ''waltz of the
flowers'' was over! I jumped down from the old
wooden stool, realizing with a wave of relief that
mrs. newton would have to choose someone else to
represent her in the august talent show. my recital
career ended, i bowed from the high school stage,
smiling broadly.

C. as i lie in bed at night, all kinds of different
fears about going to college run through my mind,
but i think my biggest fear is of flunking all of my
classes and going through a personal struggle with
myself again. the fear of failing in college has
been with me ever since i started back to college
last summer. when i first came to the university of
akron as a freshman in the fall of 1983, i flunked
out because i never attended any of my classes. in
that time i was fighting with myself because i
really in god's name didn't know what i wanted to do
in life. did i want to work at a menial job for the

city of akron or firestone tire and rubber company
because that was as high as i could go on the
corporate ladder without a college degree? it took a
lot of deep soul-searching and many long nights of
crying myself to sleep to really find out what i
wanted to do, but i still don't know. i love to work
with children and have thought about becoming a
teacher, but i also love the business world and
might like to follow in my father's footsteps as a
stockbroker. i made the decision to go to college
and try to make up my mind there instead of later in
life when it's hard to start all over again. well,
i'm here, and i'm trying my best, but as i take each
step forward in school, i'm afraid of the failure
and the indecision that lurks around every dark and
untravelled corner of my journey through college.

Lesson Eleven

Punctuation Practice

PROOFREADING FOR PUNCTUATION
WITH JOINING WORDS

In the following paragraphs, some of the punctuation used with joining words has been omitted. Supply this punctuation where needed. If you are unsure of the rules, refer to pages 7 (joining words) 14 (*long* joining words), and 37 (series).

A. Throughout my life I have always been an independent individual. Out of all my close friends, I was the first to get a job, to get an apartment and to get married. As the result of divorce, I acquired my own home but home ownership still did not reduce my drive for independence. My next goal was to live in Florida consequently I sold my home and my possessions and moved to the ''sunshine state.'' I had dreamed of this move nevertheless my happiness bubble soon burst. I was unhappy without needed close friends and comforting family members nearby. When a crisis situation arose, there was no one to turn to and I became very unhappy, depressed and lonely. The lack of higher education limited my earning potential where I was living consequently I never seemed to have enough money. Not feeling very independent, I moved back home to Akron, Ohio. I had discovered the importance of family, friends and acquiring a college degree. At this point in my life, independence has become a secondary goal for me.

B. Working as counter clerk at a dry cleaner's is a big responsibility. One of my duties is pleasing customers. I have to try to answer all their bothersome questions and make sure their orders are filled properly, which includes making sure they are receiving the clothes they brought in. Another rendered service in answering ringing phones taking messages and providing correct information to customers over the phone. Also, I have to make sure customers' special requests are granted, such as removing difficult spots pleating or sizing garments and sewing on buttons or snaps. Another responsibility is writing invoices up accurately. Three invoices are written up for plant workers bookkeeping and the customer therefore they have to be written accurately. Tagging in clothes is also an important duty because if the clothes aren't tagged in, they could become lost. Another obligation is providing a clean working area. Included in this duty are sweeping floors and cleaning counters, which is done by the counter person. My last duty of the day is closing the store. I close the register down count my money make sure the deposit is correct put writing utensils away place the money in the safe put the burglar alarm on and lock all doors and windows. I never take my counter person's job lightly.

PROOFREADING FOR PUNCTUATION OF SERIES

In the following paragraphs, some of the punctuation used with series has been omitted. Supply this punctuation where needed. If you are unsure of the rules for punctuation used with series, refer to page 00.

A. In my opinion, a library is one of the best places to study to think or to get done something that requires a lot of concentration. Upon entering the library, I find the quiet inside similar to that inside a church. ''No loud talking'' is strictly enforced, and most people talk in soft, muted tones when they do speak. The smell of books reminds me of long-past visits to the library as a child, and that familiar smell is somehow warm and comforting to me now, like a link from the past. At the library, there are no ringing phones no chiming doorbells or no distractions from the television set. There is only the atmosphere of reverence awe and silence. The people come to study to write or to reflect. If one needs a dictionary an encyclopedia or an opinion from a book, the reference material is there to be used at almost any time of the day. I escape into the world of books for pleasure knowledge or comfort when I have a problem.

B. Although the home reeks of poverty as it sits snuggled in the valley between two lush green hills, it looks well cared for and loved. If I look closely, I can see a boy a girl and a shaggy sheep dog deep in some fanciful play. A young teenaged girl and a woman in her middle forties are standing watching the children with amusement on their faces. As my gaze shifts to the weather-worn house, I notice the rough lumber that makes up the exterior. On one side the unpainted lumber is uneven because it has never been trimmed, and I wonder why. The house looks as though it were once box shaped with a section added later. The front of the house rests on logs because of the uneven ground. The people I see in this picture in my mind are my mother my sister and my brother. I am the small girl, and this is where I lived until I was nine.

PROOFREADING FOR PUNCTUATION WITH *WHO, WHICH,* AND *THAT* CLAUSES

In the following paragraphs, some of the punctuation used with *who, which,* and *that* clauses has been omitted. Supply this punctuation as needed. If you are unsure of the rules, refer to pages 132 (*who* and *that* clauses) and page 142 (*who* and *which* clauses).

A. One experience in junior high school that I will always remember came from my ninth grade algebra teacher who was an older, short, German man with greased-back hair and horned-rimmed glasses who wore suits from the 1940s with colors that never seemed to match. He would always say things to me in class about not doing my homework. One afternoon while I was sitting in study hall with nothing to do and not one book in front of me, he marched in and told me to go to my locker, get my algebra book, and meet him in the library. When I got there, he took me to a small room that was used as a group study room. He then, shaking his short, fat finger in my face, told me he was going to flunk me in algebra if I didn't buckle down and do some work or show him that at least I would try. I didn't believe him and said that he couldn't flunk me because my test scores were good enough to get a passing grade, and then I walked away. When grade cards came out, my mouth hit the floor. I looked down and saw a big fat ''F'' on my report card. When I took it home, my parents, who were very upset with me for letting this happen yelled at me and told me that if I didn't bring up my grade to a ''C,'' I couldn't play football in the upcoming fall. The next day I walked sheepishly into his classroom and asked him if he would please help me to understand algebra. He looked at me and asked if I was sincere, and I replied quietly, ''yes.'' That day after school I met him in his room to start learning from square one. He was very businesslike at first, but after two or three of these meetings, he let his hair down and became very friendly with me. I learned he was an avid fisherman and a professional football fan. As a young boy who really never thought of teachers as real human beings I learned that he was, and I also learned that algebra wasn't that hard. While doing all my homework and extra credit work, I received a ''C'' in algebra, but I also found a friend in someone that I never thought would be one. A few years later I ran into him at the shopping mall. He came up to me and shook my hand and told me he was proud to see my name on the honor roll in high school. This really made me feel good, but I felt it made him feel good also. He retired last year, and that was the last time I saw him, but I feel he would be happy to see me finally going to college.

B. My first day of high school was not only a memorable one but a terrifying experience. No one seemed to notice me as I stood alone as the older students who seemed like giants jostled me about in their mad rush. I who already felt small was afraid of being trampled. I began to panic. I knew what it felt like to be a small child who was lost on a New York subway during rush hour. The voices seemed deafening as they talked, laughed, and yelled to each other. I became desperate as I frantically looked for someone that I could recognize. Then in the throng I saw a face that caused the ''giants'' to become just bigger kids. It was that of Bruce M. who was a friend I had known since grade school days. He came toward me, pushing and shoving. The noise which had been so overpowering drifted into the background as we became engrossed in conversation of our own. The terror ended as we made our way inside the building.

PROOFREADING FOR PUNCTUATION WITH DEPENDENT CLAUSES

In the following paragraphs, some of the punctuation used with dependent clauses has been omitted. Supply this punctuation where needed. If you are unsure of the rule, refer to page 24 for guidance.

A. One of my most embarrassing moments happened on a beautiful warm day as the sun beat down and the water glistened. It was a perfect day for waterskiing, and I had a new gold sequined bathing suit that had been given to me. There was only one problem. The top was too large, so being the ingenious sort, I decided to fix the problem by filling my top with panty hose. After I put one in each side I surveyed myself and thought the effects were very satisfactory. I was then ready to ski. When I got up on my skis I knew that the sequins on my suit sparkled, and I felt proud to be wearing it. I noticed two men in another boat looking and pointing, and I was flattered to think that they were admiring my suit until I noticed that something was wrong. You guessed it. One of my faithful helpers was flapping at my side like a banner in the wind. Needless to say, I quickly dropped into the water so that I could hide my embarrassment.

B. Never getting a chance to say good-bye to Cindy was a painful experience. When I met Cindy in the fifth grade, it was difficult because she was angry and wouldn't let me or anyone else get close to her. As soon as someone tried to get close to her she would become angry and snap at them, telling them they were just wasting their time. I was told the same thing; only I didn't scare easily. We became the best of friends although some people couldn't understand that. You see, Cindy had a terrible heart condition. Her heart was enlarged and was still getting larger, but since her condition made it hard for her to get around and breathe the other children didn't want to play with her. I was determined not to let her get away from me because she was going to let me be her friend even if I had to pester her for years to come until she stopped fighting me. We became inseparable; days, months, and one year went by. We ate lunch together, sat together on the playground, and called each other on the telephone as soon as we got home from school. I never thought of Cindy dying; however, deep in the back of my mind I knew that she would, so why should I think about it when we had each other and still had time. I guess you could say we made each other feel special, for she needed me, and I certainly needed her. On Tuesday in May of 1978 I came to school, noticing Cindy in a wheelchair. She looked very sick; however, I knew better than to tell her that. That day seemed to drag on forever, and I couldn't bear to see her in pain. Holding back my tears was a battle in itself; however, I did it because I had to be strong for Cindy and for myself. I would let her squeeze my hand when she had a painful cough. I truly admired her because she never cried. Cindy was the first one dropped off the bus after school, and I was second. She waved goodbye to me for the longest time; it seemed forever for the bus to take off. Cindy never returned to school after that day, but I tried to call her for two days, and there was no answer. I was finally told Cindy had died; however, I knew this already. For some strange reason, I needed to hear it. I didn't cry because I was angry that I never got the chance to say good—bye. After the anger wore off, I did cry. I cried for the good times we had, then I smiled. I thought back to when she waved good—bye to me for the last time and how she waved for so long. The bus seemed to move in slow motion, and I realized we had said our good—byes.

PROOFREADING FOR PUNCTUATION LEARNED IN PART ONE

In the following paragraphs, some of the punctuation you learned in Part One has been omitted. Supply punctuation where needed. If you are unsure of the rules, refer to the following pages for guidance: page 7 (joining words), page 14 (*long* joining words), page 24 (dependent clauses), page 37 (series), pages 103, 111, and 116 (phrases), page 132 (*who* and *that* clauses), page 142 (*who* and *which* clauses).

A. While my mom and dad and my brother and his fiancé danced on the dance floor in an expensive restaurant in Princeton, New Jersey I sat at an empty table with the lonely feeling of being the ugly little brother. When I lifted my eyes from my napkin on the table I saw an older woman staring at me. Suddenly she turned away toward her husband and said something to him. I looked back down at the table and played with my swizzle stick in my drink thinking about what she said to her husband. Did she say I was ugly did she say I looked too young to be drinking or did she tell her husband that her meal was delicious? I didn't care what she said but I knew I had to get out of there. I got up and walked to the bathroom thinking about what kind of girl I would like to have with me at dinner. By the time I got to the bar I made up my mind that I would take any girl in the world to talk to. I sat there feeling sorry for myself and smoked a cigarette. I walked slowly back to the table just in time to see my dinner being served by a cute waitress. I ate my dinner quietly only talking when I was spoken to. I thought about what my friends were doing back home and couldn't wait to get to the hotel just so I could get out of that restaurant and maybe get out of the feeling of being the little ugly tag-a-long on a night that was made for lovers.

B. Riding home each day from school on the city bus provides me with many chances to observe people who are unique and interesting. One unique daily rider is a very large, ill-smelling woman who can best be described as loud and self-centered. Extremely overweight wearing tennis shoes and a ragged scarf over greasy hair and usually eating a candy bar, this woman climbs on the bus with all the grace of an elephant climbing a tree. Even if I were not watching the passengers on the bus I would know that this woman had boarded when I heard her sandpaper voice grating against my nerves like fingernails on a chalkboard. Without a pause for air, she tells all of her business to everyone who is on the bus whether they want to listen to her or not. I am aware that this complete stranger has painful arthritis is divorced from a drinking bum has three lazy children and one no-good son-in-law however she sings her praises of herself as a mother and a person. Daily I hear why she is downtown why she is going home at that particular time and what she is going to do when she gets home. She always goes home to watch her favorite soap operas. Everything she loudly says in that grating voice revolves around the word ''me.'' Using a whole bus seat just for her parcels, this woman covers another whole bus seat with her body consequently any person needing a seat is left hanging onto the aisle bus rails while this woman selfishly occupies two seats. While impressions can be misleading I feel that this woman is a loud, self-centered individual who has no regard for anyone but herself.

C. I believe that anyone caught drinking while driving should not be allowed to drive again. I was severely injured in an automobile accident when my Volkswagen was struck broadside by a vehicle driven by a drunk driver. Because I was immediately knocked unconscious by the impact of the collision I was unaware that I had even been involved in an accident until I woke up in a hospital emergency room. Panic confusion and disbelief at what had happened to me took hold and I sank back into unconsciousness. When

I woke up I saw that my family had waited outside
the emergency room for hours to see me and the sight
of my family made the present seem more real
consequently I fought to stay conscious so that I
could speak to my family about what had really
happened. When I learned of my injuries hate towards
the drunken driver who crashed that stop sign and
smashed into my car filled my heart. Although I
feared a permanent head injury I was lucky all my
injuries were minor. The man who hit me had a long
list of drunk driving charges therefore I strongly
suggest the changing of local and state drunk
driving laws.

Index